NORTHERN SOMÁLI LAND.

Map N° 3

Reduced by permission of the Government of India, from
the original routes of Cap.t H. G. C. Swayne R.E. and Cap.t
E. J. E. Swayne 16.th Bengal Infantry. These routes were
reconnoitred for the Government of India on a scale of
4 miles to 1 inch, by Prismatic Compass and time
measurements, on a framework of fixed points obtained
by triangulation or by continuous chains of latitudes
and azimuths from star observations with a 6 inch
transit theodolite.

Note The signs . do not indicate villages but
camps or stations of observation

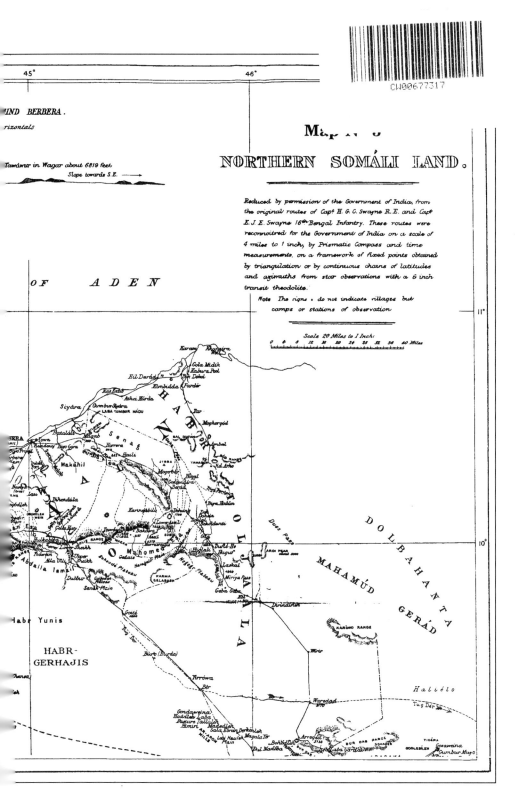

IND BERBERA.

rizontals

Tamánur in Wagar about 6819 feet.
Slope towards S.E. ⟶

OF A D E N

Scale 20 Miles to 1 Inch.

45°   46°

11°

10°

HABR

TOLJÁLA

DOLBAHANTA

GERÁD

MAHAMÚD

KARÍMO RANGE

Haliélo

Tug Der

BUR DAB RANGE

Habr Yunis

HABR-
GERHAJIS

Berbera

EARLY DAYS IN SOMALILAND
AND OTHER TALES

The author in his tent at 7,000 feet at Golis, Somaliland

Early Days in Somaliland And Other Tales

A Pioneer's Notebook

COLONEL H. G. C. SWAYNE C.M.G. R.E.

The Pentland Press
Edinburgh – Cambridge – Durham

First published in 1996 by
The Pentland Press Ltd
1 Hutton Close
South Church
Bishop Auckland
Durham

ISBN 1-85821-257-X

Typeset by Carnegie Publishing, 18 Maynard St., Preston
Printed and bound by Bookcraft Ltd., Bath

Contents

VOLUME II 1896–1902

VOLUME III 1904–1913

APPENDICES

Introduction

M Y SISTER and I decided to publish this book in memory of one of the last of the early explorers of Africa, and of a well-loved grandfather. He had an extraordinary and exciting life, and an unusually optimistic view of the world, and seemed to enjoy being alive more than anyone else I've met, even though I knew him only as an old man.

In his youth, Harald Swayne was fascinated by adventure in wild and unknown places and later became gripped by the thrill and excitement of hunting big game, for which he endured danger, discomfort and hardship. He was amongst the first Europeans to visit and map huge areas of Somaliland, the interior of which was quite unknown in the West. In spite of his privations, and bouts of fever as a young man in sometimes extremely difficult and dangerous conditions, some of which are recorded here for the first time from his notebook and diaries, he remained a remarkably fit man up to his death in 1940 aged 80.

As well as an expert tracker and hunter of big game, Harald was an extremely competent surveyor and engineer, thanks to his training in the Royal Engineers. A man of many parts, he was also an excellent artist and photographer. He could draw animals and people in action with just a few strokes of his pen. An example of his work is shown on the dust cover of this book, a small part of a 20-foot-long frieze showing Somali hunters on camels moving camp and hunting lions on horseback using spears.

At one time Harald studied art in Paris, and shared a studio there with his younger sister Dagmar, who became quite a well-known sculptress in France. However, the call of the wild set him on a different course, but his letters to us were usually decorated with pen and ink sketches of people and animals and they were always a joy to receive.

This book mainly describes his hunting trips and adventures as a young army officer in the Royal Engineers, both on duty and during some of his leaves. He regarded one such trip to the Issutugan River in April/May 1887, as a "red letter" trip (and takes 19 pages to describe it).

The trips he made up to 1887 he called the "prehistoric period". It was not until the 1890s that sportsmen and others began to flock into these areas. Many of the heads of the animals he shot were brought back for presentation to museums in England. He also presented two young lionesses to Clifton

Zoo. They had to be transported in wooden cages on the backs of camels in order to reach the port in Africa, and he had to provide minders and a herd of goats to provide meat for the lionesses on the way. The cost of doing all this, and shipping the lionesses and the remnants of the herd of goats to England, used up all his available money, and he was in debt for many years afterwards.

However this volume is not just about Somaliland. It includes visits to Portuguese East Africa, Zanzibar and Mombasa in 1885, and he notes the enormous differences in these countries where he returned in 1904.

Of particular interest is an earlier visit to Burma in 1889/90 when he took part in the Chin Lushai campaign at a period when part of Burma was in rebellion against British rule.

Later, stationed in India, his zest to combine duty with pleasure is well described, as is the great Durbar to celebrate the visit to King George V and Queen Mary for their coronation in Delhi in 1911/12 - a major celebratory event in the history of British India.

He married Aimée Holmes in 1884, and took his wife and baby daughter Helen on some of his trips.

If the reader wants to take himself or herself back in time 100 years, they will enjoy reading this book. It depicts so well the life of a young army officer and the thrill and skill of the hunter in a then sparsely inhabited country, his ability to navigate by the stars and his good common sense in dealing with awkward situations. His rapport with his own followers and those strangers he met on his travels are a tribute to his innate kindness and love of people of all kinds and races.

Many things in this book may shock and surprise the present generation of readers. Views have changed so much since it was written. One has to remember that Africa was teeming with game at that time, and several sub-species of animals found were unknown to the West. Harald made a careful study of all the animal life, and identified seven new sub-species of antelope, two of which are named after him. The excitement and danger and skill involved in stalking and hunting big game gripped the hunter in a way that perhaps is difficult to understand today; and to have an animal named after the person who first positively identified it as "new" was a unique honour, hotly sought. The hunter in those days was usually well supported by the local native people, who were often preyed on by the larger carnivorous animals. They also encouraged the hunter in every way as a means of getting free fresh meat from his success.

All that was soon to change. At the time, years later, when I knew Harald Swayne, he often said to me, "If I had my time over again, John, I would shoot with a camera, and not with a gun!"

After he lost his second wife Kitty, he took my sister Aimée on a memorable trip around America shortly before the outbreak of the Second World War. She was only 18 at the time, and he was 78. He particularly enjoyed seeing the Grand Canyon and the great California redwood forests. Afterwards, with his usual humour, he said: "I was like a tortoise, led by a greyhound."

I must thank my good friend Bob Harper for his great enthusiasm and help in going through the 4 large volumes of manuscript notebooks and photographs that Harald had left in 1940, and who with the help of his son Michael Harper, produced the typescript that forms the basis of this book. They both spent many hours of work producing it. I must also thank my sister Aimée and her husband, Captain John Gower, DSC, RN, for their help and assistance in proofreading and ideas, and to the publisher for their forbearance and co-operation in producing this volume. Lastly, I am greatly indebted to my son Paul for his help in the final stages of preparing this book for publication.

John Winder.

Volume 1
1884-1892

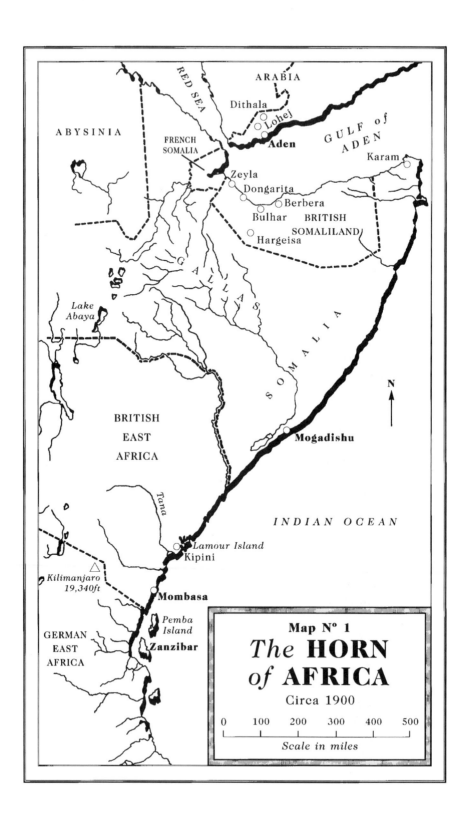

ARABIA

RED SEA

Dithala

○ Lohej

Aden

GULF of ADEN

ABYSINIA

FRENCH SOMALIA

Karam ○

Zeyla ○

Dongarita ○

○ Berbera

Bulhar ○   BRITISH

SOMALILAND

○ Hargeisa

G A L L A S

Lake Abaya

S O M A L I A

N
↑

BRITISH

EAST

AFRICA

○ Mogadishu

Tana

INDIAN OCEAN

○ *Lamour Island*
Kipini

△

○ *Kilimanjaro*
19,340ft

Mombasa

Pemba Island

Zanzibar

GERMAN
EAST
AFRICA

Map Nº 1

The **HORN**
of **AFRICA**

Circa 1900

0   100   200   300   400   500

Scale in miles

Chapter 1

Garbadir, Somaliland
4th to 15th January, 1885

SOMALILAND was scarcely known to white men in 1884 when I landed at Aden in command of a company of Madras Sappers. Across the Gulf of Aden was 'Africa' where no one goes but where there *ought* to be splendid big-game shooting, We knew the country around Aden – the Arabian deserts, the tribes armed with match-locks – and British territory extending only three miles from the shores of the harbour. Vague recollections were there of Burton's expedition about thirty years before in an attempt to penetrate Africa from Berbera, ending in the first entrance to Harar, and the attack on Burton at Berbera by the Habr Awal – Shojan being killed and Speke wounded in forty places, which 'healed up like cuts in an india-rubber ball'. Before Burton's ill-fated trip, a few Englishmen did go over and it is on record also that Colonel Merewether, Resident, shot an elephant in the hills behind the Coast.

To go back to Indian scenes, it was in April '83 that I landed at Bombay and climbed the Ghats in the train with a Major Williamson of the 43rd. Being a good shot and an enthusiast, he sketched the delights of 'shikar' as we topped the wonderful ridges bathed in sunset. At the first Bangalore auction (Johnson's, I think – 12th Lancers) I bought a .500 Express, bidding it up to the skies and carrying it home in triumph. I went down to Closepet and only managed to make an oil sketch of the river there. There were tigers reported, but they had gone so I returned to Bangalore. Then being ordered to Aden in command of No. 6 Coy. Sappers (Madras), I sold my .500 Express, being told: 'There is no sport in Aden'.

After a two months' privilege leave trip to Havre and England, I came out again to Aden just in time to meet Major Heath, the Brigade Major at Aden, who with Surgeon Captain Monks had just come over from shooting elephants in the hill country behind Berbera. They had shot six elephants and had a very exciting time, and described the bush leading up the high Ghauts, thirty miles in, as very beautiful and wild. They described the people as wild and uncertain and had one or two risky incidents which added zest to their trip. We at Aden were very keen on going. I had an inkling of the trip before going to England and came back to Aden with a .500 Express by Jolly and a 4-bore. I had also a double gun, a Paradox by Holland (12-bore).

With Captain Saunders of the R.A. I made preparations for a ten days' trip to the Ghauts where Heath and Monks got their elephants. We were to be the first in Somaliland after those two, who were absolutely the pioneers of recent sport there.

Meanwhile, in common with other Sudan garrisons, the garrison of Harar was to be withdrawn to Egypt and the place left to the Mussulman Emir, Abdillahi. The Somali coast, also under Egypt, was now being handed over to England, as represented by the British-Indian authorities at Aden, working under the Bombay Government (General Blair being Resident and Colonel F. Hunter 1st Assistant at Aden). Walsh, one of the Assistant Residents, had gone over and with a few policemen was consolidating British rule over the turbulent Somali tribes. An Egyptian Pacha with a half battalion and some guns had left, giving up the whole coast to Walsh and his policemen at Berbera and Captain King, British Consul and some policemen at Zeila. The people at Berbera were surprised because Walsh used to go out and shoot gazelles in the Berbera Plain alone, whereas the Pacha always had a strong escort whenever he left his house at Berbera!

F.L. James and his brother and Lieutenants Phillips and Aylmer were at this time already in the interior on their great trip, the first exploration to the heart of the Horn of Africa. Dualla Idris, Stanley's man, was with them.

Saunders and I, finding the weekly steamer (an Egyptian steamer called the *Khedivi* full of black masked sheep, trading between Suez, Suakim, Somaliland and Aden) did not start at a suitable date, arranged with the nakoda, or captain, of a Somali bagala (dhow) trading between Aden and Berbera to take us over. We started at sundown from Aden harbour with our guns and baggage stowed in the hold of the bagala, and we ourselves took the poop. We had 150 miles to go due south to Berbera. We were very ill, and arrived next night only near enough to have a distant view of the Egyptian lighthouse, but owing to contrary winds, had to anchor. There, next morning, the longed-for African coast appeared, a long strip of yellow sand from horizon to horizon and behind, a towering line of blue mountains rising step above step to the clouds, the lighthouse very tiny in the distance. All day we lay becalmed, the lazy Somali boatmen droning dismal melancholy chants. Rats and cockroaches had disturbed us at night, running about the rigging between us and the moon. Once I had woken up (I am speaking of the night before) with a Somali's foot over my face; he had rolled in his sleep. How we longed to get away from the stinking bilge water in the rolling, tossing ship lifted on the oily but heavy groundswell. The sun beat down pitilessly through the thin awning of Somali 'tobes' (long sheets) put up by the sailors for our benefit. At last, in the afternoon, a breeze sprang up and moving slowly at first, then more quickly, we sailed inside the sand spit which forms the harbour, and tied up our dhow to the pier-head. The pier, like all at Berbera, had been built by the Egyptian Government.

We landed and made for the Pacha's house, now owned by Walsh. A beautiful garden in the quadrangle with a fountain. Lovely Egyptian baths in the house, very large with plenty of water brought in pipes from Dubar in the Maritime Hills eight miles away – by the Egyptian Government, of course.

Walsh sent me out, or rather took me out, on the afternoon of the first day into the Berbera Maritime Plain, with its pebbly ground for three miles (as far as the lighthouse), then its sand and stunted flat-topped mimosa bushes, its flocks of goats herded by old women and girls and its gazelles. Charming bright wide-awake little creatures, those gazelles, with their whisky little tails and impudent way of standing to gaze and then hop and away, just as you are taking aim. How difficult they were to see on the pebble-strewn ground. Walsh got one by stalking from behind a led camel, and I missed another, my first rifle-shot at game! I was so excited that I would not wait but must pull the trigger too soon, in a hurry, thinking he was off. I could have waited ten seconds more! I have been hundreds of times since into this interesting plain after these bright little gazelles and the sport never palls. They are very hard to bag and the .500 was a clumsy weapon for them, though good for larger game.

Next morning, Walsh, having kindly arranged everything and having been the best of hosts, told us the camels were ready. Saunders and I on our ponies, his brown, mine a cream-colour or rather strawberry cream, if there is such a colour. About ten camels and as many followers, cook, body servants and shikaris, mostly Somalis of Somaliland, wild and unkempt, with the long tobe, shield and spear.

We marched up the dry desert bed of a river between barren mountains – the Maritime Range – yellow with bright points of mica and white gypsum and we camped at Lau, just a few feet above the level of the sandy floor of the river-bed. We were soon knocking in tent pegs, and great was our joy as we came out after dinner to smoke a cigarette and contemplate the river-bed below and realise this was our first camp in Africa, with hundreds of miles of the unknown Highlands stretching in front of us, inhabited by tribes which had never seen a white man. We got a view in the next morning's march, through ten miles of awful tumbled wilderness of gypsum hill, of a beautiful blue peak, of a rich deep indigo, shaped like the Matterhorn. We did not know the name then and called it Golis, but later experience identified this as Deimolah Wein in the Interior Plain, under the Great Golis Range, and in a valley embraced by horns of that range. The rare beauty and mystery of this towering peak of dark blue, rising above a wreath of snow-white mist, in the gap made by a break in the red sandstone barren hills which composed the foreground, is ever a vivid scene. Just as we caught sight of the great peak, some nomad Somalis with shields and spears, leading camels, came down the stony caravan track and said 'salaam aleikum' (peace!) to our own men, and then we passed them.

At the start from Lau we had a difficulty with our lazy camelmen, who refused to march so early, but by unstrapping a rifle the ringleader, who had bolted with his camel in the Berbera direction, was induced to bring the animal back. We foresaw trouble but this was almost the first and last trouble I have had with Somalis. They did not know the Ingres (English) in the early days of '84 and '85 and had only been used to Egyptian rule. Ever since '85 they have been pleasant enough to us, and all over the country have shown us marked cordiality and good nature.

As we advanced through the barren Lau Range and began to descend towards the interior plains, the country began to open up. Bushes became larger and more plentiful, and from among the scrub growing between the great boulders of rock, hares and beautiful little antelope rather smaller than a hare (called the sukaro or dik-dik) sprang up in couples and scurried away. As we began to descend, the broken plains in front were found to be undulating and covered with transparent mimosa bush and larger thorn trees, thickening into a dense dark forest at the further side, six miles away, where the interior plains began to rise to the great blue mass of Golis towering over the valley in front. From the forest rose some isolated peaks and koppies, the whole forming a lovely picture of African mountain scenery.

How we banged and banged away! Saunders was good with the guns and got most. I, blazing away ineffectively with the .577 Express rifle at the dik-dik – pretty graceful little things that got up in couples, male and female, and went off with two or three sharp whistles, and then stood and gazed behind a low mimosa bush!

I lost the caravan as we entered the dense bush on the further side of the valley and shouted for my followers, disturbing a long-necked red antelope which Saunders was aiming at, if I remember right. It became very beautiful as we got deeper into the forest, the splendid 'guda' or camel thorn throwing out its masses of green tracery between us and the evening sun. We got into grassy glades where there were sheep and goats and women tending them, and later we found cows round our camp. We pitched camp at Armaleh Garbadir in a bay of the Golis spurs, in lovely scenery, and knocked in the tent pegs as dusk came on. We were not very comfortable the first night as the camp was full of thorny branches scattered about to restrict the wanderings of the flocks. But soon they brought us milk and mutton and we slept in what was to be our shooting camp for four days.

Our camp was at the edge of some rocky ground which formed the foot of a spur of Golis with a canopy of guda trees overhead and glades of very green grass cropped short by the flocks and herds. We each started before dawn with shikaris, mine was Deria Hassan, a tall spare Somali with broad shoulders and lean keen features. We took opposite directions, I towards Gurkaweni, a koppie rising a hundred feet above the flat tree-tops. I hoped for a leopard, but suddenly Deria pointed to a slender bush over one hundred yards away and I had seen my first gerenouk (Waller's gazelle) standing half hidden, its long red neck craned forwards to look at me. I got this one with the .577 and I shall never forget bringing it home at noon to our camp, the slender head and neck and the thick black perfectly ringed horns, beautifully hooked at the ends. In the evening near camp in the rocky ground, I heard shouting among the servants and what I took to be a donkey rushed down into the glade where I was standing with Deria Hassan. He said: 'Dofar,' (pig) and I rested my rifle against the upright stem of a tree (a fatal thing to do and a fruitful source of misses owing to the recoil being delayed by friction on one side throwing the muzzle over to the right or left) and fired – first a miss then a hit and the dofar lay in all its ugliness on the short grass – ugly but how I admired it! My shikari would not touch it, nor the knife I had used to cut off its head.

Saunders and I next morning went after another dofar, but being too keen I insisted on firing and spoilt his shot. Next morning I went eastward to Gurkayer, another koppie, and in a sandy nook where a stream gurgled between bright green reeds I saw the broad track of a huge lion, the first lion track I had seen. I wounded a gerenouk and ran after it over the undulating rocky ground till I nearly fell exhausted, and then, finding it standing with haunches behind a tree stem, shoulders clear of it in front, I fired at the shoulder and finished it. Another head to bring home! Saunders had got one too. How we compared! I got a great liking for hunting this curiously slender antelope and soon came to understand its peculiar symmetry and the strong character of its appearance. It is the animal that gives the bulk of everyday Somali sport, for it is more often seen in marching than any other and once one has understood its habits it is not too difficult to hit.

The Garbadir forest was cut through by dry river beds with scarped banks of red sand, overhung by the beautiful guda thorn trees giving a delightful shade. The people were civil and obliging, and Deria Hassan seemed to be a great favourite with the old women who minded the donkeys and goats: a good thing, for there is nothing like an old woman for showing one pig! The wart-hogs root up the ground for nuts near the well and the old women go to draw water, hence the propinquity of the old women and pigs.

Deria Hassan pointed to some moving bush and I got the .577 to my hip and my finger crooked ready to steal to the trigger but I waited, saying

I would not fire till I knew what I was firing at. The excitement grew. Deria whispered: '*Maro*,' (shoot) in Hindustani but still I declined. A rustle and up jumped a dark object. I stood motionless, my finger twitching, then I saw clearly the object which went down and rose again. *Oh Deria, Deria*! It was an old woman gathering sticks for her man's fire! Lucky I didn't shoot! I told Deria he would lose his 'backshish' (present) if he ever did that again.

Another old women came to Saunders and offered to show us, for backshish, a dead pig. When Saunders and I had gone after a pig a day or two before, I had spoiled his shot. There was blood on the stones, and we had followed the pig up a rocky path into a network of thorns, finally pulling up at the mouth of a low cave into which Deria Hassan would insist on crawling, spear in hand, to look for the pig. He came out, unable to see the animal, and we gave up the chase. The old woman now led us in the direction of this previous hunt, and there, outside the same cave, lay my wart-hog, dead, having been hit by my hurried shot and since come out to die. I gave the old lady eight annas for finding the pig.

This part of the country was owned by the Aysa Musa, Hali Awal, always civil to travellers and owning plenty of cattle. They gave us milk and sheep in plenty, and excellent mutton it was. Saunders shot some beautiful guinea fowl, if I remember rightly, on this trip. They are found in all the forest where the guda tree and aloes are present and are a prominent feature of all Somali journeys. While in camp at Armaleh Garbadir we often heard the spotted hyena howl round the camp at night, and a dismal long-drawn note it was, ending in a squeal. Among birds, there were vultures, small partridges, the ever-present kites and crows. Some of the small birds were of very brilliant plumage.

Towards the end of the fourth day at Armaleh our camp began to present the appearance of a hunting camp. Vultures and kites abounded on the flat-topped trees around, scraps of meat were drying in the sun over the sleeping place of the native camp followers and trophies were to be seen about the camp in all stages of preparation: pigs' skulls in ants' nests; gazelle skulls in buckets of cold water with the horns sticking out in the air; skins spread out to dry in the shade, hair side down, a paste of alum and wood ashes rubbed into the exposed side.

Each morning before dawn we sailed out dressed in khaki, sometimes east or west along the foot of the Golis spurs, sometimes straight up the hill above camp, in brambles and rocks, looking for pig, and often out into the plains to the south-east and north-west looking for the gerenouk in the flat glades of short grass under the lovely guda thorn trees, with an occasional search for a leopard along the base of the small koppies of granite which dominated the forest.

Deimolah Wein,[1] the hill like the Matterhorn which had so struck us when marching through Lau, lay out in the level forest to the north of us in the centre of the broken interior plain, majestic each morning with a wreath of white mist for a necklace. As we left camp each day, the dew was hanging on every twig, making the jungle glitter as if festooned with diamonds. Lovely flowers of the Aruns creeper hung curtained from the branches of the guda trees, making a perfect midday retreat for the children and goats. By Major Heath we had been led to expect elephants, but four days was not long enough; they had gone, the Aysa Musa said, to the plateau at the top of Golis, for some reason, though we had been assured the cold would drive them down. Elephants never are where they are wanted at the right season and the native explanations are contradictory.

We had now seen the country which had been shot over by Major Heath and Monks and had tasted the charm of it, and had plenty of pleasant experiences with which to confirm their opinion of the Sportsman's Paradise when we should return to Aden. My bag was two pig, five Wallor's gazelles, six Pelzelus' gazelles, a total of thirteen; and Saunders got nearly the same value for his trip. For me, the wonderful mystery and charm of the country and of the sport had sunk deep, and this was to be the first of a series of journeys here lasting thirteen years.

We got back to Aden by the Egyptian steamer *Khedivi*, walking across the backs of the closely packed sheep to get to the companion ladder and mount to the Egyptian captain's little deck-house. At Aden, Saunders introduced me to a gunner who undertook to cure the trophies.

1 Lit. 'The great place of deima trees.'

Chapter 2

With Walsh to inspect a police post
7th May, 1885

BULAR, a small Somali village forty-two miles west of Berbera, of which I had never heard before, had been inundated by the coast rains about Christmas time, and Walsh came over to Aden soon afterwards on business connected with Berbera. While at Aden he asked me to come over with him and look at the Egyptian police post there, reported to have been washed away by the inundation. A suggestion had been made to have the post repaired by sappers and miners. I was placed on a few days' leave, and went over with Walsh to Berbera by steamer. We then took a bagala and shipped a stout reliable Somali, by name Mahomed Dosa (called Dosa, I believe, because he could eat a sheep at a sitting). He was a great help to Walsh and appeared to be his right-hand man.

We anchored outside the shallow water where there is a sandspit exposed at low tide, separated from the shore by a lagoon half a mile wide.

A great brown plain of thorn bush backed by blue hills, comparatively low and forming a circle round the plain of twenty miles radius. To the west, near the coast, a group of sharp high peaks called Elmas (possibly two thousand feet high or more). In the foreground, a tiny mat village, three or four whitewashed rubble blockhouses situated as detached forts to protect the village from the inland tribes, very turbulent here; between the village and the sea, a long line of yellow beach fringed by white breakers. A mile to the east, some waving date palms.

A lovely and mysterious plain, a vast sea of thorn bush, nearly flat but rising to the mountains gradually, varied by scattered glades. To the west, for the first few miles near the coast, a prairie of open grass, level near the sea, undulating and sprinkled with low bush about a mile inland. Such was Bulhar, to be in future my residence for many months.

Walsh and I landed in a surf boat at high tide and had our servants and bedding brought to the little white police 'chowkie', dirty and full of rats and cockroaches, close to the village, separated from it by a dry creek. In the evening we wandered about and chose a site for huts or 'pendals' for troops, to be erected by the Madras Sappers. We then retired to rest in our uncomfortable quarters, proposing a hunt for 'aoul' on the morrow.

My first aoul hunt, when I went out into the plain with Walsh, was unsuccessful. We saw about fifteen aoul, of a light yellowish fawn colour, male and female alike having horns, grazing on the open undulating grassy plain, and in my eagerness, as we crept up to them stooping low under the shelter of a swell in the ground, I fired too soon, thereby spoiling Walsh's shot. I missed of course and it was not the only miss by any means during those hot days.

But next morning, going out alone with one of Walsh's Somali policemen as shikari, I managed to wound a buck aoul and started to run after it at the top of my speed at about noon in the very hot May weather. At last the aoul stopped to rest under a bush, I being under another. I got in a shaking hurried shot with the .577 and the aoul sank, to rise no more. I was so done I positively could not go to him at once but threw myself down upon the dry scorched grass gasping. Then I walked up and saw my prize, a beautiful aoul buck with graceful lyrate horns about fifteen inches long, beautifully ringed. They are longer and thinner and perhaps more graceful than the horns of the gerenouk but both antelopes have a very distinct character. I gave many a view-helloa before my shikari, who had lost me in the undulations of the ground, could come up with a knife to perform the Mohammedan 'halal' and mutter the Mohammedan 'Bismillah'. We carried the aoul back to the police hut where Walsh was busy hearing complaints of robberies from the village people, who were mostly of the Ayyal Yunis tribe. Some chiefs mounted on sturdy little ponies, their saddlery covered with red tassels, had ridden in from the interior to see Walsh and very wild-looking they were.

We got into our dhow and were just weighing anchor when a policeman arrived from Berbera with news of the French flag having been hoisted at Dongarita, seventy miles to the westward. We divided a tin of sardines and some biscuits and parted, Walsh and Mahomed Dosa, with revolvers, on ponies with pillows strapped on instead of saddles, to ride one hundred sixty miles and return to Berbera with the offending flag if possible. I, to return quietly by dhow.

Chapter 3

With the Sappers at Bulhar

Auol bucks at play

THE SAPPERS arrived at Bulhar on 27th September 1885, to carry out the work of building huts for the Native Infantry to be stationed there. A dhow full of materials had been sent on, containing poles, lime, etcetera. We came ourselves in the I.M.S. (Indian Marine Ship, as it was called then) *Amberwitch*, in which I was to make many voyages. We were about thirty-five strong: myself, a subadar, jemadar and thirty-three rank. We pitched camp on some open ground near the police hut (built by Egyptians) which had been rendered ruinous by the floods, and which was to be supplemented by long huts of Zanzibar rafters (rough poles) and bamboo trellis filled in with lime to form the walls. We started a brick kiln for making a defence wall surrounding the quadrangle of huts, and burnt our own bricks, finding good clay in the small nullah bed close by. At this time Bulhar was almost empty but we used to have war-scares – we heard incidentally that ten thousand men were coming down from the mysterious mountains of the interior to attack us. So the subadar and I went out onto the plain to reconnoitre and devise a scheme for defence and we made a clearing round the camp. But things went peacefully on, the only incident during the next few weeks of any importance being another flood, which drowned us out. I found a sentry standing at his post knee-deep in water, and the men all groping about with torches looking for boots, clothes and accoutrements. When, after some three weeks, the work had made considerable progress, I was able to leave it sometimes in the afternoons, and used to go out with my shikari, Ali Hursi, of the Sheridone clan of the Ayyal Yunis sub-tribe of the Habr Awal, into the flat bush-covered plain to look for hares, bustard, dik-dik, antelope, oryx and aoul. We looked long and anxiously for oryx, sometimes going out before dawn, walking about five miles out into the bush, and returning in time for working parade, but at first I was uniformly unsuccessful.

Of tracks there were plenty; fine large tracks, well defined in the dewy sand, well pressed-down showing the weight of the animals. Every moment I used to hope to see these grand animals themselves and the longer the supreme pleasure of seeing them, and perhaps getting a shot, was deferred, the more keen I became. Of dik-dik antelopes there were plenty and a few bustard. It was when firing at a bustard that I disturbed a party of robbers from the hills of the interior, who had come down to sweep the Bulhar plain for camels.

I had gone out at about two p.m. and had walked on and on through the flat bush country and glades of sandy soil, with an occasional tuft of grass. I had fired at a dik-dik and a bustard, missing the latter, with a .577 rifle and turned to go home. It was about four p.m. As we neared Bulhar and emerged from the thick bush, we saw a crowd of about one hundred and fifty Ayyal Yunis with spears and shields advancing over the plain towards us at a quick pace.

Two or three came on running and shouting, and I recognised Walsh's friend Mahomed Dosa who had come to Bulhar for a few days. It appears Walsh had sent some police to Bulhar to look out for raiders of the Abdul Ishak who had made a descent on Berbera and taken some camels away from the Ayyal Ahmed tribe. The Bulhar people knew the direction raiders were likely to take, and as I had gone in shooting right across the line of retreat, the village people had come out to bring me in.

I took a few men and went back on my footsteps, and coming to where I had fired at the bustard, we continued on into the bush. We had only gone thus for six hundred yards or so when we found tracks of horsemen going south-west, and it was here that the raiders had heard my shot and made off at a gallop, thinking the police were come up with them. It would have been awkward if, instead of retiring, they had taken it into their heads to advance, for I had been alone with Ali Hursi and besides my Express there was only his spear. A few days later I got a note from Walsh upbraiding me for 'frightening away his robbers' whom he had made such elaborate arrangements to catch.

Bulhar was now (at the beginning of October) beginning to fill up for the brisk trade season. The plain became covered with flocks and their attendant women and children and herds of camels, some quite young with soft hair, and though there were plenty of aoul, it became almost unsafe to shoot with a rifle. Far out, however, on the oryx ground (at least eight miles from Bulhar) the plain was still uninhabited, and I had one or two hunts there, getting up at three in the morning to go there in time to get back for the daily work at the coast. Young grass was springing up everywhere from the recent rain and tracks abounded.

With the arrival of the trading caravans and pasturing flocks at Bulhar for the season, there also came from Berbera Mr. David Morrison, Deputy Assistant Political Agent, and a small force of Somali police. Morrison was thenceforth the magistrate in charge of Bulhar for many years until his sad death in '91 of sunstroke. It was a great boon to have the society of another European after the somewhat solitary time I had been having.

Morrison and I occupied the two ends of the Residential hut, one of the new quarters which the Sappers had built, and there was another open hall between the two ends which we used as a dining and sitting room. Here Morrison also heard cases and settled disputes, so I saw a good deal of the natives and made the acquaintance of many of the Ayyal Yunis chiefs who came to see Morrison on tribal matters – ankal or akils, they are called, i.e. wise men (Arabic).

Morrison and I rode about the plain a good deal together and one night we sat up for hyenas near the outskirts of the village, but without result as we could only shoot in one direction for fear of hitting someone if we fired anywhere towards the village. These animals (the spotted hyena) swarmed around Bulhar at night and made the dark hours hideous with their howls. They stole children and in one case killed an old woman while I was there. Curiously enough, she had been badly bitten by a hyena when a girl, in the thigh. Jackals were also very numerous about the Bulhar Plain and some of the patches of bush stank of them. I wounded an aoul one day and lost it, and next day I saw it not far from the spot where I had lost it, sitting in the open with a circle of half a dozen jackals crouched in the longer patches of grass about a hundred yards away, watching it.

On some evenings enormous flights of sand grouse came to the open grass plains near the sea, at the wells three and a half miles west of the town, to feed. Their cry is peculiar – you hear 'tuka-tuka-tuka' then 'tuka-tuka' and look up and see them flying overhead. When they have decided to come to the ground they drop very suddenly after slanting down for some distance.

In one of my wanderings to the oryx ground I came upon a scene which quite changed my tactics in regard to the hunting of this glorious animal. With my two hunters I was plodding along straight through the flat sandy bush country some eight miles from Bulhar inland, looking, as usual, for oryx, when I came upon a dozen men standing under a tree, and was furiously attacked by a lot of pariah dogs. Going up to the tree, I saw the magnificent head of a bull oryx, with grand rapier horns nearly three feet long, standing against the trunk of the tree, freshly severed, while at a fire the men were roasting the flesh. Others were cutting up the carcase and throwing scraps to the quarrelling dogs. Occasionally a dog which was too forward received a kick in the ribs from a naked foot.

These people, I found, were Midgans, the inferior outcast race of Somaliland, who live by hunting. They make shields from the thick hides over the withers of the bull oryx. We were not long in making friends of the Midgans, and they promised to take us out oryx hunting with them next day if I would sleep in their kraal and start at 3 a.m. for the shooting grounds. This I did, with my two hunters and my cook, taking nothing and sleeping on a blanket spread upon camel mats in the Midgan kraal out upon the Bulhar Plain.

We woke at 2.30 a.m., silently loaded the camel and got off without waking the people in the kraal, and at early dawn had reached oryx ground some ten miles from Bulhar, where my new Midgan friends assured me we should find oryx. It was not, however, till the afternoon that we came upon any. We had rested from our search while I had some sandwiches and cold tea. One of the shikaris was up a thorn tree, where I had put him to watch for oryx, when suddenly he stopped his afternoon prayers and jumped down from the tree, running and pointing and snapping his fingers and whistling to the dogs. They all followed, and the rest of the men coming up, we were soon in full swing and after running for some minutes through thorny bush, till I was nearly beat, we entered a glade whither we had been attracted by the barking of our dogs in front. There, at the further side of the glade, were about fifteen oryx at bay, charging the dogs which were trying to get at an oryx calf. As we got to the edge of the glade, coming up silently but at a great pace, the Midgans let off a flight of poisoned arrows, apparently aiming for the calf, for that was all they got, while I, aiming hurriedly at the shoulder of the nearest, dropped it in its tracks. It turned out to be a cow, but as the cows have horns as long as and generally slightly longer than the bulls, it is very difficult to tell them apart. The wounded calf got away for a time, but it was afterwards pulled down by the dogs. We then returned to Bulhar with the trophy.

About four days after this I went out again with the same family of Midgans and the same dogs, this time to Jebel Elmas, about fifteen miles from Bulhar, a mountain with several bold peaks overlooking the sea. We saw a good many herds of aoul in the open ground beyond Dimis, and we passed Elmas in rear, leaving it between us and the sea, and as we skirted the base of the mountains we passed several gorges running up to the peaks on our right. At the head of one of these we saw some oryx but they saw us at the same time and were off over a spur. We followed at top speed, the usual whistling on of the dogs and snapping of fingers beginning the chase, for the dogs must view the game, generally, before they will begin to hunt. This was a fearful run, the sun being very hot, at about 11 a.m., and I was utterly exhausted when we came up to the herd and so shaky I could not hold the rifle steady. They were at bay on a saddle of the mountain, between a spur and the main mass, the dogs barking around them. But, as is usual, directly we showed ourselves the herd scattered in every direction like a bursting shell. I fired at a bull standing broadside on and only twenty yards away and felt fairly steady but missed for some unaccountable reason, probably the severe run I had made and the sweat pouring into my eyes obscured my view. One calf passed me within a yard as he galloped full speed down the spur.

As we returned to Bulhar in the afternoon we rested under a tree and waited for the cool of night before continuing our march. It was a large tree (I forget the variety) and its position at the eastern base of Elmas Mountain is impressed on my memory from what occurred there two nights afterwards.

This tree was the scene of a horrible murder, as two days after my visit to Elmas, sixteen people of all ages and sexes were murdered whilst sleeping under it.

My hunter Hirsi, who belonged to the clan which had suffered, promptly asked for leave to go to the interior to see his sick father who, he said, had suddenly and unaccountably been taken ill. This afterwards proved to be incorrect, for Ali Hirsi, being the son of an akil or elder of the clan, had found it necessary to answer to the family call to arms.

My friend Morrison soon found his hands full with this feud between the two clans of the Sheridone Yunis, Habr Awal, which were called respectively Boho Sheridone and Ba-Gadabursi Sheridone. As trade stops in feud time, it became Morrison's duty to restore the peace.

A few days after Morrison's arrival, a messenger came running in at dawn one morning to say that the Boho had seized the Bulhar Wells, three miles west of the town, and were that morning going to be attacked by the Ba-Gadabursi from Elmas, each side about five hundred strong. Morrison and I, with his interpreter and a sapper muleteer, rode out to dissuade the Ba-Gadabursi from attacking. At the wells we came upon the Boho halted. Here was Ali Hirsi, my hunter, sporting a 'khaili' tobe and with a good nag decked out in war saddlery and red tassels grazing knee-haltered close by. He came cheerily up, no longer a servant, and shook hands. Asked after the sick papa, he said with a bland smile that he had got well again and he pointed to where an old grey-beard, Hirsi Ali, sat crouched, shield and spears in hand, a boy holding his horse, also covered with red tassels.

We rode on crossing a bare undulating plain, over which we had often shot sand-grouse and hunted aoul, and a mile beyond the Boho were the Ba-Gadabursi, actually advancing to the attack! It was a stirring scene! About two hundred horsemen and three hundred spearmen on foot were advancing in a long line facing to the east, coming towards us. The horsemen formed the left wing, along the flat sandy plain which stretched down to the raised sea-shore bank on our right, which, though we could hear their roar, hid from our view the white breakers of the Gulf of Aden beating upon the yellow sand. On our left the plain rose to low sand dunes covered with scrub and grass, and along these came the right wing, the footmen, extended at a pace apart, in a good line, each carrying his shield and spears and wearing his white tobe wound round his waist. Most of the horsemen wore the red and blue 'khaili' tobe. The plain over which we had ridden stretched behind us to Bulhar, four miles to the rear.

Our party of four cantered to meet this array. Now and then a horseman darted out from the line and scurrying round in a circle, threw his spear and picked it up again while at full speed. As we approached they set up a battle song, to show us, I suppose, the business for which they had collected, but they stopped when Morrison rode up to one of the ankal[1] and demanded a halt. There was angry shouting and the crowd of horsemen pressed round us in a dense mass, arguing and gesticulating so that we could only extricate ourselves by showing our pistols. They now saw we were in earnest about the business we had come upon, and the elders turned to the crowd and exhorted them to hear, at any rate, what the 'Sirtol' (Indian 'Sirk ar') or Government, had to say to them. There was a man called Warsama Dryal, 'Good news from the fight', who, though a noted firebrand and a distinguished chief, did us good service in getting us a hearing.

When quiet was restored, Morrison, by the help of his interpreter, explained that if an armistice could be agreed upon he would try and arbitrate about the blood money due, etcetera. He only wanted them to put off the attack for a day and if after that they decided to fight, they might do so provided

Spoiling for a fight

1 Ankal = elders.

they fought nowhere near Bulhar or the caravan routes. Meanwhile I sent in Khoda Bux, the muleteer, for my thirty Madras Sappers and this sporting Punjabi boy started off on his four-mile ride. A Ba-Gadabursi brave galloped close on the heels of his mule, till headed off by Morrison with a pistol. About this time, seeing the infantry creeping forward, I took Warsama Dryal and cantered off to stop them. When they saw me on a kicking mule, with a revolver which I had forgotten to put in its holster, waving vaguely in the air, and old Warsama excitedly yelling at them, they began to laugh and good-naturedly squatted down on their heels, the butts of their spears firmly planted in the ground, blinking over their shields and the line of hillocks in front which hid the wells, and the Boho, from view. They begged me to let them advance fifty yards 'just to the top of the next rise', so that they might see the Boho, for they were thirsty and sick of drinking camel's milk and the sight of the wells would do them good! They did not want to hurt any Englishmen, all they desired was just to wipe out the Boho; it was so little to ask, so easy to grant.

Morrison at last got the elders to agree to send back the clan bodily to Eil Sheikh, themselves coming into Bulhar under our escort to try and hold a meeting with the Boho 'dukal'. After a long delay, the Sappers came out at about nine o'clock, and a dozen elders accepted our escort through the Boho line. I extended a section on either side, marching in single file, while Morrison and the elders rode bunched up in the middle. We passed the Boho line in this order, having sent the interpreter on to explain. The Boho looked savagely at our protegés but were too level-headed to attack us for the sake of slitting the throats of a few ankal, so not a horse was mounted and all passed serenely.

Arrived at Bulhar, Morrison rode out and brought in the Boho elders, and after two days' talking in a tent outside Morrison's hut, the feud was temporarily settled, though it broke out again a week later, giving Morrison an infinity of trouble and anxiety. Twice my little force was called out in aid of the civil power, as we had to turn the Ba-Gadabursi out of their huts and pull them down, Morrison having ordered the tribe away. I was lucky enough to notice a Mullah dancing and preaching to a crowd of men watching our work and I promptly jumped on him with the aid of two Sappers and took away his sword ('bilawa') and made him a prisoner. I had him round the waist when I saw his skinny old hand clawing among his folds of tobe for his bilawa, and only seized his wrist and got possession of the weapon just in time.

Morrison ordered the tribes to live apart, the Ba-Gadabursi fourteen miles to the west of Eil Sheikh, the Boho fifteen miles to the east at Geri, the elders meeting occasionally at Bulhar for a conference. It was only a question of blood money, but what a question! We always knew how things were going, for when relations were a bit strained the two semicircles of old men,

A herd of Oryx

seated on the ground, would shroud their faces in the ends of their tobes, allowing only a slit to look through and adding the supreme insult of shading their eyes with their hands when they looked at the opposite side. When things were improving they looked their enemies frankly in the face.

About this time it was found necessary to have some of the neighbouring country surveyed. Walsh and Morrison had many murder and robbery cases to settle, but as they took place up country and the interior was unmapped and unvisited by white men, a little surveying was necessary to give some idea in settling these cases.

We decided to begin with the Bulhar Plain, and I had many tramps with the Sappers and a rope chain carried on poles which I had invented so as to clear the low 'khansa' thorn bushes, making our base a hill called Gerigoan, fourteen miles from Bulhar, to which we 'chained' twice. Finding, however, this work unsuitable to the requirement of the case, I arranged with the Resident at Aden to allow me to take as survey escort part of a detachment of Aden troop which had just come to Bulhar. I took fifteen Sabres and started on a week's mounted reconnaissance straight into the interior through the mountains, by way of the Issutugan River, the main route to Hargeisa, a mullah town we had heard of as lying a hundred miles due south. Its other name is 'Little Harar'. But where all was unvisited by white men, our information was very vague, resting as it did on euphemistic Somali gossip. This Aden troop trip was the first important journey of exploration of a long series I was afterwards to make in the country.

Somali water-hán, milk vessels, bow and quiver etc.

It was about December 1st 1885 that I started on this trip, but first it is necessary to describe a chase after robbers I made with the Aden troop. One day Morrison and I got news of a raid into the edge of the Bulhar Plain, by the Jibril Abokr, I think, and we got off at once with fifteen Aden troop. When we had ridden a quarter of the way across the plain, seventeen miles across in this direction, we saw a hunting leopard disappear in the grass, and as we were nearing Selei, at the edge of the plain, I turned back and remarked to Morrison: 'Someone is lighting a big pipe in Bulhar.' A column of smoke was visible, black smoke, issuing straight up from the site of the town, which is built mainly of matting and bamboo. Morrison rode back at once to find the town levelled and in ashes, and had to convict twenty people of theft of property during the fire, which was quite an accidental one. With the Aden troop, I held on my way to Selei, a beautiful gorge where the Bulhar Plain runs up into the mountains. The river bed was strewn with white pebbles and these in the evening light contrasted strongly with the sombre frowning hills and dark thorn bushes. We tethered the ponies in line beside a rippling stream at dusk and went out to look for tracks, but instead of tracks of looters, the only evidence of human occupation was an old woman and a donkey laden with water-hans.[2] Next morning we rode back into Bulhar, stiff after our dewy bivouac without tents.

---

2 Hans = the local name for water (or milk) containers.

Chapter 4

Up the Issutugan
Seven days hard forced marching

(See Route Plan R1 – Appendix 1)

THE TRIP to the Issutugan, or Straight River ('tug' meaning a river) began about 1st December 1885. It was the first of a long series of mountain reconnoitring survey trips and, being the first, its every scene lives vividly in the memory.

On the first day, going about four and a half miles, mounted, with fifteen Suvars of the Aden Troop under Rissaldar Abdullah Khan and with the dogs' rations up and fodder on fast Aden camels permanently attached to the Aden Troop, we made So Midgan, twenty three miles from Bulhar, in two marches, one in the morning and one in the afternoon.

The Aden Troop is a force of Indian Cavalry (embodied, I believe, as an offshoot of the Central India Horse), very smart. Stationed permanently at Khor Maksar, about five miles from Aden, an outpost protecting Aden from attack by the Arab tribes and situated at the junction of the flat isthmus of sand with the mainland of Arabia. The Aden Troop make many expeditions into the interior of Arabia, keeping caravan routes open and punishing turbulent tribes. Nice fellows they were, the picture of what Indian soldiers are at their best, tall and slight, very intelligent and gentlemanly looking with the best manners in the world.

During the morning march across the bush-covered Bulhar Maritime Plain, a suvar let his pony go at one of the short halts and failed to catch him. Off it went with an Aden Troop saddle and holsters containing a pair of pistols. The Rissaldar detached two troopers and some Somalis to recover the pony and continued the march.

We halted at noon near the shoulder of the hill 'Gerigoan' (literally 'solitary hill'), a landmark I had noted in my surveys of the Plain with the Sappers, and a point in the bush for which I had often steered when oryx-hunting out in the distant parts of the plain. It is very barren but overlooks the broad bed of the Issutugan River where it emerges with a grand breadth of eight hundred yards from the Maritime Mountains to curve over the Bulhar Plain and reach the sea at Geri, fifteen miles east of Bulhar.

When I say reach the sea, no water is visible above ground lower than So Midgan, twenty-three miles inland. There are only brackish wells at Geri.

Our noon camp at Gerigoan was very hot, as is the whole of the Maritime Plain at this time of day, and the march up the dry broad sandy bed of the Issutugan, between earth (or sand) banks about eight feet high, was simply boiling. There is no water after leaving Bulhar till you reach So Midgan, twenty three miles inland. I was surveying, so had no time to look for game, indeed I got none of any importance this trip. The trip was none the less exciting, for it was my first exploring trip and I had, being still only two and twenty, the whole responsibility of the journey, absolute freedom of movement and absolute control of the escort of Indian Cavalry, in a country unknown to Europeans, but known to be infested with wild raiding tribes, almost constantly at war with one another. The prospect of being the first to explore this new country filled me with delight and awakened my faculties. At that time we believed Somaliland to be the desert home of bigoted and ferocious savages. Happily it has proved not to be so, but if it had been, I am sure my Aden Troop escort would have been the first to find it out and to prove in our own persons that it was so.

On the second day we marched over a saddle in the hills, avoiding the almost impassable narrow gorge of the Issutugan, and descended into the river again at a reed bed named Alalo Dadab ('alalo' meaning reeds). On the way, on trap rock formations, very arid, we had seen a beautiful herd of wild asses, which followed us with the greatest curiosity, but I did not fire as I was not keen on killing them. At least, I don't remember having fired but I think I allowed one of the Aden Troop to try a shot. At Alalo Dadab, or just before it, were very bad quicksands, the stream there flowing over sunken rocks and the sand being held in suspension just above them. The ponies sank nearly up to their girths in the wet sand and the camels showed great nervousness.

We ascended by an awfully rocky pass into the mountains again, among weird scenery, the peaks showing interesting shapes, some flat, some pointed, evidently the result of denudation on a large scale. We caught a glimpse of a grand bull kudu climbing a rocky hill but he was going hard away and had seen us. I ran after him and nearly broke my heart with disappointment in losing him, for he disappeared in the intricate labyrinth of hills. He was the first of this grand antelope I had seen, and it was to be more than a year before I was to see another, in spite of my extended wanderings over hundreds of miles of country. This vision of the bull kudu filled me with desire to shoot one and hang his horns upon my walls.

The camp at Gal Hedigaleh (star gully) was on a lovely island in the wide sandy bed of the river with beautiful spreading thorn trees overhead.

Half a mile up the river was a well in the rocks, forming a pool twenty feet wide. Gal Hedigaleh takes its name from the fact that the stars can be seen reflected in the pool, a thing unusual in Somali wells as they are generally small and deep.

On the third day we marched over much the same country, now over shoulders of the wild hills through which the Issutugan cuts, now dipping down to cross the sandy stream bed itself, to a moderately wide wooded valley called Aleyalaleh, a favourite home for that much-sought-for Somali game, the African elephant. A beautifully wooded valley it was, at the edge of which our camp was made.

On the fourth day we left the river at Aleyalaleh and marched over the barren Damel Plain, all trap rock having the appearance of having been rained on by a shower of black stones, to Eil Demet. Here we again struck the river at a very pretty spot. There was plenty of water running over the sand in a stream and a huge fig tree to shelter my party from the sun. What added to the interest of the river bed here and its tributaries, was that there were plenty of lion-tracks printed fresh in the soft damp sand. I spent the afternoon searching for lions but without success. I should mention that back at Gal Hedigaleh, at dusk, I had gone out alone to look for gerenouk (Waller's gazelle), which I had been so successful with at Armaleh Garbadir early in the year. When I came to a small tributary stream, I found in the reeds the tracks of eight lions together, of all ages and sizes. They looked so fresh that I examined one to see whether the water was still oozing into it or not. At Eil Demet it was just the same, but the lions were impossible to find. They wander up and down the open sandy river beds at night and lie up in the larger patches of reeds by day. They feed on oryx and kudu and pig, of which there are plenty on the banks of this river, higher up towards Hargeisa.

We had now cut through the Maritime Hills and emerged onto the open Damel Plateau, a part of the Interior Plain between the Maritime Range and the Great Ghauts. Here, however, owing to the Damel Plateau being canted up towards the south, the Interior Plain rises gradually to Hargeisa, which is five thousand feet above sea level, and there are no sudden ghauts like Golis further east, behind Berbera.

On the fifth day we returned north-west over the Damel Plain to Dararweina, some miles west of Aleyalaleh, in order to return to Bulhar by the Dowai Route, leaving the Issutugan two days' march to the east. Dara Dowanleh is a small stream cutting a deep gorge in the trap plateau and is very remarkable, the gorge being half a mile wide and very abrupt. We saw a herd of oryx as we approached Dara Dowanleh, but as the only animal within range was a calf, I did not fire.

We went to Dowai on the sixth day by a steep descent of some two thousand feet and on the way we disturbed some guineafowl and I shot one.

One the seventh day we made a morning march to Selei, the scene of my hunt after robbers from Bulhar some weeks before. From Selei, where we halted at noon, we made an afternoon march across the Bulhar Plain and arrived at Bulhar after a march of seven days and one hundred and twenty miles, the whole route being surveyed in detail. I found Morrison well and laying out new streets in Bulhar, with the aid of the Sappers, in place of the old crooked narrow lanes of the burnt town.

Chapter 5

The Bulhar Fights
January, 1886

AFTER THE Issutugan trip I returned to Aden to prepare for further explorations in the Habr Awal country, and at the end of December 1885, arrived at Bulhar with three suvars of the Aden Troop (Duffedar Goolshere Khan, Hurmut Shere Khan and Sheikh Hussein), mounted Punjabi Police raised for the purpose, and ten sepoys of the Bombay Infantry, in all a survey escort of twenty-five men.

Although we were ready to start the survey by January 1st, the Bulhar tribes were in such a disturbed state that Morrison, finding it necessary to utilise whatever troops came to hand, was obliged, in his official capacity of Magistrate in charge of Bulhar, to ask me to remain and give him the benefit of the services of my little force till the tribes should have become more settled.

The Sheridone feud had broken out again, and some of the Boho having managed to get into Bulhar to buy food, the Ba-Gadabursi were reported to be coming in from Eil Sheikh, fifteen miles away, to attack them in Bulhar. Morrison promptly sent out notice that if they did come they would be fired at.

One morning, soon after this, while Morrison and I were at breakfast in the little verandah of the Bulhar quarters, news came in that the Ba-Gadabursi array was actually in sight, advancing to attack the town from the Eil Sheikh direction, over the plains where we had often hunted sand grouse and where we had together stopped the fight near Dimis less than a month before.

I jumped on my pony and rode out alone to reconnoitre, and seeing the Ba-Gadabursi sure enough, within a mile of the town, with outlying scouts circling on the yellow sand only half a mile from the nearest huts, I turned round my pony and cantered back. Passing the sepoys' quarters I called out to the Duffedar to turn out my fifteen mounted men. When Morrison and I could get into our saddles, ready with revolvers, sword, etcetera, we found the Aden Troop and Mounted Police dressed in sleeping clothes and turbans, with cartridge belts hastily around their waists.

Thus accoutred, we crept out under the shelter of the town in Indian file, and when clear of the huts we deployed into single line in the open, and there in front were the Ba-Gadabursi, over a hundred in number mounted and a dozen or so on foot, advancing on the town. So we reined in and fired two irregular volleys from the saddle, the distance being seven hundred yards, then returning the carbines to their leather saddle-buckets, we drew swords and advanced at a gallop.

The Ba-Gadabursi halted at the first shots and their horsemen were soon lost to sight in the haze of the Maritime Plain, while those on foot, seeing themselves abandoned by their comrades, tried to hide in the long grass but were all caught by my men. Only one, a man run down on the plain by Sowar Sheikh Hussein of the Aden Troop, was slightly wounded by a sword point through the arm.

With the men were captured seventeen spears and several shields thrown away in their flight. The prisoners were given back theirs by Morrison the next day when he released them. The rest I kept as a memento of an interesting day.

The Ba-Gadabursi were quiet for a week after this, and then, on another morning, a man came running in to say that they were again coming in, in larger force, mostly on foot. Our ponies had all been knocked up scouting for hill raiders in the Selei direction on the previous day, so we called out all our available men on foot. Morrison took command of the fifteen dismounted policemen, while I collected my own survey Bombay Infantry sepoys (9th Bo. Inf.) and an infantry guard of the same regiment now at Bulhar, in all about thirty, and awaited the signal. We had arranged that if Morrison fired with the police, I should follow suit with the infantry.

While the Ba-Gadabursi were still quite a thousand yards away, Morrison, having drawn up the police party along the seashore, gave the signal by firing two volleys along the sea beach at the distant line of natives. They bolted at once, and I had a skirmish, running and firing for half an hour over two miles of grassy plain till they got so far away it was useless firing. I finally fired a dozen shots at a man in a white tobe, a small speck in the distance, at some one thousand two hundred yards. This turned out next day to have been old Warsama Dryal. I found great difficulty in preventing the men who lagged behind from firing past their comrades' heads in front, endangering their lives.

We found some fifteen men hiding in the grass and many spears, and a lance-naik of the Infantry saw two men out swimming in the surf, and, wading out with his rifle into the shallow water, he threatened to fire, with the result that he disarmed them both and marched them in front of him triumphantly into the town.

As I lingered looking at the fast-disappearing specks, I heard some low groans in a patch of grass close by, and going up with half a dozen sepoys, found a Somali of the Ba-Gadabursi clan sitting in the grass with a wounded foot, a bullet having passed through the instep under the bone. The sepoys rushed up to him calling out delightedly: '*Ek Admi Mila! Sahib! Ek Admi Mila!*' (We've got our man! We've got our man!) and the wretched man thought his last moment had come.

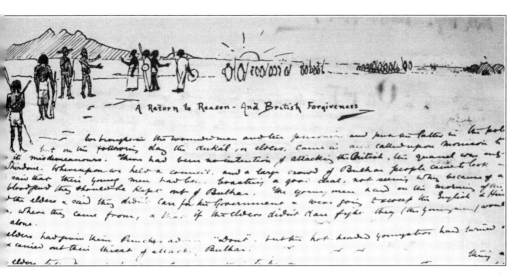

A return to Reason – and forgiveness

We brought in the wounded man and the prisoners, and put the latter in the police 'chowki' but on the following day the ankal came in and called upon Morrison to forgive the tribe its misdemeanours. There had been no intention of attacking the British, the quarrel was only with the Boho Sheridone. Whereupon we held a council and a large crowd of Bulhar people came to look on. The elders said that their young men had been boasting a good deal, not seeing why because of a trifling little blood feud they should be kept out of Bulhar. The young men had on the morning of the attack roused the elders and said they didn't care for the Government and were going to sweep the English and Hindis into the sea where they came from and that if the elders didn't dare fight, the young men would go and do it alone.

The elders had given them Punch's advice: 'Don't,' but the hot-headed youngsters had turned a deaf ear and carried out their threat of attacking Bulhar.

The elders told Morrison he had fired on their tribe, a thing not easy to be forgiven, but he hoped that there would be no further bloodshed (for they had taken away a few wounded with them) and that the boys would be quieter next time.

We made friends with the ankal, and old Warsama showed us a bullet splash on the blade of his spear which had been carried by an attendant during the fight of yesterday. I said nothing but remembered my ten shots at one thousand two hundred yards at the old man in a dazzlingly white tobe and thought he had had a very lucky escape!

Poor Warsama. A noted firebrand and a clever chief, he lost his life two years later through buying a French revolver. In a fight with the Boho, or the Ru Hared Fibril Aboker, another family of 'tough ones', he allowed his enemies to come to close quarters and then coolly drew his revolver. Being of cheap construction, it refused to revolve and he fell, sacrificed to his confidence in the white man's weapons!

The wounded got well and Morrison stopped the fighting for a while, only for it to break out again some months later.

Chapter 6

Survey to Argan, February 1886

(See Route Plan R2 – Appendix 2)

O N 1ST FEBRUARY, things were sufficiently quiet at Bulhar for us to start on the Government surveys. I had been appointed DAQMG and placed at the disposal of the Resident, Aden, to survey the Habr Awal country so as to aid the officials at Berbera, Zeyla and Bulhar by the production of a map which was to be of great service in adjudicating on raid, robbery and murder cases. These make up the bulk of the work before the officers in charge of the Somali Coast.

The party consisted of seventeen mounted police on Somali ponies (chiefly Somalis and a few Indians, three being Aden Troop drill instructors) and ten 9th Bombay Infantry. The latter I gave ten donkeys to ride or carry their valises on – Aden donkeys, and our baggage was on eighteen Aden hill camels, weedy delicate creatures, and they were tended by Arab camel-men of the Aden Troop. The Aden animals were not acclimatised to Africa, went very slowly and eventually, I believe, all died, if not during, then after my three trips. I had to shoot several of the camels myself and leave them on the road for the vultures. Since the above experience I have never imported any animals from Aden to Somaliland except the thoroughbred trotting camels which, if properly acclimatised by three months in the country, become invaluable.

On 1st February we set off to So Midgan, a distance of twenty-three miles. The intention had been to go in by So Midgan and Eil Anod to the Interior Plains and thence to strike through the Maritime Range to Berbera, a thing that had of course not yet been done by any white man. At this period, the German Lainer Menges, and James' party and that of Major Heath, had been the only travellers since Burton in the hinterland of Berbera and Bulhar. I omit Revoil because his journeys were along to Cape Guardafui, many hundred miles east, and were never far inland. I met Georges Revoil afterwards in Paris and a Somali opened his front door (this was in 1887), and on my asking '*Sircal Ki me?*' – Where is the sahib? – he collapsed into a grin, left the door open and yelled: 'Monsieur, a sahib from Somaliland,' and Revoil came out, gripped my arm and led me into his library and straightaway began doing the honours, his photos, his sketches, his curios; such is the freemasonry of travel!

On 2nd February we went to Eil Anod, a journey of ten miles. We expected to come upon the Habr Gerhajis tribe (this was the large tribe which had sent down defiant messages when first I camped with the Sappers to make the quarters at Bulhar, six months before). They were supposed to be mildly hostile to the British and addicted to raiding. As we passed the spurs of the Sarar-awr (camel back) plateau, on the way to Eil Anod, we saw the tops of the hills white with sheep and lined with men shouting down at us. They felt secure, for cavalry cannot climb hills. Later we came upon a karia (or kraal) with only a few women left in it, and they laughed and said all the men had run away, thinking we had come to loot them, and the women might mind their huts and property till they returned!

These women, finding us harmless, went and got their men, and the flocks were driven down into the plains again. This was a 'jilib' or family of the Habr Gurhajis (Abdullah Ishak clan) and soon an intelligent young man, who had lost one leg, came mounted on a pony; he bent over and shook hands with me. He was Deria Shire, son of Shire Sherimaki, an important elder of the Abdulla Ishak, whom I was to meet again when elephant hunting a year later and experience great hospitality at his hands. Of late I have heard more of Deria Shire, who, though well mannered, is a bloodthirsty scoundrel and a prince among looters of caravans. The last news I heard was that he had speared his old father through the leg!

Deria Shire came with us to the wells, situated in a river bed surrounded by thick guda jungle. He remarked that he was unaware of the object of our visit, that his clan were suspicious. No other white man had ever come here before and it was not apparent why I had brought soldiers.

The men at the wells received us with black looks, and taking possession of one well, we posted a sentry over it, reserving it for our own use. Deria Shire left us, warning me that he would not hold himself responsible for any actions of his tribe but he hoped we would leave them all alone. Meanwhile, my interpreter Sumunter, who, poor fellow (he was killed by a lion some years later when out with an English sportsman), got the 'funks' on board, and going down to the wells, came back with the alarming intelligence that he had reliable information we were to be attacked that night so I had better order a strong 'zeriba' to be made and not leave camp, or allow my men to do so.

There being game about, however, I determined to fortify the old zeriba we had occupied, leave fifteen men inside under the Duffedar, and sally out myself with the ten Bombay Infantry and walk the jungle for game. Making a circuit within two miles of camp, we returned in the evening with three hares and six dik-dik antelopes. As we entered the zeriba at dusk, carrying our game, we filed past a large guda tree, under which were collected a hundred and fifty men, all with spears and shields, and a few saddled ponies grazing. They took no further notice than to scowl at us as we passed. I came back from the zeriba with two sepoys and the unlucky Sumunter Shirmaki, and walking straight up to the crowd, used the usual Arab salutation: '*Salaam aleikum*', (peace be upon you). No answer for some time and then an old man with a white goatee beard and a wicked-looking bald skull, stared surlily and mumbled, '*Salaam*'. Then he lowered his gaze and spat on the ground and fell to absent-mindedly scratching the earth with bit of stick and then smoothing out the marks with his hands.

The crowd remained silent, sulky, and mischievous – some staring rudely, others shading their eyes with their hands or hiding their faces behind the folds of their tobes. My interpreter asked why I had been received so coldly – there was a pause before two old vulture-like ankal cleared their throats and looked at each other, then without rising one spoke. His spear shook more from hate than age and he said (beginning with '*Warya minki Frinji*', i.e. 'I say foreigner') he and his clansmen wanted to know why I had brought soldiers into the Habr Gerhajis country, whether to steal cattle, for if so we might go back as they had only sheep. There were plenty of cattle to be seen among the other tribes. We answered that we had come to see if trade routes were safe and report to the Resident at Aden. So, after a long discussion, the old man who had mumbled 'Salaam', becoming more friendly, said they didn't know what the word looting meant, had never looted a caravan in their lives, all the sub-tribes around looted, but his clan, oh dear no! I might tell the Government this. ('*Sirialki Wahetdrada*' – how well we know that phrase at the Coast Magistrates' courts). Though these were the worst of all looters, steeped in the blood of innocents, I promised to convey the message, and the old man became happier. Peace was now restored and though I had made all preparations for an attack, all passed off quietly, and before dawn, putting fuel on the fire – for it was cold – we warmed the handles of our spears in the cheerful blaze before starting, and bid a pleasant goodbye to the elders, filled nearly to bursting with new milk brought us by the women of the tribe.

We marched on 3rd February to Argan and camped under the fig tree of that name. Here a fearful thunderstorm came down upon us from the hills. We were camped between two forks of a dry mountain torrent, which the rain filled and left us encamped on an island. The hail was of great size, nearly as large as a pigeon's egg, and soon all our tents were blown flat on top of us. Our ponies got loose and careered about the country, not being recovered till nightfall. The water here was a pool in the torrent bed and all the ground was rocky. Hyenas disturbed us at night with their weird howls. We halted to do some more surveying and to dry our clothes and tents, which were heavy for the camels in their soaked condition; and on the 7th we marched to Abdal.

On this night hyenas came to the stream, at the sloping side of which our camp was pitched in thin forest. The crickets and bullfrogs suddenly stopped, and steps were heard of some animal coming down the opposite bank to the water. The men had woken me about 11 p.m. and I had come to sit by the sentry, rifle in hand, and watch the water.

Then I saw in the dim light a large animal and the sentry put grass on the fire, and by the light of the blaze, I fired. Down dropped the animal into the water, dead! A large spotted hyena. I had heard the lap-lap as it drank just before I pulled the trigger. Before morning another hyena came up our bank and stood only fifteen yards away. It was very dark and I fired and missed and it bolted. As it made off it looked so large that, having lions always in my thoughts, I mistook it for a lion. I saw another great yellow object still standing where the animal I had fired at had been and fired again at what was, I thought, a second lion. It proved to be a block of grey-yellow rock with my bullet mark in the centre!

On the 9th February we marched to Hedd through the same beautiful aloe country, and on the 10th to Dalaad, making a turn to the left as I intended to strike north-east to Berbera through the Hegebo Plateau. At Dalaad we found tracks of leopard. On the 12th we marched to Arroweina and on the 13th to Deringalolo. This is a curious and forbidding-looking gorge surrounded by flat plateaux of black trap rock, the tops of the plateaux being covered with black stones. The plateaux are cut through by river-beds some five hundred feet deep. At the edges of the escarpments are jagged rocks and thorn bush, and here the great kudu is occasionally to be found. There are also wild ass and oryx and below in the river beds are gazelles of different kinds. My men having tracked some kudu and arranged a hunt, I climbed to the top of the plateau from the Deringalolo gorge and walked across the flat plain on the top, over the black stones, stepping from stone to stone. Long tufts of feathery grass grew from between the stones. As I neared a horseshoe bend in the plateau my men, who were ahead, dropped onto the stones as if shot and beckoned to me. I ran crouching up, and there, across the gorge, were three grand kudu. I fired, and two made off across the open plateau, but the third jumped down into the gorge and tried to hide. I fired across and missed but the kudu sprang down in great bounds, crash! crash! crash!, and seeing a native, whom my shikaris had sent round early in the morning to stop the mouth of the gorge far below, he charged him. The native sprang out of the way, throwing his spear, but the kudu broke by and escaped. It is the only instance I had known a kudu charging, but we saw it very distinctly.

We next marched on the 15th February (the day before, the 14th, –

Valentine's Day – having been my birthday) to Malgui, a fearfully hot valley strewn with pebbles where a river bed had been. There was a little water here in wells several feet below the pebbly channel, but there were many tracks of wild asses and it would be interesting to know whether they climbed down into the well to drink or dispensed with water altogether.

On the 16th and 17th we marched to Baba, at the edge of the Berbera Maritime Plain and across it to Berbera, having made the second route survey which was to help us make a map of the Habr Awal country, and having been the first white man to go from Bulhar to Berbera by way of the interior plains.

I had now seen the Interior Plains in many parts and the charm of the forest of high guda thorn trees, with undergrowth of 'hig' and 'dar' aloes, had taken possession of me. Golis Range always rose blue above the guda trees in my memory and I only longed for the day when I should again wander through those wonderful Interior Plains and perhaps, with luck, bag a kudu. At that time we did not know of a great or lesser kudu but only of one kind, consequently the specimens of the latter we shot disappointed us, as we thought they were only young kudu. We were, however, to be later undeceived in this matter. At Berbera I put up with Walsh and refitted for another survey trip.

Chapter 7

Survey to Jerato and Syk
March, 1886

(See Route Plan R3 – Appendix 3)

A Herd of Plateau Gazelle

WE LEFT Berbera for the Interior Plains on March 15th and made a halt at Baba. Next morning we marched on to Malgui, seeing a beautiful specimen of the Somali wild ass (which I would not shoot) on the way, gazing down on the passing caravan from the slopes of the Hegebo Plateau.

At Deringalolo, camped in the centre of the gloomy gorge of that name, I shot a hyena in rather curious circumstances. I was woken up by the sentry at midnight saying hyenas were about and he led me into the Sowars' tent and told me that by lying down inside the tent and watching the fire from under the tent I would see a hyena come to the fire and warm himself!

This he actually did and as I shot him he fell among the glowing ashes. I cannot explain why he came to the fire – there may have been old bones thrown into it from the cooking – but that is the explanation the men gave. Next day as we marched, I found an oryx in the tamarisk bush in the river bed and followed it, wounded, a long distance and eventually bagged it. It proved to be a cow.

On 22nd March we went to Mandeira, threading our way along little paths between the lovely Sansaveria aloes, bright green and yellow, at some seasons carrying beautiful red and yellow flowers. In some places this aloe grew so thick it was impossible to move along the paths without spiking the ponies' legs and bellies as the aloes grew to some five feet and they give, as I know by experience, a nasty wound, for which the Midgans have vegetable antidotes.

As I looked in front in the direction of our march I saw a most lovely scene of African mountain country ahead, Gan Libah and the bluffs of Golis overlooking the beautiful Interior Plain covered with forests of dark, flat-topped guda thorn trees, dark sombre poison bushes and bright spines of sansaveria. There were misty wreaths of vapour shrouding half of Gan Libah ('Lion's Hand Mountain') making the dark bush at its base look the more mysterious. Out of the forest between the base of Gan Libah and Kenweina, rose several kopjes (to use the South African word as the most appropriate to properly describe them), abrupt bosses of rock or isolated hillocks, most prominent among them being 'Todoballa' (the rock of the seven robbers from Todoba) so called because seven Jibril-Aboker raiders were there surrounded and starved and then attacked and all slain with spears by the irate Adan Aysa, Aysa Musa, who had lost sheep at their hands. Lovely was the jungle at its base, the home of the lesser kudu, the appropriate home of the most beautiful antelope in Somaliland.

From Mandeira I made a dash for the plateau above, leaving most of the men in camp and taking only Sumunter and seven troopers with me, armed to the teeth. We went by daylight for fear of attack and filed up the Jerato Pass. Every man, including myself, had a carbine in the saddle bucket, a pistol in his holster, and a belt well filled with cartridges. We took also our food, I a roast guineafowl and cold tea in the left holster, unoccupied by pistols – the Indians took chupattis or unleavened cakes made with ghee (clarified butter), while those troopers who were Somali took simply a handful of dates, one of them also having a skin of sour milk at his saddlebow. Each after his own kind!

The vegetation became very peculiar at about 5,000 feet as we topped the Jerato Pass. A curious root was to be seen growing into a huge mass some feet across, grey and having the appearance of rounded rock. As we began gradually to descend on the long southward slope which is the top of the Golis Steps, I saw some Speke's or plateau gazelles which have longer hair than the Pelzelni's or coast gazelle. They are very pretty little animals and their horns, I think, are slightly better ringed than the gazelles of the low country. These high-level gazelles have a bunch of loose skin over the nostrils which has sometimes caused them to be called by naturalists 'big-nosed gazelles', but there is no fleshy protuberance as some have endeavoured to make out, only folds of skin.

We seven rode on, after I had shot the Speke's gazelle, and four miles beyond the top of the rise we came to a huge fig tree overhanging a watercourse, called Darei-Ka-Syk (the Syk fig tree). Here were some ankal or old men of the Kasin Ishak, Habr Gerhagis, by whom we had fully expected to be attacked as they are a brother clan of the Abdul Ishak of Eil Anod. But they had milk ready for us and welcomed us, saying that they had heard from the Abdul Ishak that they had met us at Eil Anod a month ago and we had done no harm, so that was alright! The figs were full of maggots but my men ate them with avidity.

The Aden hill camels being unacclimatised and unaccustomed to the Somali vegetation, richer than that of Arabia, had fallen ill and a halt was required at Mandeira to recruit. I was able to triangulate in the Interior Plains by ascending the kopjes round Mandeira and taking various angles, and spent a delightful three days here. We then marched to Laferug. Here, before marching next morning, I ascended the stony Hegebo Plateau to look for oryx, and dipping into a small depression, saw across it a magnificent wild ass. My Somalis said 'shoot' and I yielded to the temptation though I have never done so since. He was really a magnificent animal and our Aden troopers were struck with astonishment when they saw his hoofs – hard as nails from scrambling unshod over the awful iron stone plateau of Hegebo.

We marched on to Hamas where there is a curious double-pointed rock and two or three date palms overlooking a torrent-bed and where we found lion tracks but no lion. In that dismal stony 'karoo'[1] -covered desert called Deregodleh (ravine of caves) we found caves, very full of ticks from sheltering flocks, and plenty of little dik-dik antelopes in the low scrub. We then marched to Nasiya 'the resting tree' out on the Berbera Plain and on in the evening, reaching Berbera on March 29th 1886.

---

1 Karoo = A high pastoral inland table-land, e.g. the "Great Karoo" desert in South Africa.

Chapter 8

To survey the Interior Plains and Sheikh – May, 1886

(See Route Plan R4 – Appendix 4)

- Dik-Dik and Aloes -

ON 26TH APRIL 1886, we marched from Berbera to Bulhar by the coast road. Though I call it a road, it is only a camel-track worn in the soft alluvial or sandy soil by caravans. Halfway is the Gedki-jia or Daba-da-jialeh (the jia tree, or the hillock of the jia tree), shooting out as a spur of the Alola Jifeu Plateau, which is a northern continuation of Hegebo on the coast side. At the very extremity of these low hills is a solitary bush, a jia tree, and this has been used since time immemorial as a watering place for caravans passing along the coast track which ribbons out in the dust four hundred yards or so in front and below it, between it and the sea, on the flats where in places the brackish water from below has, in subsidence, left a glistening salt deposit, looking like snow by moonlight in patches, across the coast track. Aysa Musa marauders used to use this tree and pounce on caravans from it, and it always has a weird aspect, whether viewed by dim moonlight or by the glare of day. As you pass there at night, the rifle butt is gripped involuntarily and the pistol loosened in its holster. In those days the chance of an encounter was ever present; now British rule has made the coast road perfectly safe.

It was forty-two miles from Berbera to Bulhar without any but brackish undrinkable water. Pretty thorn bush, some of it, but all weird, inhospitable and lonely. Morrison and I used to ride from Bulhar to Berbera by night, doing it on one pony in nine hours, and I have once ridden from Bulhar to Berbera and back the next night on another pony, eighty-four miles in two successive nights and a busy day in between.

The march was an exceptionally severe one if carried out by day. I have made it considerably more than a dozen times and every time it has been more monotonous, and the distance without water and with very little shade, always heartbreaking! How glad we used to be to sight the minaret at Berbera or the flag over the old Egyptian quarters at Bulhar; or if travelling towards Berbera by night, or just before early dawn, how delightful when first seen shining over the black mass of bush was the ray from the Berbera lighthouse, first seen seventeen miles from its position.

But those were the early days of Somali exploration, and I must confess to a feeling of excitement each time we passed the jia tree by night along that road, where one looked for an enemy under every bush and gripped, unnecessarily of course, the stock of one's rifle at the sighing of the land wind in the thorn bushes! The coast road, for all its intense dreariness and monotony, its distances on tired nags and its dark grey powdery alluvial soil, is a most interesting memory of a good old time.

There was not much business to detain us at Bulhar, so on 29th April we said goodbye to Morrison and marched to So Midgan. We found oryx in the open plain near Gerigoan Hill, and as we arrived in the river bed opposite to the entrance to So Midgan gorge I saw a leopard spring into the river bed from the bush on the left bank and disappear into the rising bush-covered ground on the right bank. I followed and looked for him until nightfall, but without success. There were plenty of lion tracks here and some of my camelmen going to water returned with empty water sacks on their camels, as they had seen a lion and were afraid to draw water in the gloomy gorge now that it was getting dark.

So, after my dinner, I went back with them, carrying my .500 Express, and sat on a rock overlooking the spring while they drew the water and loaded the mussacks (goatskins) on the camels. We were already halfway out of the gorge when the first man in the procession must needs drop the one hurricane lantern. This was too much for the nerves of the others, now at high tension, and the dropping of the lantern was the signal for a 'sauve qui peut' and we all scuttled out of the ravine together, never stopping till we reached camp. I got in last because the Somalis can see to run in the dark while I cannot. However, I managed to bring the lantern in which rather lessened the disgraceful nature of our retreat.

At midnight we were woke up by a freshet,[1] the Tug Issutugan, coming roaring down onto the dry sandy bed in a great wave, and running all night and next morning. Ninety yards wide and three feet deep. When we marched I strolled along the edge of the swollen river to look at the 'lion gorge' as we now called the main rocky gate of So Midgan, and the water was rushing through in a foaming cataract twelve feet deep. I lost several things, among them the iron top of my quicksilver bottle, for the artificial horizon I had brought for finding latitudes (since discarded for the theodolite). This flood was my first warning (and we have had many since) that it is not good to camp in the dry bed of a river, however smooth and enticing the stretch of sand may be.

We halted at Weil-a-warab (calf's drinking place) for a couple of days to recruit the camels and I had some walks in the lovely aloe jungles between Weil-a-Warab and Karira Kopje, three miles away, a good survey point.

In the last trip a lion had been reported there. It was delightful to get back into the Interior Plains again. I went out for a stroll with my .500 Express, some water and a belt full of cartridges and walked to a mile beyond Karira, and in a beautiful aloe-strewn ravine I shot a lesser kudu buck, a perfect pair of horns with a gimlet twist. I carried the rifle and the head and skin home with a light heart, though I had no attendant to help me. What days they were! In marching from Weil-a-warab to Mandeira and surveying from kopje to kopje (for I had to ascend many to get records of angles), I got altogether four of these lovely antelopes, two between Weil-a-warab and Karira and two in the ravines near Gadoballa Rock and Mandeira. As to long dry dissertations on the spot where the bullets hit, their smashing power, the way the game was standing, measurements of animals and their horns, I can say little at this distance of time. Records there were, some still holding good, but measurements shrink as the horns dry down in the stored collection. I shot a twenty-seven-and-a-half-inch lesser kudu, base to tip of horn in a straight line, and after seven years' exposure in a museum the horns only measured twenty-six inches! I prefer rather to remember the marvellous beauty of the scenery, of the wild aloe jungles overhung with thorn trees festooned with shady bowers of the lovely

1 A sudden flow of water in a dry, or nearly dry, river bed.

'armo' creeper, the bright cheerful shock-headed Somali hunters and camel-men, and the clever intelligent service willingly and ungrudgingly given. Their sympathy with the sport, disappointment in my disappointments and enthusiasm at my success. One shadow there was: I had not yet got my elephant or my lion.

We marched on to Barkassan, where we found guineafowl, and thence to Lafarug where there is an excellent view over the Henweina valley in which the Tug Henweina, which supplies the Lafarug wells, takes its rise. Garbadir, the scene of my first shooting trip with Saunders, where I had such good sport. I was glad to see the dear old place again and had some adventures with pig. To Lasadowao, beyond the Garka Wein Rocks, thence to Hulkaboba. The character of all the country from Lafarug to here had changed from the aspect of the Interior Plains at Mandeira and Weil-a-warab. The aloes had nearly ceased and there was more undulating rocky arid ground. Once out of the guda forests, always beautiful, there was little to interest the eye.

At Sheikh there is a very long gently sloping gorge winding up into the Golis range. A stream flows along the centre of this gorge, which is very narrow, and by the margins of the stream are little plots of green turf which have a refreshing effect when the halt is made there after coming along the

Rock Rabbits

rather arid road from Berbera. But you must beware of the fleas, for if the sheep have been resting on the grass plots they abound with them and with ticks.

As we were riding towards the Sheikh Gorge from the plains a huge warthog went away in front of us. We had no spears, and the ground moreover in all this Guban country is not suitable for riding pig, except at Teyla on the Maritime Plain. So I jumped off and dropped him as he bolted into some high grass one hundred and twenty yards away, with his tail sticking straight in the air over his back, a habit of the warthog when disturbed in his mind!

From Sheikh we marched by Gelok to Bihendthola, and from Bihendthola to Berbera, arriving about the 26th of May. As we approached Bihendthola I was amused at my Somalis: they were all smearing their hair with reddish clay and ashes mixed together, to make their hair curl before they should put in an appearance at Berbera. They let it dry in the sun and keep it on about twenty-four hours, then dust it and the result is a head of interesting little curls. There is no dandy like your Somali on occasions! Thus ended my first series of trips in the immediate hinterland of Berbera and Bulhar. As yet I had only touched the higher tableland at Jerato and Murgo.

Chapter 9

Gadabursi Hills
October, 1886

(See Route Map R5 – Appendix 5)

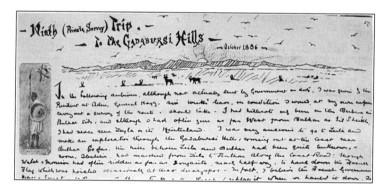

IN THE following Autumn, although not actually sent by Government on duty, I was given by the Resident at Aden, General Hogg, six weeks' leave on condition I would, at my own expense, carry out a survey of the route I should take. I had hitherto only been on the Berbera and Bulhar side, and although I had often gone as far west from Bulhar as Eil Sheikh, I had never seen Zeyla or its hinterland. I was very anxious to go to Zeyla and make an exploration through the Gadabursi Hills, coming out at the coast near Bulhar. So far, the hills between Zeyla and Bulhar had been quite unknown and no one, I believe, had marched from Zeyla to Bulhar along the coast road; though Walsh and Morrison had often ridden as far as Dongarita, nearly halfway, to haul down the French flag which was hoisted occasionally at that dreary spot. In fact, I believe the French Government kept a Somali there on 10R a month to keep the flag up and replace it when we hauled it down. It led at last to the 'Dongarita Incident' and the usual apology to the Foreign Minister in London and the packing away of the French flag by Morrison and its eventually, I suppose, being put under lock and key by the First Assistant Resident Aden. From Bulhar to Dongarita is about sixty miles, so the ride from Bulhar to Dongarita and back to Berbera is about one hundred and forty-two miles. This Walsh did on one of these occasions (my first visit to Bulhar) on a Somali pony with a pillow strapped on to do duty as a saddle, a box of sardines, five biscuits and a revolver being his other accoutrements, and Mahomed Dosa and the half leg of a sheep and another revolver and his own fat carcase acted as orderly!

We reached Zeyla (Captain Godfrey and I) about 1st October and put up with Captain King, then Assistant Resident and Consul at Zeyla. We used to sleep on the flat-topped roof of King's house, overlooking the huts of the town, a French Consulate and Mission and Egyptian guardhouse being the chief remaining buildings.

I did not lose much time in going out to Warabili for pig (warthog) and I was successful in getting one there, but sad to say, by the rifle as I had brought no spear. At that time Mills had not, I think, started the noble sport of hog hunting and I was unaware that it could be done in Somaliland, most of the mountains where pig exist, Golis etcetera, being unrideable.

I was back again in Zeyla within two days and our caravan was nearly ready. King was to start on an official exploring tour of his own, taking Phillips, the Superintendent of Customs at Zeyla, with him, so with Godfrey and myself there were four of us and, but for the hardships of the trip, we had a very jolly time of it.

Our caravan (I forget the number of camels) started about 7th October, and we marched to Warabod, the first water, and next day to Udawadiri, the last water before the passing of the great waterless grass plains of Zeyla. We had a day's rest before attempting the stretch of about thirty-five miles to Garisa, at the edge of the Eilo Mountains, on the further edge of the plains. We had of course only native report to go by in estimating the distance to Garisa, and as we only had one day's supply of water with us and several ponies (which drink a good deal) we were a little anxious about this distance. No white man, so far as we knew, had yet gone into these mountains.

We started from Udawadiri by the light of the stars – there was no moon till midnight – and it was not long before we got lost. Our guides and Zeyla camelmen had made some arrangement amongst themselves to turn us back to Zeyla. They feared looters or something, and they wilfully pretended they could not find their way over the plain in the dark. So at last King and I took to path-finding, King striking a match now and then to consult his compass (we ought to have been able to go by the stars but I was not an adept in those days). Well, we led them fairly correctly, thanks to the bearing I had taken on Gambur har Garisa before starting from Udawadiri. The grass was about two feet high and the ground full of holes and we stumbled on. At last, after some hours, we missed half the caravan and we all scattered (the officers) to find it. I was so excited at the treachery of the rascally guides I spurred my horse at full speed over the plain over ground I would have hesitated to cross at a canter by daylight. Then I turned to go back to King and as I turned I thought I heard voices to my right front and at once galloped there and found the missing half of the caravan, but making straight back for Zeyla!

Mindful of the usefulness of the same course of action some twelve months before when stopping a Sheridone fight, I pulled out my revolver and ordered the leading camelman, an old ankal with a bald head and grey goatee, whom I knew to be the greatest scoundrel of the lot, to turn back towards Garisa. He swore Garisa was in the other direction (pointing towards Zeyla) but by threats and by a great deal show of the revolver, I got the whole lot of them right about and at last heard welcome voices, those of King and the rest of the caravan. Thus united we pursued our way, and when the moon rose we halted for a spell and then went on again. At about dawn (if I remember right) we halted and formed our camp. There was, I think, no water and we used up our supply. Plenty aoul grazing near. In the visions of memory given me of this march come vividly one of Phillips and myself coming on a large sounder of warthog in the scarped river bed of the Tug Sallul, one of the rivers crossing this great grass plain and with its snake-like course marked by thorn trees. How they ran! How we peppered them, knocking the dust up all around them but hitting none! Another scene there is of two oryx stalked (only to get away) on the edge of another river bed, the pony left tethered at a stump (gari – we used often to bark our shins against the galol gari or stump of galol wood), and how the pony was nowhere to be found when I came back. How a search revealed him out on the plain and all the wiles we had to employ to catch him! Phillips was generally my companion on these rambles and a very entertaining one he was. He had hunted in Swaziland and Delagoa Bay, so was experienced in the wilds and an enthusiastic Africander!

The Author's campsite in the Gadabursi Hills

We made another march to Garisa, the last four miles being through tolerably thick bush, and we camped at the side of the river bed under huge guda thorn trees, a lovely spot. The Gumbar Garisa hillock, half a mile upstream, is where I had a hunt after Waller's gazelle but at this distance of time I can't recall whether I got one or not. That is of little moment, it is the scene, the beautiful jungle, the light graceful red beasts skimming through it, that is indelibly engraved on the memory. We climbed the Gumbar har Garisa and I took compass angles. On up the bed of a lovely tug or wadi with a very large thorn forest on either side. Tracks and signs of elephants but none to be found. How excited we were as we marched up the wide long stretch of yellow sand between the lines of forest. We skirted the Eilo Range and reached Salak. In the Eilo Range is a cave, first explored by Captain King and it should be called King's Cave as there is no other name, but I have called it Eilo Cave in the map, I believe.

At Salak King and Godfrey decided to turn back for Zeyla, there being no sport for Godfrey (it being a bad dry season) and no further business for King. I forgot to mention our Sudanese escort whom King took from Zeyla. These were the old Egyptian black garrison of Zeyla and capital fellows. Ten of these under a native officer (whom we called 'Effendi') were told off by King to go with Phillips and myself. For I had determined to push on in spite of all the reports of Jibril Abokr looters ahead, scarcity of water, etcetera, being loth to give up my project to explore the hills and reach Bulhar by the interior route. Phillips, like the sporting chap he was, cheerily offered to accompany me and King kindly allowed him to do so, to my delight.

King and Godfrey (who had been slightly ill from a touch of the sun in the awful Zeyla plain) left for the coast by a roundabout route (Buk Gego I think) leaving Phillips and myself to organise our little caravan at Salak.

A sounder of Warthog.

Ever since Garisa we had heard of proposed attacks by the Jibril Abokr, the most turbulent clan of the Habr Awal, and these rumours had been increasing in intensity till there was almost a panic among our Gadabursi followers, excepting of course the stolid black Sudanese soldiers. These were fine tall men in long shirts reaching to their ankles, no other uniform, only their belts and rifles and an embroidered waistcoat for the Effendi. Good-humoured, thick squat faces and a soft thick speech. They are good men and true in a quarrel.

Phillips and I marched from Salak to Banhir, all by picturesque and grand scenery and finally reached Kabri Bahr whence we could see the mountains round Bulhar. After Salak we had no guides and spent several days marching through the Eilo country entirely on our own guesswork, finding water at last at Kabri Bahr by chance and searching for it without any help from anyone who knew the country. The bush was empty and we were in constant expectation of meeting the raiding Jibril Abokr. We came on tracks of elephant and lion but on our forced marches in search of water we had no time to stay and hunt.

From Kabri Bahr to the Bulhar side I was the sole guide. When at Salak I had ascended with Phillips a hill from which, hazy in the far distance, we could see to the north the great Zeyla Plain stretching away beyond Garisa – and turning to the east-north-east towards Bulhar to my delight and astonishment I caught sight of Elmas, good old Elmas with his three peaks, dim by reason of the fifty miles or so which separated us, and to the east and south-east were the Golis Mountains, yes, the bluffs of Gan Libah and Banyero, one hundred and twenty miles away (as I found out some years later when our surveys were compiled). I now knew that without a guide I could take my men to Eil Sheikh or Dinis if only we could find Kabri Bahr water. For I had hunted over every inch of ground on the further side of Elmas when staying at Bulhar, and Bulhar lay only seventeen miles on the further side of the great mountain.

We hit upon the Kabri Bahr well quite by accident and instinct of my followers, for having no Jibril Abokr, or any Bulhar men with us, we had to guess where it was. I filled up at Kabri Bahr well what water vessels we had, and we started with some misgivings for a tramp through a ghastly plain of fearful khausa bush. We were to traverse over seventy miles of this plain and past Elmas with only three pints of water per man, and Phillips had to ride by the camels pistol in hand to conserve the water. As we neared the sea after two days my men rushed into the waves to suck the water through their parched skins. I failed to find the Eil Sheikh wells, and at Dinis we at last found water. The mules and camels rushed into the well and I had to shoot my pony from the effects of the thirsty march, the day after we reached Bulhar.

Chapter 10

Issutugan and Zeyla
October and November, 1886

WHEN WE had rested at Bulhar for a few days after our terrible march and forgotten our sufferings from thirst and our haunting anxiety of the last three days, Phillips and I decided, as I had a few days' leave to spare, to make a push up the Issutugan River on my old exploration route to Gal Hedijaleh, before returning to Bulhar and Zeyla. To the latter place we intended to go by the hitherto unexplored coast route, which I was also to put into my map.

We started from Bulhar about 1st November and marched up the Issutugan to Gal Hedijaleh, the only incident being at the latter place, the terminus of our journey, where I heard of a leopard having killed a goat. Following the trail where the brute had dragged the dead goat over the huge rounded boulders and rocks (some being thirty feet across) we reached a kopje full of caves, and there under the shadow of a rock at the mouth of cave formed by two other rocks leaning against each other, was the goat's carcase. In the mouth of the cave were many bones of former suppers of sheep and goats. We retired to camp and returned at 3 p.m., when I posted lookout men on all the prominent rocks, and I had a splendid hunt. It began by the leopard, after his midday sleep, coming out to hunt at about 3.30 p.m., when he was sighted by my lookout men, and a most interesting chase began, Phillips and I directed by the lookout men, jumping from rock to rock to try and get a sight of the brute. He had apparently changed his mind and determined to return to his cave, for after some ten minutes of this sort of work, Phillips and one of the men saw him and pointed him out. He was just strolling round the corner of a rock towards his cave, his long tail drooping over the path, and taking a hurried snapshot at seventy yards I fired, leaving a cloud of dust on the path where he had stood, but he must have disappeared with one spring. There was no blood and his tracks led into the cave. After some consultation, Phillips and I crept in, Phillips, by the way, going first, owing, as he claimed, to his Cape and Swaziland experience of these brutes. As we crept into the narrow entrance, stooping, a cloud of bats came out and Phillips and I, who both had loaded rifles, involuntarily stepped back a pace or two, our rifles clashing together, for we thought in our hurry that not bats but a wounded leopard was on us. We never got him for we went in and explored the cave through and through and found the tracks led out by an outlet above to the top of the hill, and as the ground was very stony and night was coming on, we had to give it up.

After we reached camp a huge torrent came down onto the dry sandy river bed in three waves, rolling boulders four feet in diameter down over and over as if they were pebbles. It went about five miles an hour and would have swept away any men or camels crossing the river at the time. For six hours afterwards, instead of the bone-dry yellow sand, there rolled three feet deep and fifty yards wide a grey-brown turbid river, and next morning it was only damp sand and a rivulet six feet wide and a foot deep, a channel winding from bank to bank. Stranded trees and new boulders strewed the river bed.

Finding there was no sport, we now returned to Bulhar and reorganised our caravan for the desert coast march to Zeyla. It is a terrible march, the road from Bulhar to Eil Sheikh, as I of course knew, then there was a terrible sandy desert track to Biyo Foga (distant water) and at last, after about one and a half days, we arrived at a place called Armaleh, where there was low salsola bush, a huge jungle of it, about six or eight feet high, evergreen, the earth being burnt umber, powdery alluvial soil, impregnated with salt, and very disagreeably covering the clothes with dust. We had a very exciting midnight hunt after a sounder of pig in the thick scrub, there being a full moon; and later as I went for a very serious stroll far out into the bush, and as I was walking along one of the deep watercourses which intersect this hummocky country, I heard a twig crack, and looking down into the watercourse below me I espied the skin, grey with white stripes, of a magnificent lesser kudu. I couldn't see what I was aiming at, but was certain it was a kudu and a possible shot at his shoulder and I pulled the trigger. There was a crash and a struggle, and there the beautiful buck lay still. My feelings were very triumphant as I walked home through the dusk with the lovely trophy, quite a record, twenty seven and a half inches from base to tip of horn. Phillips and the men were delighted with my success when, shouting with joy, I returned and showed them the head.

We completed the survey to Zeyla and then, leaving Phillips there, I marched back to Bulhar to take back some men (police) I had borrowed from that place. I did it in four days, one hundred and twenty miles, the fastest marching I have ever done for any length of time with Somali camels. We marched on to Berbera and I took ship to Aden, there to complete my map.

Thus ends what I call the prehistoric period of my visits to Somaliland – the records I have not, to my great regret, kept, and I have had to trust to memory. In future I shall have my diary to trust to.

Chapter 11

Précis of trips prior to 1887

I HAD NOW surveyed the greater part of the Habr Awal country, the hinterland of Berbera and Bulhar so far as Guban, the lower country west, and had produced a 'Map of the Habr Awal Country', three miles to one inch. I had also surveyed Eilo Range and the Bulhar to Zeyla Route and produced a 'Map of Eilo Range, Gadabursi Hills and Bulhar to Zeyla Caravan Route'. These maps were sent to Poona and the one of the Habr Awal Country was printed there during 1886. So far my only (and *the* only, except James' route) exploration beyond Guban (the low country) had been my two dashes to Jerato and Murgo. I had not yet shot a lion, leopard or elephant and of course had not heard of the rhinoceros. At that time we had only just discovered there are two kinds of kudu — we only believed in one kind of Speke's gazelle and thought the three kinds of dik-dik were only one. Of the 'sig' or hartebeest I first heard on my Eilo trip, but cannot imagine how the Gadabursi heard of it as I don't know of its whereabouts anywhere near the Eilo Range.

The shadowed portions of the map show my explorations so far. We had not heard of the Abyssinians, for Harar, the Mohammedan state, was between us and Abyssinia and was governed by the Mohammedan Emir Abdullahi. All the Abyssinian troubles were to come four years later. Porro's expedition had not yet been massacred. Those were the prehistoric days when the only Europeans who had visited Harar, I believe, were Burton, Colonel Hunter with Captain Fullerton, Colonel Heath and Lieutenant Peyton, and Paulitski. Generals Blair and Hogg were Residents of Aden in succession during these years and Colonel Hunter was Assistant Resident. It was chiefly due to the exertions of Colonel Hunter, L.P. Walsh and David Morrison, that the British Protectorate was consolidated in these times. They were good old days, and in spite of a comparatively slender bag of game, they were very romantic days. Every bit of the Interior reconnoitred by me was hitherto unexplored by white men and at a time when no shooting parties were in the Interior. I had it all to myself in those days. I was the sole possessor of the secrets of the interesting aloe-strewn Interior Plains, which I knew far better than any stretch of country in England. The names of the trees were more familiar to me than the names of English trees, and I came to recognise natives whom I met as old friends with old faces. I had begun the training of caravan after caravan and formed the nucleus of the shikari and European camp-followers trade which is now running so briskly and giving work to so many Somalis on the Coast and in the Interior with sportsmen's caravans. It was my privilege also to be the pioneer of civilisation in these wilds among these untouched tribes. While Walsh and Morrison were working on the Coast, I was doing similar work in the Interior, making them acquainted with the English idea. Trying and often succeeding in winning their lasting affection, visiting them as a guest in their own homes at a time when attack would probably have meant annihilation for our party. What a mysterious Interior it was! I found on coming to England in 1887 that no one knew where Somaliland was, just as I had never heard of the country until I came to Aden!

I was fated to have two more shooting trips during this state of things (to be subsequently described), the later of the two being the most enjoyable shooting trip I have ever made in a series where the happy days are thickly strewn with joyful memories. This was in 1887, later than that which I call the 'prehistoric period', but sportsmen had not yet begun to flock in. It was not till about 1890 that the influx began, at first slowly, then in 1894 by shoals. I may be expected to say: '*sic transit gloria mundi*' but refrain from it, for the aloe jungles of those Interior Plains, with the bluff top of old Gan Libah and the Bluffs of Golis rising blue above the 'guda' thorn trees, are as beautiful as ever! The game may be scarcer but with experience in other lands has come greater skill to make up for the difficulty. Prices are, however, higher and I wish I could say deeper funds are ready to meet this difficulty too! But here I stop. Money is a hard fact which no enthusiasm can mellow down by imagination – it is too inelastic. Well, well, those prehistoric days are part of the old Speke, Grant and Burton days of African exploration, gone, alas, forever, never to return. The world is getting very commonplace!

Chapter 12

Shooting in Arabia and life at Aden
between 1884 and 1887

AFTER THE first trip, to Garbadir, I brought home the Waller's gazelle heads (and pigs' teeth) and had them all cleaned and set up by a gunner skilled in setting up black buck heads and hung them up in my house (1300 rupees advance from Government, cost 1100 and then 200 more because part of it was burnt down). I had a square room only and verandah all round, dressing room and bathroom arranged by partitions in the verandah. It had a beautiful view of sunsets over Little Aden in front and was situated on Ras Jarshyne overlooking the sea. How proud I used to be of those first Waller's (gerenouk) heads!

E.J. Chevallier and I made a very fine trip to Lahej, twenty-five miles from Aden, where we shot gazelles (*G. arabica*) but I was not, I believe, very successful and only got one doe! I had mistaken a doe for a buck! What has become of that wretched little head? I don't know but I was proud of it then because it was the first thing I had shot in Asia. The ground round Lahej was sandy desert with thick low bushes surmounting sand dunes, and made the very best of stalking ground. Chevallier got a gazelle too. Then we went to Hitatum, on the edge of the desert which is visible from Aden and slopes up to the high mountains of Yemen. Here, two years before, an Austrian professor had gone to pick up shells, and wandering up a river bed too far into the desert, he undressed to bathe, laying his gun, loaded, on the pile of clothes. Up came the Bedouin and shot him with his own gun! So this was an interesting part of Arabia! There were five thorn trees in a clump here, under which we camped (I forgot to say we rode out from Aden on trotting thoroughbred Arab camels) and in the jungle in the bed of the wadi and on its banks were 'chuckori' or partridge, the largest Asiatic breed, beautifully plumaged and most exciting sport. I didn't do much but Chevallier got a lot of these and sand grouse. It was a most pleasurable trip. Chevallier had a lot of Arab servants and camelmen who were very good fellows. We got back to Lahej and stayed at the Sultan's Dak Bungalow, provided for European visitors from Aden. Here Chevallier fell seedy and we had to get back to Aden to the nearest doctor.

Just below my bungalow and eighty yards away, was the sea, and five miles across the mouth of Aden Harbour was Little Aden, a pretty mass of peaks, a peninsular rising out of the sea, picturesque but barren. Behind Little Aden were the plains covered with sand and scattered thorn bush, with gazelles and hares. British territory extended three miles inland. All the Arabian tribes had matchlocks and most tribes were very turbulent. The Sultan of Lahej, being subsidised, kept the caravan routes quiet, aided and supported by the Aden Troop, a force of Indian cavalry and camelry stationed at the outpost of Khor Maksai six miles from Aden. The Aden Troop were under Colonel Stevens, Gliggeham, Domvile, Gordon and Wardson, in succession, I believe. They often made expeditions into the interior to punish or bring to reason the wild caravan-raiding tribes.

At Steamer Point on Ras Jarshyne, where my house was built, there was generally a cool sea breeze, making it no worse than Bombay save for the barrenness. In Camp, four miles distant (between Khor Maksai, the neck of the Aden Peninsular and Steamer Point) lay the Crater, the volcano itself, its seaward wall on the side furthest from Steamer Point, broken so that the town of Aden is built on the floor of the crater and overlooks the sea. Between the Crater and Khor Maksai was a tunnel going through the walls of the volcano into a fortified gorge called the Isthmus. Between the Isthmus and Khor Maksai in the mainland was a long stretch of sand and one white road.

Often on Sundays from the RA Mess one or two of us made expeditions up Jebel Shunnshunn, the peaks of the volcano. On the Steamer Point side it is nearly inaccessible, the way being by Gold Mohur Valley (where there is a stunted gold mohur tree) and I never really got to the top of that side. But on the Crater side, near the famous tanks, a zigzag path leads up to the signal station at the top of Shunnshunn, and as you go up this path you get buried in ravines in the brown volcanic rocks, and the scenery, with little stunted bright green scrub trying to look cheerful, is like that in the barren Law Range of Somaliland, the Range of which we had crossed for ten miles on the way to Gadabursi. Here on Shunnshunn were no expectations of oryx or leopard, but I liked these little Sunday trips and could forget Aden and imagine myself in the wilds again. The view from the signal station on top of Shunnshunn (1900 feet) is magnificent, with rich contrasts of burnt sienna sand, brown mountains and bright blue sky. The deep blue contrasts so well with the volcanic rocks, which are themselves varied in colour by rich sulphurous reds and yellows and greys. To an artist, even Aden is beautiful for all its barrenness.

Chapter 13

Issutugan River – April–May 1887

(See Route Plan R6 – Appendix 6)

OBTAINING leave of absence from Aden on 39th April 1887, I crossed over the gulf in a native dhow, and reached Berbera, on the African coast, after two days' sail. There is always a difficulty in getting camels at the close of the Berbera Fair season, and I was kept waiting for two days; but on the evening of 4th May, we were fairly under way. My party was made up of myself, with four personal servants, all Somalis, then two Somali trackers and one Midgan, or bushman, carrying his bow and poisoned arrows. For transport we had four camels and two camelmen. Being in search of sport, I did not wish to burden myself with a ponderous escort, so I merely armed my personal servants with Sniders as a precaution against raiding parties, should we meet with any. My butler, Nur Osman, was a fairly good shot, having being with the Khartoum Expedition as a camel-man, and there learnt to use a rifle.

With a glorious full moon, we started off to cross the Berbera Maritime Plain, in a south-westerly direction, and by 1 a.m. reached a small tree called Nasiya, or 'the resting-place', sixteen miles from Berbera. Early in the night we had passed several caravans halted round Berbera for the fair season, each circle of mat huts pouring forth a bevy of villainous-looking pariah dogs to give us a surly salute as we went by. At the last caravan I obtained a shot at a large 'waraba', or spotted hyena, but without hitting him. These halted caravans are the only villages to be met with in the interior, and are moveable at two hours' notice. They will give nothing to strangers, so that the only supplies to be counted on are grass and water. Sometimes by good luck a sheep or some milk may be purchased, the latter generally sour.

At Nasiya, we took a short sleep to refresh ourselves for the march yet before us, and at 4 a.m. we pushed on towards the first water, Deregodleh, twenty-two miles from Berbera. During this march the bare flat Maritime Plain breaks up into stony watercourses and thorny bush, and the first low Maritime Range is entered.

Before reaching Deregodleh I caught a glimpse of dark red in a watercourse some 200 yards away, and on going forward put up a herd of 'gerenouk' (*Gazella walleri*). This is a curious lanky red antelope, with a very long neck, and a face not altogether unlike that of a camel; he has a pair of black horns twelve inches long, curving over forward at the points, very thick at the base, and beautifully ringed. When an enemy is discovered, the gerenouk extends his neck to gaze, he then lowers his head and dives into the bush at a long swinging trot; then he stops for a subsequent look when he thinks himself safe, and this is the time for a shot at him, generally from 150 to 200 yards; he is very shy and gives good sport. At the same time, this is one of the commonest wild animals in the interior, and frequently seen. I was fortunate to drop the buck of the herd by a rather long shot from my Martini rifle.

We reached Deregodleh at 10 a.m. This is a rocky watercourse, the water trickling from the rocks and losing itself in the sand of the river bed below. There is a little gorse-like cover on each bank, containing hares and great numbers of the tiny 'Sakaro' antelope, a little beast about the size and colour of a hare, and having a reddish tuft on the forehead, from which peep two charming little horns, 1 inch long. It is a very common thing to put up as many as forty of these little antelopes in a day's march, but they are difficult shooting, and can best be got with a gun and No. 4 shot.

We left Deregodleh and camped a stage further on, marching on 6th May to Mandeira, a delightful headquarters. It is a valley about three miles wide, nestling under the great Gan Libah ('Lion-hand') mountain, one of the Golis range. These mountains rise to a height of nearly six thousand feet above sea level, and run parallel to, and thirty-five miles from, the coast. They form a gigantic step, the northern or coast face being precipitious, the southern face sloping gently towards the far interior in a series of open rolling downs. This high country beyond the Ghauts is called Ogo, the low country, including the Maritime Plain, Guban. The climate of Ogo is deliciously cool. At the foot of the Ghauts, on the coast face, is dense high tree jungle, with generally a thick undergrowth of cactus, aloes, and thorny bushes. Here are found a few lions, leopard, and lesser kudu, gerenouk, and wart hog are numerous; also the large kudu, with his immense spiral horns, is found here and there in the gorges and on the mountain sides. In the open stony country between the Ghauts and the Maritime range, are found oryx, wild ass, and a few shy ostriches. Spotted hyenas are very common, striped hyenas somewhat rare; gazelles (spekii) fairly plentiful; they resemble the Indian and Arabian gazelles.

We reached Mandeira on 6th June, at midday, and found the valley occupied by a section of the Habr Gerhajis tribe, a fine race of bearded hillmen, who keep flocks and herds. These people have very sketchy ideas of caravan rights; however, as I had had some previous experience of them to go upon, I was not molested in any way.

I will pass over quickly the next few days. We went to a place where I was visited by a bevy of eight ladies of the Habr Gerhajis tribe, who insisted upon turning over everything in my tent, and making hay generally; they tried to annex my looking-glass, and they were very funny in their criticism, amusing the camp greatly!

While at the same place I shot several gerenouk, and a lesser kudu buck, and missed a splendid bull kudu, which crossed a ledge of rock two hundred feet above us. Besides this, we ran to earth a black snake 6 feet long; all the stones which we heaved at it missed, and its tail disappeared under the root of a tree before the gun could be brought up.

The lesser kudu buck is, I think, the most beautiful wild animal in the Somali country; his coat is fairly long, of a French grey colour in old males, and nicely marked with white bands on the body; horns spiral, about twenty-five inches long; and he has a bushy tail tipped with white. When disturbed, he goes off in great bounds, flying over the bushes and clumps of aloes, and presents a most difficult shot.

Hearing of elephants near Little Harar, I made my way to Gulanleh, about twenty miles short of that place and about ninety miles south-west of Berbera. At Gulanleh the country becomes open and undulating, the Golis range ceases, and the Guban country rises gradually to Ogo. Hargeisa (Little Harar) is situated between Guban and Ogo, on the Damel Plain, a vast expanse of open rolling downs covered with stones and thorny bushes, traversed here and there by tributaries of the great Issutugan river bed. This is a fuimara[1] (sic) some eight hundred yards wide, which cuts through the Maritime Range and reaches the sea near the port of Bulhar, fifty miles west of Berbera. The tributaries which cross the Damel Plain are generally dry and sandy, with patches of dense reeds, and are bordered by belts of high tree jungle about a mile wide. These reeds, often ten feet high, are infested with lions, which do not appear by day but leave plenty of their tracks in the sand at night.

I had determined to make Gulanleh my headquarters, and to send my two trackers, who were mounted, together with a Habr Gerhajis horseman we had picked up by the way, to all the large elephant coverts within twenty miles. Meanwhile, I remained at Gulanleh. Here I was lucky enough to kill two very fine bull oryx and two cows, all four having very long straight horns. A few buck gerenouk and gazelles followed, and on the second day of my stay we put up nine ostriches, two cocks and seven hens. I fired at them with my Martini-Henry at three hundred yards, as they sailed away, and knocked up the dust all round them without hitting any. Three times we fell in with ostriches, but always found their vision too good for us. They look very funny, streaming away at a great rate, like a lot of immense

A Herd of Oryx

1 'Fuimara' meaning uncertain. Probably a wadi, or the dry bed of a torrent.

fowls. At Gulanleh we also came on a herd of wild asses, which halted fifty yards from us and grazed. They have striped legs.

On May 13th my patience was rewarded by the arrival of my three horsemen with the news that they had found a large herd of elephants at Jalelo, about twelve miles away, towards Little Harar. So putting a few blankets, axes, tinned provisions etcetera on a camel, and some dates in my pocket, and accompanied by two mounted trackers, the Midgan, and two other men, I set out at 8 a.m. for the Jalelo covert, leaving the Gulanleh camp in the charge of Nur Osman. The Jalelo covert consists of heavy timber bordering the Wadi Hembeweina, the principal tributary of the Issutugan river. There are extensive tracts of high reeds in the river bed, and these are so dense that it is hard to force one's way through them, and when inside one can see nothing except in the parts where the reeds are low or very thin.

After a hot march, at about 1 p.m., we struck the Hembeweina at Jalelo, and, sending my trackers to hunt up the elephants, I ensconced myself under a date-palm, and proceeded to lunch off sardines and dates and to make myself comfortable.

The mid-day was fearfully hot, and I was just dozing off to sleep under the grateful shade of the date-palm, when my head tracker, Hussein Debeli, came bounding up in a wonderful state of excitement, brandishing a big spear and dancing round me in circles. I felt inclined to kick him for being such a fool, but knew that his news was good, so, after a pause to take breath, he said that he had suddenly seen an enormous bull elephant in the bed of the river only half a mile below our palm tree. Packing everything quickly on the camel, and leaving orders for it to be brought on slowly after us, I took Hussein Debeli as guide, and, shouldering my heavy rifle, a double 4-bore, we started off to look up the elephant. On rounding a spur there he was, walking down the centre of the river bed below us, turning his great head from side to side as he moved along. He looked rather disturbed in his mind, and must have suspected danger; the wind being from us to him, blowing straight down the river. Going as fast as we could lay legs to the ground, we ran along the high bank to intercept him, and get below him to leeward before commencing the attack, but as we got nearly abreast of him he either saw or winded us, and broke into a shambling trot. Seeing he was escaping us, I opened fire with the 4-bore, though the range was at least seventy yards, and too great for much execution. At the shots he spun round and turned upstream again at a great pace. Bathed in perspiration from the mid-day sun, and suffering for a drink, I followed as fast as I could, and at last, in the distance upriver, appeared my two horsemen, with red bows flying and spears flashing in the sun, galloping down *ventre à terre*, with whoops and jeers, to head the elephant. This had the effect of making him plunge into a vast expanse of reeds, where he pulled up, comparatively secure from the attack. It so happened, however, that he had chosen a spot where the steep river bank overlooked the reeds, so that on going to the edge and looking down I could see his head and the ridge of his back rising above them. The range was far – about sixty yards; but this was preferable to trying to approach him in the reeds; so, aiming for the temple, I opened fire with the 4-bore. Bang! bang! answered by a loud, unmistakable crack and a swish as the second bullet went over the mark and sped innocently through the reed tops. However, the first shot had told, having bored a clean hole through the flap of his ear and entered the skull, far back. He merely gave a shrill trumpet, spread out his enormous ears, and spun round facing us. Then he resumed his original position. Bang! at the place where his shoulder ought to be. Up went his trunk, and he subsided gently, disappearing into the reeds like a sinking ship. Then up again, standing as before, but this time looking very dejected, musing over his hard fate. This would never do; so, climbing down the steep scarp to the lower level, and edging gingerly round the reed patches till I got the opposite side of him, I went a little way in, following the path he had made into the reeds, and found him lying on his side, one tusk being 4 ft. long and very thick; the other had lost a foot from the point, possibly broken off while uprooting a tree. He was a fine fellow, and, bringing a tape later on, we found that he measured 10 ft. 6 in. perpendicular height at the shoulder. Returning towards where we had left our camel, we brought up axes and at once set to work to cut out his ivory. I found the Somalis very feeble at this work, for by sunset they had only removed one tusk, and seemed thoroughly exhausted.

(A month or two later C. Chevallier made a similar expedition and got to Jalelo at the identical place where I had fired at the bull from the high bank. He picked up several of my 4-bore cartridges on the top of the bank; just where I had been standing at the time.)

Then a heavy rainstorm burst upon us, and the setting sun left us all wet through, shivering under a thorn bush, the river valley turned into an immense marsh, and worse than all, no moon. We had seen many fresh lion-tracks in the river-bed during our hunt, which did not tend to improve our tempers; adding to this, my five men were all too exhausted to collect dry firewood, and lay like logs, looking the very picture of misery.

After poking at them for about ten minutes, and being only answered by grunts, I began to lose my temper, too; and then they foresaw a possible diminution in pay, and sulkily helped me gather firewood, the rain having stopped. They said that Allah would keep the lions away, and that they were too wet and miserable to care whether the lions came or not. However, they were my best men, and not altogether such bad fellows, so they began to warm to their work, and collected a goodly pile, and, digging out a box of matches from my bag, we soon had a blazing fire, and made a thorn fence or 'zeriba' round our bivouac, which began to look fairly comfortable, with our clothes hanging in festoons upon the surrounding trees.

The Somalis were soon snoring under my blankets, which I had to lend them; but I had no intention of going supperless to bed, and sat up for two hours longer, cooking a formidable dish of soup and a pot of cocoa, and thoroughly enjoying myself. The consequence was, that when we woke up next morning at the disgracefully late hour of 7 a.m., I was fresh as a daisy, while my companions did nothing but grunt and mutter strange oaths from beneath their blankets. However, by noon we had cut another tusk, and packing everything upon the camel, we set out to march down the river to Hembeweina, distant about four miles.

During our march to Hembeweina we saw kudu, oryx, and gerenouk; but I was unsuccessful throughout the day, and we again bivouacked without having found the main herd of elephants, of which we were in search. Next morning we returned to Gulanleh, intending to bring back our camp and strike the river again at Sobaat, twelve miles above Jalelo. This we accordingly did, forming an encampment at Sobaat beneath the great rocks through which the stream trickles at this spot. Below our camp, the river opened out into a broad, dry, sandy wadi, without weeds, and bordered by dense forest with undergrowth of aloes. This river, from Sobaat down to Hembeweina, contained plenty of grass and water, and therefore, game, and the nearest Somali kraals were those of the Habr Gerhajis, twenty miles to the south-east.

The morning after our arrival at Sobaat, I was rudely awakened from my sound sleep by Nur Osman poking me up and informing me that elephants had been heard trumpeting in the jungle, a short distance from the tent, evidently afraid to come to the water. It was still dark, but by the time I had lit a candle and had a wash and breakfast, the dawn was just beginning to break, and we sallied out. We expected to come on the fresh spoor at once, but had searched the jungle round for at least half a mile from camp before one of my men, who had gone farther afield, came running back, and said he could show us the herd. So, topping the next rise, we looked about us, and there, in the thickest part of the forest belt, we saw several dark masses, which, on closer inspection, proved to be the ears of the elephants moving backwards and forwards as they flapped them occasionally to keep off the flies. Walking cautiously round them, we reached a small hillock which overlooked the forest below their wind, and proceeded to examine them. While so doing, we looked round, and we found that the herd was a very numerous one, one or two cows which we had overlooked being actually to leeward of us.

None of the elephants at first appeared to notice us, but we must have become careless while looking for a tusker, and shown ourselves too much. We had been watching them for nearly half an hour, and a very pretty sight it was. The herd numbered something like sixty, and seemed to consist entirely of cows and young ones. Hitherto they had been browsing comfortably, and seemed quite at home, as if the forest belonged to them.

Now, however, they slowly but surely began to move away. Whether they had discovered us, or whether they merely contemplated a change of quarters, was not quite clear. In a short time a line began to be formed, and they filed away in full view, travelling down the wind, so that we did not quite know what was the next thing to be done. They were moving at a steady walk, and we amused ourselves counting them and examining each individual among them, as I did not wish to shoot cows more than I could help. I regretted much not having the means to photgraph them as they solemnly went by, without fuss or noise, treading gingerly, each small calf running along under the shade of its great mother's hind legs. All the cows of any size seemed to have tusks. Whilst I was admiring the herd disappearing like a dissolving view, I was reminded by my gunbearer that we had come to destroy elephants, and not to stare at them; so directly they had gone we followed in their tracks through heavy timber, with bad cactus undergrowth, sometimes hearing a crash as some elephant playfully broke a tree ahead of us. Once we followed too close, and a prolonged crash in our direction told us that an old cow was investigating the taint in the air. We, of course, gave 'leg-bail,' not wishing to disturb the herd yet; and when all was quiet we resumed our way. At last, after a tramp of one mile, we again sighted the elephants standing at the edge of the forest in three large groups, and looking uncommonly suspicious. Beyond the forest the ground became higher, and, circling round at a respectful distance, we reached a position very open and exposed, but otherwise good, being down-wind and within sixty yards of the nearest group. The ground we stood on was a spur of the Damel plain, covered with loose gravel, and studded with a few small bushes at intervals. After looking round to fix upon a line of retreat, should such a course become necessary, we began work. Bang, went the four-bore at the biggest elephant, followed by a indescribable commotion as the three groups dissolved into a long string of elephants rushing headlong past us, squealing and only intent upon escape. The big cow fired at was half-hidden in a cloud of dust for a moment, and then, making a semi-circle, she went off after the others, her stern quite closing up the pathway. Following on in her wake we caught up some of the herd which were lagging behind, and fired at what seemed to be a young bull, bringing it down stone dead, the bullet having caught it behind the shoulder as it ran by. Unfortunately, on inspection it proved to be a cow; then following on in the direction taken by the herd, we at length espied the cow first standing within forty yards of a large tree, and, stalking up to the tree, which was to leeward of her, I fired for her temple. Down she went and rolled over on her side, the Somalis running up with a yell to jump on her back. Suddenly I shouted, 'Look out, she's getting up,' and I had scarcely time to cover her temple from where I stood, twenty yards away, before she was on her legs, looking

Elephant, taken in rear

about her. Bang, went my heavy rifle, and she fell dead. I must have been standing wrong, for as I fired something gave way in my right leg, and I dumped down into a sitting postion onto a clump of aloes, unable to rise, and looking ruefully towards the elephant. I was laid up in camp for three days, but on the fourth was able to limp about very creditably, and killed a fine warthog boar near camp, beides putting up five hyenas from the rocks near our water. Having cut out the tusks of the two cows, we resolved on trying fresh ground, and, getting astride of my mule, I marched with the whole camp away to Hembeweina, sixteen miles lower down the river. At Hembeweina we found the tracks in the sand of six lions, of sizes, which had been prowling about in the river bed, and in the reeds which bordered the river close to our camp we found the half-eaten carcase of a spotted hyena which they had caught. The oryx and kudu had all left the vicinity in conseqence of the lions.

The day after our arrival at Hembeweina I was again disturbed before dawn by Nur Osman, with the report that a lot of elephants had been heard during the night trumpeting at the water, and after a good breakfast we started in search of them. After going up the river for three or four miles we came to the patch of reeds at Jalelo, where I had killed the first bull eight days previously, and, getting on to the identical spot on the high bank from which I had fired at him, we proceeded to examine the expanse of reeds. The air was much tainted as we approached the edge of the bank, but we did not care to go down into the reeds and investigate further. Looking over the sea of yellow stems, we at once saw two large cow elephants, accompanied by one calf, standing under a palm tree well out in the reeds, some two hundred and fifty yards away from our bank. Wishing to get a bull, I decided not to attack them. My Somalis were advising me to advance upon the three cows, and we were sitting on the edge of the bank intently gazing at them, when an indescribable feeling made me look round, and there was an enormous tusker standing right over us, quietly blinking his eyes at us, and balancing his right leg, undecided whether to go on along the top of the bank behind us, or to take a path straight down into the reeds. He must have come up very quietly behind us, for no one had heard a sound, and my looking round had been quite accidental. Meanwhile, as we were on the edge of the scarp, and in a bad position for a charge, we crouched under the edge of the bank, keeping as still as mice, and watched the enormous brute making up his mind. He was cogitating deeply, turning over the pros and cons of the matter; then after swinging his foot once or twice, he took the path down into the reeds, treading softly, as if on eggs, and looking very gravely towards us out of the corner of his eye; when he was well round the bank we drew a breath of relief, and began consulting as to what was to be done; then we peered over, stood up, and prepared for action.

On reaching the lower level he seemed to scent the dead elephant, and began walking out into the reeds. There was no time to be lost, so, aiming quickly as he moved, I fired my heavy rifle at the root of his ear, hitting him just a little too far back. A fiendish change at once came over him, before so calm and solemn. Out went his great ears, standing at right angles to his body like sails, and with his trunk curled up tightly in front of his chest, and giving a short trumpet, he raised his head and went crashing through the reeds, going up the river bed, and presenting his broadside to us. Aiming for the shoulder I again fired, and struck him in the ribs, in a good place; this turned him across the river straight away from our bank, and he dropped into the wake of the three cows, which, on the shots, had left the palm tree in alarm, and were already sailing away through the reeds in fine style. My leg was still not sound, and until the mule came up I had to content myself with watching them disappear in the forest on the farther side of the river. While they were crossing the reeds the wounded bull occasionally gave a squeal and charged off at a tangent, pounding imaginary foes, and looking the picture of annoyance. As the four disappeared into the trees they were joined by two strings of cows and young ones which we had not seen before, followed by two more enormous tuskers. I regretted then that we had left the horses in camp, for they would have been most useful for turning the elephants. We had to wait some time for my mule to come up, and it was 9 a.m. by the time we took up the tracks of the wounded elephant. The sun was beginning to get very strong, and it was hard work making our way over the fallen reeds, even in the lane made by the elephants. However, the spooring was not difficult, as the reeds in the path of the bull were bespattered with blood. But when we reached the forest on the further side of the river the blood ceased, and the tracking became a serious matter, as the footsteps of the wounded one were becoming mixed with those of the other two bulls. It was dreadfully hot, and for more than two hours we toiled along through aloes and thorns and tree jungles, covering about six miles of ground before we again sighted the elephants.

They were standing under two or three large trees, taking shelter from the midday sun, and we advanced cautiously to the attack. We could not make out the wounded bull, so I fired at the largest elephant I could see, a fine tusker, and the explosion of my rifle was followed by a loud answering crack and a squeal from the mass of elephants, which soon became enveloped in a dense cloud of dust. We ran on after the herd, but they slipped away and crossed half a mile of open stony ground, passed a clump of rocks which overhung the river bed and stood about half a mile beyond in moderately high tree jungle. Climbing the rocks I could see them, but following them further with my lame leg was out of the question; so my two trackers offered to go round and drive them to me, provided I lent them my Express and Martini, and gave them plenty of cartridges.

Meanwhile, I seated myself on a likely rock and watched the herd. There was one very sick elephant among them, which seemed to be continually rolling, and it was surrounded by a group of sympathising friends. I afterwards found this to be the bull first wounded – our friend who had surprised us on the river bank – and he appeared to be in a dying state. While I was gazing over the forest at them, the herd suddenly began to move in my

Saving her calf

direction very fast, and a moment later the breeze carried to my position the faint reports of musketry coming from the far distance beyond the elephants. They disappeared for about five minutes and again emerged from the forest about two hundred yards from my rock, and made down the river past me.

When they were abreast of me and about fifty yards from me, I fired right and left into the shoulder of a very old bull, the biggest of the three, carrying fine long tusks. He fell and kicked about for some seconds in a cloud of dust, and then turned upstream again with the others, going very fast. They then passed round my rock again at seventy yards, and I put another ball into the shoulder of the bull first wounded, which had somewhat recovered up to this time. Poor thing! it was continually throwing water over its body as it went along, but with undiminished speed. My leg was now beginning to feel the strain to which it had been put all day, and each time I fired the 4-bore had sent me back against the wall of rock behind me. At the third discharge I went flying, and plumped down into a sitting posture on the rocks, the rifle falling out of my hands. The elephants now sailed gaily away over huge boulders and nullahs with the activity of monkeys, and soon disappeared over the brow of a low hill, leaving me on the rock nonplussed. Soon the trackers came up, and we went to examine the place where the largest bull had fallen. The cactus was crushed to bits and the sand much scraped about, but no blood. He had evidently fallen and struggled some time before rising again. The elephants had quite beaten us, and we made the best of our way home, reaching camp at dusk, after a fearfully tiring day.

For two days I had horsemen dogging the footsteps of the wounded bulls, but they returned and reported that the herd had gone past Little Harar, and might not pull up for days, having been thoroughly disturbed by the hunt; that they had followed the tracks of the bull first wounded for twenty-five miles, that he had separated from the herd, and halted to roll many times, but that at length his tracks had become mixed with those of a fresh herd of bulls, cows and young ones, and that they had at last given him up. Rain having recently fallen rendered the tracking more difficult.

Some days afterwards, in Berbera, two Somalis came in and reported that they had seen the dead elephant near Hargeisa (Little Harar), and that a passing caravan had appropriated the tusks, and taken them in to Harar itself. So, from Berbera we sent letters to Harar to request their recovery. Meanwhile we remained in camp at Hembeweina, waiting for elephants or anything that might turn up.

The night after the long elephant hunt previously mentioned, we were kept awake at midnight by two lions, which kept up a deep roaring, repeated at short intervals, which seemed only thirty yards from our zeriba, though in reality it was over a hundred, as we saw by the pugs in the sand next day. Luckily, neither my mule nor the three Somali ponies were a bit nervous, or we should have had some trouble. One lion kept upwind, giving a few low grunts, growing louder and ending in a roar, then dwindling down again. After a bit he would be answered by a rumbling sound from the lion on the other side, who seemed to be concealed in the reeds of the river bed close by. There was absolutely no moon, so we could do nothing but replenish the fires with a stock of grass and sticks which I always keep for this purpose. The Somalis jeered at my concern about the lions, and said that they were not in earnest or they would not roar. The mule seemed to take no notice of them, and the ponies merely snorted contemptuously. We had left out some meat within twenty yards of the zeriba, but found it untouched next morning, so that the visit of the lions was a dead failure as far as they themselves were concerned.

I found Hembeweina very pleasant, and never tired of wandering about near camp, examining the fresh elephant tracks in the river. On 24th May, I was on one of these rambles, quite alone, and had ascended to the top of a plateau about a mile from camp. The summit was a level plain, covered with black stones, with occasional tufts of very green feathery grass. Finding some fresh oryx tracks, I began to cross the plateau, but the spooring was difficult on account of the stones. All at once I caught sight of a large animal moving slowly amongst some bushes, evidently grazing unsuspicious of danger, and, thinking it might be a wild ass, I began to stalk up to it. This was not so easy, on account of the transparent nature of the thorn bushes; however, I got up to three hundred yards, and imagine my surprise on finding the animal to be an ordinary Somali pony, alone in this bleak spot. This plateau had a bad reputation, as the nearest tribe in that direction lived some seventy miles off, and were said to amuse themselves by raiding this part of the country and lifting cattle whenever there was nothing else to do.

By the side of the horse I could see a brown thing on the ground, which might be a man or an ant-hill. Having on a former trip been dogged by scouts from a neighbouring tribe, I determined to investigate; so shoving a couple of cartridges into my Express rifle, and loosening my revolver, I crept up to the bushes and looked over, hoping to catch the scout, if such he should be, asleep. However, the imaginary man turned out to be an ant-hill; and the horse, perfectly wild, and without tether or rope on him, gave a loud whinny and trotted in a circle round me, with arching neck, nodding his head at me in a most amusing way. He was evidently a horse which had been abandoned by some doughty chief; and I determined to catch him, use him for elephant work, and then take him to the coast to be publicly claimed. Returning to camp I brought up my people, and with

Habr Gerhajis

the help of my mule, which made a clever decoy, we at last got a rope over his head, after much playful kicking; and then he let himself be led quietly into camp.

The day after the capture of the horse two men rode in to give me news that Shire Shermaki, one of the Habr Gerhajis chief men, was on his way from his camp, some fifteen miles away, to visit me, bringing thirty horsemen with him, whom he was pleased to call his 'children'. Then followed a delightful scene. In the distance, over the plain, arose a thin wreath of dust, and under it appeared first one or two, and then about thirty, horsemen, following each other in file, and coming on at a trot. Presently, as they approached our camp, they formed into a line, and broke into a canter, the spears of the men flashing merrily in the sun, and the bright red trappings of the horses flaring out against the green bushes. Each man wore a calico 'tobe' of scarlet, dashed with blue, in check pattern, the dress of the Somali when on raid or state occasions. They came within a hundred yards of my camp, and halted. Accompanied by my nine Somalis, I left the zeriba, and advanced to meet them. Sitting on his pony in the centre of the group was Shire Shermaki, a dignified-looking old man, with a white beard, and on either side of him two or three fine fellows, in the prime of life, his sons. There were also one or two boys, armed, like their seniors, with spears and shield, and the short, straight, Roman-shaped sword, of native manufacture, which Somalis always wear round the waist, for use at close quarters. All the horsemen, without exception, looked a sturdy lot, and up to rough work.

We exchanged the usual Mussulman salaams, and one of Shire Shermaki's sons urged his pony up in front of the rest and sang an extempore song. This was a long one, but at last came to an end; then I complimented the old fellow upon his turnout, and waited expectantly for him to explain his visit. He said that, being with his people and their flocks and herds, at a spot some fifteen miles to the eastward, and having heard of my presence in his neighbourhood, he had come with some of his young men to visit me, sing songs (eat my rice), and have a good time. This was all very well, but our supply of provisions was getting scanty, and I mentally resolved to get rid of our friends at the first opportunity. I now requested the old chief to show me what his children could do in the way of equestrian exercises, and at once two or three impatient spirits galloped forward and threw their spears, then went careering round us, and ended by pulling up with a jerk. The Somali bit is very severe, and frequently the poor ponies can be seen bleeding from their mouths; but, on the whole, they seem to enjoy the fun.

Soon the whole plain around my zeriba was covered with rushing steeds, and excited riders, throwing their spears in every direction and picking them up again at full speed. Each pony raised a cloud of dust all to himself, the confusion increased, and had reached its height when the old chief raised his hand, and one by one the men galloped up to where I was standing, each rider, as he reached me, pulling his pony back on to its haunches, quivering all over. Every man, as he came up in turn, gave the customary exclamation of triumph, '*Mot, io mot,*' (noticed by Burton, in his *First Footsteps in East Africa*); and each one we all answered, as is duty bound, '*Kul leban,*' (thanks). The Somalis are very clever horsemen, and many can throw the spear about ninety yards at full gallop, though somewhat wide of the mark at this distance. They ride by balance, and I remember once, when riding by moonlight, on a fifty-mile march, having in front of me as guide a chief man, who went to sleep in the saddle; so did the pony, and, waking up suddenly as he passed a small black bush, he stopped dead, and shied away from the bush. The Somali plumped on to his head, and I as nearly as possible rode over him.

After the equestrian games we all repaired to my zeriba, and I exhorted my Somalis to prepare a sumptuous meal of rice, dates, etcetera, to put before our guests. Soon from across the plain came two more horsemen, and a boy leading a cow, which, after much mysterious whispering, was brought in front of my tent as a present, with Shire Shermaki's compliments. We killed it ten minutes later, and my men joined the strangers in a big feed, followed by a firelight dance, the men clapping their hands to the strains of a horrible reed flute, advancing and retiring as in a quadrille at home. Then a few graceful step dances, followed by songs. Most of these were extempore, alternatively in praise of the English and of the Habr Gerhajis tribe. The burden of one song was: There is nobody like us, our horses are the best in the countryside, and nobody can fight like we can fight; our old men are wise, our young men are strong as lions, our girls are the fairest in the land, etcetera. When I retired to my tent at midnight the clamour was still going on and I was roused at 3 a.m. by the departure of the whole lot; not, however, till after an affectionate farewell. By the lurid glare of our camp fire old Shire Shermaki made a speech, laying great stress on my having seen his country, and asking me to tell the English that his tribe were very good people, and never molested caravans, etcetera; to which I replied that, so far as having seen his country was concerned, he was perfectly at liberty to come and see mine, and I promised him a State 'tobe' from Berbera, and cloth for his men.

They recognised the horse which I had caught as one which had been abandoned by one of their tribesmen three months previously while on a journey. So I promised, if they would send in a man to Berbera, that I would give up the horse to the British representative officer at that port, and they must address a claim to him. Finally, I apologised for not having shown them any equestrian games on our part, saying that 'the mule was sick'. This made them laugh, and the joke had to be repeated all round for the benefit of those who were at all deaf. Then a hearty handshake with everybody, and they festively trotted off into the gloom of the night.

While shifting our camp, next day, back to Gulanleh, we were constantly in sight of game, either gerenouk, oryx, or gazelles, and we caught sight of a leopard sneaking across a nullah three hundred yards ahead of us; but he disappeared into some rocky ground, where tracking became impossible. On arriving at Gulanleh I sent my horseman for a grand tour to all the elephant covers round, and remained meanwhile in camp, ready to march at a moment's notice. Besides my own trackers, I had two parties of Habr Gerhajis horsemen also searching for elephants, each party consisting of three men.

While in camp at Gulanleh I was suddenly roused by shouts of 'Sahib! Shoot him down! Kill him dead!' So, pulling out my revolver, I looked round the fly of the tent, and found my whole camp in an uproar, men running for their spears, and, backing into one side of the zeriba, stood the Midgan (bushman) fitting a poisoned arrow to his long bow, and glaring in a very 'let me at him' sort of way at one of my camelmen, who stood at the other end of the zeriba surrounded by his friends, and holding his spear out in a menacing way at the Midgan. The situation was decidedly theatrical. I happened to be on good terms with my bushman, so, preferring to trust him, I turned my back on him and walked up to the Somali, telling the latter to sit down and give us his spears, then going back to my jungle friend I bundled him ignominiously into my tent, poisoned arrows and all, and threw him an oryx skull to clean, further stating that if he tried to escape from my tent to go for the Somali, he would probably come to an untimely end on his way. Having thus satisfactorily disposed of the centres of disturbance, I inquired into the cause of the row. During some chaff over the midday meal, the camelman had lost his temper, and had prodded the Midgan in the back with his broad-bladed spear, luckily inflicting only a slight wound. The Midgan was clearly in the right, and, going to my tent, I had a long argument with him on the subject of his wrongs. Then calling the camelman to my tent I held out my beautiful nickel-plated revolver over them, and 'persuaded' them to shake hands and swear eternal friendship.

These fights are of constant occurrence, and often end fatally; when a blood-feud between two tribes, lasting perhaps for years, is the result. The Somali is quick to anger or to laughter, and easily excited, but as quickly cools down again. I took the precaution to have neither of these men on guard that night, and we heard no more of the matter.

On May 27th, at 9 a.m., one of my trackers rode in to say that his party had struck the spoor of a solitary bull elephant in a nullah some twelve miles to the westward, and that they had followed him down the bed of the nullah for eight hours, when they had at last found him, feeding and standing about, at El-Danan. He had left his two comrades to watch the elephant. Taking one camel and two or three men, I at once set out for El-Danan, and after a hot march we struck the wadi at 2 p.m., and followed in the tracks of the two watchmen until we found them. Then, after resting for lunch under a tree, I went forward with my gunbearer, Deria Hassan, to explore the reeds where the elephant had last been seen. After some trouble we at length spied him standing under a tree at the further side of a belt of reeds some forty yards wide. He seemed a very large bull, and had a nice thick pair of tusks protruding from his lips. On the further side of him the ground was quite bare. I crept up to the edge, and getting on the roots of a tree, could see his head above the reeds. He was swinging it slowly from side to side, and all the time looking quietly in my direction, though he did not appear to see me. At last he presented his temple for a shot, and I fired as well as I could, hitting him a loud smack, and Deria Hassan fired from the bank behind me. Instantly the beast gave a fiendish shriek and charged, coming straight at me through the reeds. I did not wait for his head to appear, but ran down the edge of the reeds, to leeward, and hid under a thorn bush, Deria disappearing with equal promptitude in another direction. Then the three horsemen rode up, and, seeing them, the elephant turned again into the reeds and made off, keeping down the centre, the horsemen riding parallel to him along the border of the reeds. I followed on foot, and came up, a mile further down, just in time to see him charge viciously at the horses, scattering them in every direction. This manoeuvre was repeated twice, and then the elephant went up a side gully three hundred yards wide, choked by an unbroken expanse of very high reeds. We lost sight of him here for a time, and taking up his tracks we found much blood.

On reaching the wadi I sent the horsemen on after the elephant, and, being parched with thirst, lay down and drank from the rivulet. Before I had finished, Deria said, 'Look out!' and I heard galloping and loud shouts, and sprang up just in time to see the elephant break back and cross the stream two hundred yards below me, and take up his former position in the reeds, followed by my three horsemen, who were working admirably. When I came up, the horsemen were collected on some rising ground overlooking the reeds, hooting at the elephant, who stood, with the top of his head just visible, listening to them. Advancing to a small knoll in front of the horsemen, I fired right and left at his head. His disappeared for a moment, and then someone cried, 'He's coming!' Out he came, very silently, and I slipped away to leeward and crouched under a bush, to watch him. Off he went after the horsemen, and singling out Hussein Debeli, following every turn of the horse, he kept close behind its tail for two hundred yards, till I thought the plucky fellow would be caught, and they disappeared together among the trees. However, looking in the reeds soon afterwards, I saw that the elephant, having finished his charge, was stealing back again towards the gully he had first tried. Back came the horseman, and after a short race headed him, and brought him to a standstill, giving me a beautiful shot at the shoulder at fifty yards. Half expecting to have the watchful beast down on me like 'a thousand of bricks' at the shot, I fired; but this time, dropping his tail, his trunk hanging down, he went slowly on towards the gully, looking quite demoralised. Before he could reach the jungle I ran in close, and gave him a second shot in the shoulder at twenty yards, as he ran. Swerving at this, he disappeared in the reeds, and we heard him crashing about in them for some time, then a dreadfully plaintive moaning bellow, and all was still.

Before venturing in I fired two shots with my Express, and listened, but,

A vicious charge

hearing nothing, we determined to examine the reeds. We were not long in finding the great cutting made by the beast through them, and with rifles on full cock, and every sense on the alert, we entered. On each side rose an impenetrable wall; wherever we looked we saw nothing but reeds, and as we proceeded we had to climb over great mounds of fallen stalks. Yard by yard we advanced, every now and then stopping to listen. Along the floor and sides of the lane of reeds blood was plentifully sprinkled, and at length we began to approach the place where the great brute had been last heard to moan. I peeped round an angle and saw him lying on his side stone dead, and we walked up to examine our prize. He was an old bull, 10 ft. 6 in. at the shoulder, and had a beautiful white pair of tusks, very thick.

By the time the sun had gone down we had cut out one tusk, and returned up the river to search the plateau for a camping ground, with good grass for the horses. Leaving the main river, we bivouacked near a small grassy nullah. The arrangements were quickly made, and, spreading out our blankets under a thorn bush, we were soon all fast asleep. We had no fence, and at midnight I was awakened by a lion roaring a short distance up the nullah. Rubbing my eyes, I awoke Deria, and told him to watch and keep the fire alight. Then I dozed off again, and when we woke next morning Deria was fast asleep by the fire, which was nearly out.

We cut the other tusk, and returning to Gulanleh, my leave being up, after skirting the foot of Golis for five days, we marched by easy stages to Berbera, then by dhow back to Aden, where we were becalmed twelve hours in sight of the station before getting in.

Thus ended happily a most charming expedition. I had been in the interior a month, and besides exploring the unknown Issutugan District, I had bagged 5 elephants, 4 oryx, 2 lesser kudu, 7 Waller's gazelles, 2 warthog, 5 gazelles, 2 dik-dik: 25 head not counting the dik-dik. I had long held the opinion that shikar was the only hobby, besides painting, worthy of attention and this wonderful trip confirmed that opinion – though only one of many journeys, it was probably *the* red-letter one – for it and the one before it were my first trial with *dangerous* large game.

Chapter 14

Zanzibar and Mombasa
Oct '88–March '89

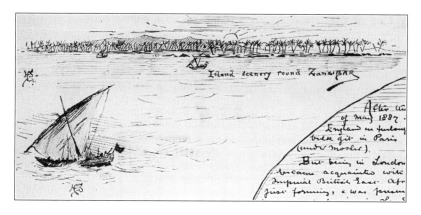

A FTER THE great trip of May 1887, I went to England on furlough, spending the bulk of it in Paris studying Art (under Mosler).

But being in London in 1888, I became acquainted with the new Imperial British East African Company just forming and was present at the inaugural dinner in London. Sir W. MacKinnon was just about to send his first caravan out, the first thing being to relieve Stanley, who had not been heard of for some time, and it was purposed to send up to Wadelai (in Emir's Province) an expedition of 12 Europeans and 900 porters, with a Maxim gun. Volunteering my services, I was chosen to command and started about a month later with George S. Mackenzie as Managing Director at Mombasa – we had a steamer chartered on purpose for us – from the British India Company – and we Europeans all went out in this vessel. There was MacKinnon, our doctor, Crawford, MacLaren, Gadge of Ceylon, Last the ex-missionary, and finally Jackson the sportsman, who has since written several articles for big game shooting in the Badminton Library. There were also Kenwick and Halloway Carew, two sportsmen.

After leaving Aden, we skirted the mountains of Eastern Somaliland, the unexplored ranges of the Warsangli Country – and my Somalis, (for I had four horsemen with their horses sent from the Dolbahanta Country to drive cattle on this expedition) paid a last adieu to these beautiful mountains with reverent eyes. There were four of them; one, Adam Yusuf, becoming my best headman in many later trips. Approaching Zanzibar, we steamed past the beautiful palm-covered islands of Pemba etcetera – the slaves are supposed to have a short life on Pemba, only averaging three years, owing to fever – and at last anchored in the harbour. A most interesting place, Zanzibar, but hot and feverish. Arab flat-topped houses, whitewashed outsides and palm trees rising over them. The call of the Muezzin from the Musjid and on every roof at prayer time: '*Allah-hu-akbar – ashamdous Allah illa ha ille-la,*' etcetera etcetera. A grotesque palace (since burnt). We went to a big reception there given by Sais Bayhashi's successor (I forgot his name), the Sultan of Zanzibar – General Matthews with his army, from European uniforms and gold lace tailing down to almost nakedness and a sword; led us to the palace, and a brass band. Then the Audience Chamber – Sultan – G. Mackenzie in the centre at the lead. We next, then the long line of Arab elders in flowing silks etcetera sherbet and cigarettes. After the first salaams, G. Mackenzie, with Persian flowery speech, said: 'The East African Company is a little flower – we men of the City of London will water it with our money; but your Highness has the important part, so be the Sun and shine upon it with your approval, so that it will grow and be admired by everyone.' Eternal sherbet.

A room with ghastly French chandeliers, and 60 clocks all ticking at once, and showing various times! After the Audience we gave his Highness a Maxim gun inlaid with silver, costing £500. We put up, most of us, at the Consulate, being the guests of Consul General Ewan Smith, a most charming host. It was a very pleasant time. We went out and made a day of it at the Sultan's summer palace at the other end of the island where he keeps his harem – if he has one.

Everything has an end and our pleasant sojourn at Zanzibar had one – Admiral Fremantle had made his after-lunch speech and we were ready for the Dark Continent. We said goodbye to the British Fleet blockading the coast (to prevent the slave trade), and sailed in our British India ship again for Mombasa. All the German coast was in open revolt and there had been heavy fighting at Bagamoyo etcetera and we were doubtful about our reception. Entering Mombasa Harbour we had a mishap, a boat falling from the davits while being lowered and getting smashed. Soon afterwards, when we were shouting with laughter at lunch in the saloon, the doctor came and dampened our spirits saying that a young naval lieutenant, who was being taken home with remittent fever, had died that moment in the deckhouse a few feet above us!

We cast anchor in this harbour, and in the evening I was the first to go ashore with the doctor. Just before our arrival, some of our Zanzibari porters, who were awaiting us, had quarrelled with the people in Mombasa and it

Street scene in Zanzibar

ended the night before in a drunken riot, swords being drawn and one of our men killed and nine wounded. I went and visited them at a temporary hospital which had been arranged. The wounded men looked very sorry for themselves and in the centre of the room on a table, with a sheet over his head, was the dead man. I saw the cut – a sword cut – it had cut his skull almost in two on the right side and extended down to his left side, cutting into the ribs there and nearly severing his back – truly an awful cut, apparently made with a two-handed sabre as he lay on the ground.

Next day we went ashore to the funeral of the poor naval lieutenant and buried him in the little cemetery of the Church Missionary Society's station among the palm groves.

We then took up our quarters in the old Mission House overlooking the harbour and were for about a week surrounded with boxes, stores, rifles and the usual paraphernalia of an exploring expedition. Last, an ex-missionary, was engaged to be a guide for us and head of transport coolies and European interpreter.

The Swahilis are light-hearted, good-humoured people when not drunk. When you walk through the fields at Mombasa in the morning, you hear cries of *'Yambo, yambo Bwana Kubwa,'* – ('Welcome Great Master') in salutation. When drunk they are impudent and combative. Mombasa grows mangoes, pineapples, coconuts, popoi and tropical fruit in profusion.

We at last set off for the interior and marched through Rabai to Jumba

– the commencement of the Nyika. Jackson was with me as second in command. We marched across the Nyika, or thorn wilderness, and got to Gulu Gulu, where we settled down to make the first permanent station. A little spot in the Nyika of Ukanbani – with a small pool overshadowed by thick trees and said to contain crocodiles.

From Gulu Gulu, where I began making a survey, I had some interesting wanderings and saw zebra, waterbuck and roan antelope – but only glimpses – I fired at the waterbuck, two of them, but was unsuccessful.

The Wakamba were good-natured actively built bush people, almost naked, the girls wearing strings of beads round their waists as their only clothing. Unfortunately, my photos all turned out badly. We got splendid views to the west, inland, of Kilina-Kibomu, the next hill and Kilimanjaro and others.

One morning, I decided to go through about five miles of forest and visit Indindi to put it in my map. I took with me Adam Yusuf and three other mounted Somalis with their spears and we were all mounted. On the edge of the forest we passed a war party of Wakamba with spears, bows and arrows running by, all war feathers and red ochre – to repel, they said, a great raid of Masai warriors. They crowded round me and asked me where I was going. 'Indindi,' I answered. 'Oh! don't go to Indindi, it's full of Masai warriors.' So I halted to argue with them, when my Somali said, 'Sahib, don't let us listen to these stupid cattle – let us go and see. Who cares for the Masai, we who are Somalis.' So we plunged into four miles of forest, and at the further side came suddenly into a village, which was Indindi. A few elders only remained in the village and they came out to greet us. They said the Masai had been there the night before and driven off some cattle and the young men had gone to follow them up. This was like good old Somaliland over again!

On another occasion while in a termporary bush camp, we heard the singing of five hundred voices or so in chorus in the bush. I was taking a photo of camp and went on with what I was doing, but all the porters (Swahilis) disappeared into the bush away from the noise of singing. My four Somalis, however, seeing something was up, came up and asked if they might bring in the ponies, which were tethered among the bushes on the side where the noise was. So they quietly came back with the ponies all safe and we sat down to await events. Soon our porters began dropping into camp again, the scare over. It turned out to be a village turning out to pray for rain and our timid Swahili had mistaken it for a war party of Masai.

About this time I went down to Mombasa on business and heard that Stanley was coming down by the Bagamoyo route so we should not be sent to Wadelai as originally intended but work into the interior slowly by making stations, Gulu Gulu being the first. This was not a very bright prospect.

Meanwhile a road to Gulu Gulu through 21 miles of bush was required. I surveyed the old native path, fixed the scale and line of the drawing by astronomical observations and on the map plotted the 'straight through' line with offsets from landmarks, such as anthills etcetera, on the old path. The result was a straight road; the beginning, I suppose, of the present Uganda road.

At this time, it being found necessary to engage an interpreter, I managed with G. Mackenzie to go on a trip to the Mission Station of Galbanti on the Tana to try and secure the services of Mrs Durant, a half-native missionary there.

Chapter 15

Up the Tana River – March '88

— *On the Tana River (Ozi branch)*

(with schools of hippos)

Tʜɪs ᴡᴀs a very interesting trip. How I got to Lamour I do not remember, but I remember being in the Sultan's steamer from Zanzibar and casting anchor in Lamour harbour. Mombasa and Lamour were then scarcely known – they were spots difficult to find on the map before '88, so small was the print and 'Isle de Lamour' was always written in French. All this has changed now.

As we steamed slowly into the harbour, we passed a patch of sand dunes on our left, covered with little scintillating white spots and streaks, thousands of them. Drawing near, we could see what they were with the help of our Captain's explanations. In former times, a great landing had been attempted by the inhabitants of Manda and Patta Island in the teeth of a force of Lamour people and the result had been a great fight in which some – I forget the number, but think 20,000 people were killed. This landing was attempted in countless canoes, but failed. There they were, skulls, skeletons, legbones, pieces of pelvis – repeated in countless number, sticking half in and half out of the drift sand, here laid bare by a scour of the sea-breeze, there nearly covered again by the drift.

After a visit to the 'Wali', an Arab Governor of Lamour, I took ship with my Mombasa porters in an Arab dhow for Kipini, about two days down the coast. We got chased, I believe for a short time by a man o' war's cutter which we saw a mile or two astern, but on running up the Union Jack, the cutter held on its way. They had no doubt mistaken me and my coolies for an Arab slave-owner running slaves over to Pemba. We eventually, on the second (or was it the third?) day, made Kipini, at the mouth of the Ozi river, at dusk. I called on the Wali of this very African village, and he, a very blind old man (a relation, like most of the Arab walis or governors, to the Sultan of Zanzibar), put me up in his house for the night, giving me a divan to sleep upon. Very comfortable, but badly lighted and plenty of mosquitoes. Next afternoon we started up the broad flood of the Ozi in a dhow, propelled by singing natives, Lamour men and Wapokomo. It was my first experience of an African river and a very interesting one.

Soon the sun set up-river in the West and we had a moonlight journey of the most marvellous beauty. Schools of hippopotami were seen across our path in the shallows in the centre of the river and I fired a few shots – but finding I could not wait to ascertain whether the bodies rose or not (it generally takes six hours), I refrained after a few shots and left them in peace. My boatman who manned the sweeps were pulling with a long, slow, rhythmical stroke, singing all the while a new song of Lamour:

'*Yambo, Yamboo, eh Yambo Miopeh,*
Yambo, Yamboo, eh Yambo Miopeh.'

This was the chorus, the song, my helmsman told me, was to the effect that 'White Men and white things (Rupees) had come to Mombasa – welcome, my brothers!' A very pretty chorus, sung as it was by sturdy, soft-voiced negroes, and sung as is their custom, with a will!

Very early in the morning we got to Karo, where the Ozi communicated with the Tana by the Belezoni Canal,[1] a very ancient work (see Rider Haggard's *She* by Allan Quartermain). It was still bright moonlight and my sleep was further prevented by the mosquitoes – perhaps the most terrible in the world! They tormented us till after daylight – in fact, we spent the day in the terrible Belezoni Canal – a small ditch made in ancient times to connect the two rivers. The mosquitoes are awful, they crawl about your clothes and get into the bottom of the boat and crawl up your legs and settle in swarms under your hat where the forehead meets the inside of the crown of the hat.

After a day of superlative misery I arrived at Tchanaa and got into the main stream of the Tana – then we poled up against the stream for several

---

1 The Belezoni Canal brings boats over from the Tana in order to reach the sea, as the Tana has a bar at its mouth, rendering it incapable of being used for navigation.

hours and arrived at Golbanti, the United Methodist Mission Station where my business was.

Howe, the missionary, was there – proved a very nice fellow and was most hospitable. I was there two or three days. We used to emerge from our mosquito curtains at 8 a.m. and return to them after an early dinner at 6 p.m. I went out into the plain after 'tope' or Hunter's antelopes (something like a hartebeeste) but was unsuccessful. They were very smart. In the light yellow grass, about 4 ft. 6 in. high, their heads looked very black and distinct, so I suppose mine did too whenever I put it up to look. Anyway, they always bolted out of shot in a long string, swishing through the grass. I mean to have another shot at them someday if possible, when the Tana becomes more accessible.

One afternoon, Howe and I went out elephant hunting, but saw nothing. Near Howe's home on the edge of the Nyika bush was the ruined and deserted dwelling of Houton (or Houghton) his predecessor, who three years previously had sent some of the Mission boys and Golbanti people to recover some cattle stolen by the Masai elmorano (warriors). The Golbanti people lost many hundreds in the battle that followed – and a few months later a band of 20 Masai burst into the compound of Houghton's house with their great shovelheaded spears. He was in the garden and Mrs Houghton in the house and they were both instantly killed. Their graves are outside in the garden side by side. In the deserted cottage is a table with one leg eaten off by white ants. The lamp with the snuffed wick (it was morning) and broken chimney still stood on the table when Howe showed me the house. The mattress had great spear holes in it where the warriors had been probing for booty.

That had happened three years before, and since then there had been a great raid of the Somalis from the north of the Tana, who are good swimmers and cross the Tana to raid Golbanti. Howe and his colleagues defended the place against them, and the Somalis withdrew. When I was at Golbanti, Howe was expecting another raid of Somalis, and borrowed some rifle cartridges from me. The double-storeyed stockaded house of the Mission, in which I was entertained by Howe, was a new one built after the murder of Mr Houghton, and was very well designed for defence.

On the Tana, I found the river population were called the Wa-Pakomos, negroes of fine physique, lorded over and held in subjection by the warlike Gallas.

The Gallas at Golbanti a few years before my visit numbered between one and two thousand souls, rich in cattle, but latterly they had been annually raided by the Masai from the south and the Somalis from the north – till the village of Golbanti itself had dwindled down to about one hundred and fifty inhabitants. Only Howe's presence kept the village going at all. The

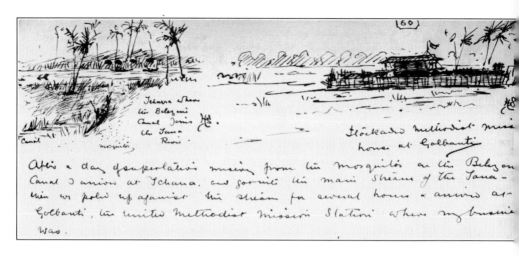

Stockaded Methodist mission house at Golbanti

Golbanti Mission was founded, I believe, by Mrs Wakefield, and is of the United Methodist persuasion.

After the murder of Houghton, when the Somalis came down, they first had burnt the German station of Ngai, a few miles upstream, and the German missionaries had taken refuge in the Golbanti house, They saw the flare of their own Mission burning a few miles away. The Gallas at Golbanti said they feared the Somalis even more than the Masai as the former, being good swimmers, the Tana River was no obstacle to them.

The Southern Somalis are very bold and are said to raid cattle from the Gallas and take them to Lamour, on the east coast, to sell them. Lamour is a mixed Galla and Arab town. As the Somalis have horsemen, they are said to be able to cope with the Masai, whom they sometimes meet when both are raiding the Gallas near the Tana. We saw a few of the Southern Somalis walking about Lamour. They are rougher, more savage-looking, and finer men than the Northern Somalis. The Gallas of Golbanti were well-featured men, very quiet in manners, brown in colour with thin lips and spare, slight physique. The Somalis are very like them, but rather bigger and better built, and the only difference once could observe was that there appeared to be some Arab blood in the Somalis.

The Gallas on the Tana are wedged in between the continually advancing Somalis from the north and Masai from the south, the apex of the wedge being near the Tana mouth and the base at the souces of the Juba. The effect of this pressure is perhaps driving the Tana Gallas up the river to the countries where they are numerous and can hold their own.

We could not manage to engage the services of Mrs Durant as she preferred to stop with the Methodist Mission.

After a very pleasant stay with Howe, I got into my canoe – very seedy, by the by – for the return journey down the Tana and Ozi. Was it going up or down that I slept a night ashore at a village and the people lit fires and danced all night to keep off mosquitoes, beating each other with cowtail whips all the time? At one spot on the Tana a hippo blew below us; we floated down over him, the Pokomo boatman prodding at his body; and after we had got down 100 yards, he blew again at this same spot, so that we passed in the shallow water only 3 ft. over his body! I had many adventures with hippo but was too weak to take much trouble in hunting them, and not having time to wait and see the effect of my shots, I bagged nothing. Back through the awful canal again and down the broad sweep, the canoe being followed for miles by a school of inquisitive hippos or 'kipini'. By this time I was very bad with remittent fever and glad to find the MS *Stork* surveying ship (Captain Pullen) at work here making a survey. I was put on board and soon in the hands of the European doctor and taken to Mombasa. Poor Pullen died of fever a few years after, I believe on this coast.

After staying at Mombasa a week or two and finding the remittent fever so obstinate that doctors recommended my leaving the coast, and finding that there was to be no Stanley relief expedition after all, I seriously thought of throwing it all up and returning to India. My leave (six months) was drawing to a close. I had asked under what conditions I would be granted a year's further leave, and on the authorities replying that I would have to pay 100R a month for the right to an Indian pension, I asked for my passage to India and threw up the appointment.

On the whole, it had been a very interesting trip with vivid impressions. I brought my four Somalis safely back, though they had had very bad fever. The fact is, Mombasa is not very healthy.

I got into a little British India Steamer at Zanzibar and was one of three first class passengers – the others being O'Neale, Consul of Lake Nyassa and his wife. A deck passenger, a deserter from Natal, formerly a Hussar Sergeant Major – an Irishman by name of Denis Murphy – took occasion to sleep in a first class cabin, get drunk and beat a Portuguese steward. On my going to the Captain, he said: 'All right my fine military friend, one more sweet night and we shall be in Aden, when I'll jump on your chest, me bhoy, "For that's the way they die!!"'

Chapter 16

Henweina and Golis
March and April 1889

A CAPITAL TRIP — I had still some time left before my six months' leave
(which I had received) to serve with the East African Company, I
should explain — so, ill as I was with remittent fever and jaundice, and as
yellow as a guinea, I crawled out of the British India Mail Steamer at Aden
and, going to Cowasgies', booked my passage by the next steamer for
Berbera for a three-week trip to Somaliland. How my Somalis, also down
with remittent fever, had gazed at the mountains of the Warsingili country
as we had steamed up the Gulf of Aden!

Landing at Berbera in due course, I marched to Deregodleh, Hamass and
Laferug by the old shooting route, and then turned off southwards to the
beautiful aloe-strewn Henweina Plain under the foothills of Banyero and
Gan Libah sections of the Golis Range. This was a red-letter trip. A quiet
modest, lively little shoot. I was chiefly after warthog and lesser kudu, and
the great kudu itself. So I made my first camp at Garasleh Henweina, where
I shot some guinea fowl and a couple of magnificent warthog boars. It was
a lovely camp and I took several photographs with a French camera I had
bought in the Rue du Château d'Eau, Paris, and got some successful results,
especially of the guda and aloe forest in the Henweina plain.

I only took a boat sail on this trip and we stretched it over gypsy poles
to form a sort of small Somali hut. Leaving our camp at Garasleh Henweina
full of guineafowls' feathers, we climbed up into the mile-wide ledge of

Mirso and formed camp at Kulmaye on a stretch of green sward with forests of euphorbia trees all round, and a splendid view to the west over Mur Aderyu (the Hill of Kudus) in the great bluff of Gan Libah. Birds and butterflies and wild flowers abounded and it was quite respectably cold. Nightly a lion roared – but never got a chance at him, though I sat on an old platform in a tree, built I believe by Francis & Wood or by Lieutenant Phillips, to try and circumvent him. My followers, only about eight in number, including old Hussein Debeli, who had been with me on my elephant-shooting trip up the Issutugan; Tana and Hassan Midgan; Adam Yusuf my trusty horseman who had followed me to Mombasa; and several others. A good lot. We were therefore a jolly little camp. It was cold on Mirso, being about 5,000 feet, but I had given every man a blanket.

After many hunts after large kudu round the hill, Mur Aderyu, I had to give it up. We were shown a stone called Dagah-shabil – the panther stone, from which a man-eating panther was said to lie in wait and spring on passers-by. It was curiously hollowed out at the top, just in the form of the crouching body of a panther! It was said to have killed a hundred people in a year. But we never came across it.

We climbed up Golis (Banyeri) one day and found magnificent cedars on top – a lovely forest all smelling of the pencil cedar-wood, one tree was about 4 feet diameter and 100 feet high. Nothing could exceed the wild beauty of this climb. Tracks of kudu everywhere, but not to be seen. I came down to camp again in the evening well satisfied with my explorations. I had had no luck with the kudu. That was to come on a later trip – three years later, in fact – but I had seen what I still hold to be the most beautiful spot in Somaliland – the gorges above Kulmeye in Mirso. There is nothing to touch it, in my opinion, anywhere in the country, except in the Harar Highlands. The great red weathered limestone and sandstone precipices at the edge of the Banyero Bluff were particularly fine, and at their base huge rocks had fallen from the top – forming caves and recesses grown over with moss and maidenhair fern.

We marched down to Garasleh Henweina again and had another turn at the game there, and I got two very fine lesser kudu bucks, one of which held the record for many years – nearly 28 inches in a straight line from the base to the white point, but it has shrunk over several years in a museum, as they always do. It was a grand prize and I remember my joy as I stooped to measure it. I took a photo of Hussein Debeli and the other shikaris skinning it among the aloes and with the beautiful thorn jungle overhead. My camp at Garasleh had now taken on quite the appearance of a successful shikari's camp. There were the old guinea fowl feathers from my sojourn of ten days before, and now there were also the head and skins of the warthogs and lesser kudu drying in the sun, flesh side well rubbed with a paste of alum and wood ashes, hair side sprinkled with turpentine – my invariable and very successful device for temporarily preparing skins in the bush. The skulls were in buckets being daily scrubbed clean.

This had been a most successful little bit of shikar and I now marched to Berbera and took my passage to Aden a new man, having shaken off most of my fever. Such is the wonderful power of an absorbing interest like shikar, good alike for mind and body, and a sure fore-runner to a strong, virile old age. It is the best tonic in the world! I returned to India a happy man – I had at last got a really good warthog and a record lesser kudu!

Chapter 17

India
A short trip to Closepeth – and
Bangalore sports generally

WENT FOR a few days in May 1889 to Closepeth, 30 miles by train from Bangalore, Mysore, to shoot bear and tiger – with Roe of the Madras Sappers. (While myself quartered with the Sappers at Bangalore, the regimental headquarters.)

A terrible trip – nothing but disappointment – but jolly all the same – coconuts in abundance in the villages, an obsequious though rascally population who gave us roast chickens when there was nothing else handy – a bad thunderstorm, and much hedge-hopping – crow shooting &c in camp. Searched and drove for bear without result, pretty bamboo jungles and wooded country, great rounded rock 'koppies' rising abruptly, forming a crick of hills, and very picturesque country all round. How hard we worked! But we came away empty-handed. I spent a very interesting but uncanny night in the bamboo jungle far from camp.

Roe and I were in camp together when we hear of a 'kill' of a heifer by a panther or tiger. We drew straws and I won the chance of sitting up at night. We went to view the body of the heifer and found it lying on the side of a shallow nullah about 9 ft. across. During daylight this did not seem to be a propitious place for sitting up on the ground with a thin zeriba to watch for a leopard, though it was separated by 3 miles of dense bamboo jungle from the camp, so that anyone sitting here alone would be 3 miles from the nearest human being. It looked so different by day!

Well, we made a tiny shelter into which I could just crawl, of flimsy brushwood some 3 ft. high, on the same level as the heifer which was about 30 ft. distant but then I was practically sitting on the ground without protection. About an hour before sunset I sent the men, who had made these preparations, back the 3 miles to camp through the heavy bamboo jungle, and there I sat on the ground alone, waiting for the sun to go down. A long watch – silent, motionless, finger on trigger and every sense on the alert – a pool at my back somewhere in the low scrub where I could hear bullfrogs and occasionally soft footsteps – this went on till 1 a.m. – when the glorious moon had reached the horizon and was just taking the final plunge. Then light got dull, the earth was streaked with mile-long shadows, anything more lonely cannot be imagined – all nature stood still. I could still see very dimly the faint gleam of white on the heifer's body, but I could not see the foresight of my rifle. Suddenly the thought of what killed the heifer oppressed me. Could it be, not a leopard, but a tiger? Even the soft footsteps had ceased and as it grew pitch dark all the jungle lay absolutely silent. Then, as I could see nothing, not even my hand or the rifle I was holding, much less across the nullah, which now seemed miles wide, to the heifer, I hoped the tiger would not come. It would be perfectly useless if he came. So, as I believed I began to hear soft footsteps again and splashing in the marshy jungle behind me, I took to coughing softly at five-minute intervals to scare off any marauder. At last, I don't know quite when, I lay down with my cheek on the stock of the rifle and that again on my shoulder and lying on my right side on the ground, the muzzle betweeen my curled-up knee, and I slept – say at 2 a.m. – and did not awake until broad daylight – then my fears seemed absurd – the men at last turned up after an unconscionable wait (as I was feeling hungry for breakfast) and I walked into camp, telling them I had had a very pleasant time.

And that was the end of our trip – we got nothing at all, and had gone through some very hard work; on the whole, though, we enjoyed it.

Chapter 18

India
Mysore
June, July and August 1889

Three old friends

BACK IN Bangalore by May 1889, I began to think of Shinurja in West Mysore where a friend had told me tigers were plentiful. So when a requisition came down from the Intelligence Branch, Simla, for an officer willing to travel round Mysore and report on roads and camping grounds for the Intelligence Dept., on regimental pay of a subaltern (265R a month), I volunteered for the job. Without the maps it is hard after 10 years to identify the camping grounds. I generally had two chestnut country-bred ponies 13.3 high, and 3 bullock carts, I sleeping in one, at night, on a foot of clean straw and my Madras boy, Monisamy, and a small boy to help him, and my baggage, in the other 2 carts. We got round 1,000 miles that way in the 3 months and in spite of the rains being on, I saw a great deal of the black-buck, especially at a place called Jagabur near Chitaldrooj. But the horns in Madras proved over-small, my largest being 19½ in. but an equilateral triangle formed by the horns – a very pretty head. There was a place called Bamagondanakere, 30 miles south of Billary, where I was lucky enough to shoot my first bear. Molkalmurin, rather, for Bamagondanakere was the name of the nearest village on the road where there was a travellers' bungalow. At another place, Shikaripur near Shunoja, a python 12 ft. 6 in. long. Several black-buck and Chinkara and a shot at a bison very nearly, but he saw me and was off before I was ready.

I went to Gersoppa in the burst of the monsoon and saw the 900-ft. falls. In the course of these travels, I went all over the Konally Gold Mines with the manager, drove unsuccessfully for tiger, bear, and pig, shot a doe chital by mistake in dense forest, and visited Sagar, where I got some beautiful Hindu sandalwood carvings of gods, and the Falls of Gersoppa, where a river falls 900 feet sheer, in 3 parallel falls, into Canara, some thousands of feet below. Good fishing at the pool at the foot of the fall. Near a large tank or lake (3 or 4 miles in circumference) I met John and C. Silk, coffee planters from the Baba-Budrum hills, Kadur District, Mysore, and we foregathered. I was afterwards to taste of their hospitality. The whole trip was most enjoyable. I sold one of my two ponies to John Silk!

The Mysore country, with its open cultivated plains of black cotton soil, and hills dotting the level here and there, and its forest-covered mountains in the west, is a sportsman's paradise. It is from 2 to 3,000 feet above sea level in the plains and about 6,000 feet at the tops of the hills in the west. I am not talking of Ootacamund — that is another region.

I was still in Mysore with my Madras cook and 2 bullock carts when I heard of my promotion, and almost immediately afterwards I was ordered (via Bangalore) to the Chin Lushai Campaign in Upper Burma to command a company of Madras Sappers (No. 6 Company). It did not take me long to pack up and go — a few days — but on arriving at Mandalay, we had some delay before finally getting off.

The spirit of the Mysore shooting grounds had got hold of me and I resolved to come back and have a good trip there later on. At this time, I had shot neither lion or tiger. That was to come later on and it forms a dramatic story even for shikar.

Chapter 19

Burma
Nov. to Feb. 1889-1890

IN JULY 1889, while completing my surveys of Mysore Camping Grounds for the IntelligenceDept., I received orders to rejoin at once at Bangalore and go to Burma in charge of the No. 6 Coy. Queen's Own (Madras) Sappers and Miners, Evans, Hutton and Ainslie being the 3 subalterns. The Company was to proceed at once to Mandalay to join a Field Force under the command of Brigadier General Symons, to then enter the Chin Hills from the Burma side and co-operate with the Lushai column from the Chittagong side. The point of meeting was to be Tashon Goma, the capital of the Bangshe Chins, and we expected considerable resistance at that strong point.

We took the Prom-Mandalay railway. On the way we came to a gap where a bridge had been washed away and had to take over all the Company baggage, entrenching tools, stores, rations and kits by hand in trollies. The rails and sleepers were hanging over the gap and the trollies were run across on the rails. One sapper was trundling a trolley across it when it ran away with him and his steps over the sleepers got quicker and quicker till he fell and barked his shins fearfully. At the sides of the railway was jungle with grasses 12 ft. high, teak trees, bamboos and palms – very beautiful it was. Some of it looked very tigerish country. I sent some of the high grass home to London to Rowland Ward, and I think it was put into the jungle scene in one of the Earl's Court Shows.

We slept in and around Thebans Palace, the citadel of the town of Mandalay. It was about a year or more before this that the British took Mandalay under Sir Harry Prendergast. Everything was still very primitive and I remember I slept alone in a remote corner of this palace, laying my blankets on the bare boards, huge wooden columns painted in red and gold rising to a canopy, under which was a golden throne, studded with coloured glass. It was very weird. The rats scampered behind the wainscotting and between the walls and I got my sword (which lay beside me) and pinned a rat through, I think, in the boards, holding him prisoner. Then I called my Madras boy and said: 'Monisamy, get my big shikar knife while I make an end of him,' and changing my mind, gave the hilt of the sword to

A Burmese Girl

Monisamy to keep him pinned there while I groped for the knife. But Monisamy was half asleep and the rat wriggled out from under the sword and escaped. I remember the incident as if it were yesterday!

Outside my room under a large shady tree dwelt the King's carvers, the cleverest I have ever seen, creating beautifully bold teakwood mirror frames etc. for tourists. I kept them hard at work and sent a good deal of these carvings home. The Club is in the 'Queen's Room', and those who fitted up this room with its great red and gold throne and red pillars of wood were artistic enough to arrange everything to match, even to the punkah, beams and frills. Burmese tourist parties from all parts of Burma were allowed to come and visit the Palace and used to troop in in the evenings as we, the Club members, sat in our long arm chairs.

They came prettily dressed, and in one of these parties was a Burmese girl with one of the most beautiful faces I have ever seen, very straight well-chiselled features and a sweet expression, and some Members said they had often see her there, though her people were Burmese she had Armenian blood in her veins – that accounted for it, as most Burmese girls have anything but regular features.

In November we left Mandalay and went by boat up the Chindwin river to Minggan, a large military station, dry and healthy, on the banks of the Chindwin, and containing barracks for two regiments and a base hospital. As we steamed up the Chindwin, we could see the steep scarped earth banks being undermined by the swirl of the river (about a mile broad) and huge masses of earth, carrying tufts of high grass, were falling in showers into the muddy water. Of course the river would be silting up on the opposite side. But I never anywhere else saw this action of the water so rapid. We crossed the Chindwin and eventually steamed up it and disembarked at Pokkokku where General Symons had assembled his big force into a huge camp. I went to report the arrival of our detachment and the General sang out from his tub and sent me off to work. In a few days we marched out of Pokkokku, my company forming the leading detachment. Colonel Henry (then Major I think) accompanied us as C.R.E., also Dofield as Adjutant R.E.

Chin-Lushai head-dress

Officers wore 'Mashibur' (I don't know – or no –) hats – a very sensible head-dress. When we got in the enemy's country the whole of the officers of the column, I think, were allowed to discard their swords and carry dahs, or Burmese kukris, for cutting down jungle with.

We marched across upper Burma – still in process of subjugation but yet not quite an enemy's country – about 160 miles from Pokkokku to Kan; that is, from the Chindwin River to the Myitha River. As the Chin Hills where we were going were almost impassable for animals, even the officers had to walk, and a very hot march it was, lasting some 10 days. At Kan we were on the pretty Myitha River, which we only had to wade across, waist-deep, to get into the enemy's country. Kan was a very pretty little village overlooking the steep banks of this little river. I'm afraid we used to use dynamite to catch fish for the sepoys and got about 40 lb. of fish one morning – luckily there were no means or time to fish them properly – the fishermen came up afterward with the main column and weren't they savage! I also shot some fish, or rather, shot at them, with a 12-bore 'Paradox' gun which I carried throughout the campaign hoping to get some of the wild buffalo etcetera that abound on these hills (though it was not the best weapon for buffalo) but the advantage was it took both shot and ball. On the day we crossed the river and entered the enemy's country, I fired at a beautiful jungle cock but missed, and got nearly sat upon for firing off the first shot of the campaign (and letting the Chins know of our arrival) though luckily no one heard the shot I think, as I had wandered a bit to one side through the jungle.

It was a very pretty march through rising ground and bleak forest to a small thick forest at the foot of the hills, where we formed our first camp and where about a month's road-making was done. About 20 miles away was the serrated range of peaks behind which lay Yashon Gorma, the great Chin stronghold, our objective. At this camp I met my cousin (Eddie) who occupied, I think, the same hut for a day or two. He had come up from the Somersetshire Regiment, as a special signalling officer.

This Yanylih Camp was the last camp reached by me before being sent down. It was fired into every night but I wasn't there at night. I shall never forget the road-making up that valley – about 47 river crossings in 20 miles – the road took us many weeks to make and we all had fever, there were always 33% of the sepoys and 50% of the European officers and soldiers on the sick list. I went to sleep through weakness while finding my way to a working party, and found they had gone 2 miles and I had been asleep, absolutely alone, on the track we had made, the prey of any Chin who chose to be out reconnoitring. Had I been seen, my head would undoubtedly have been cut off with one stroke of a dah. Unutterable weakness assailed the whole Force. There was always, however, a spice of danger to keep our spirits up and at Taungtek, 10 miles on, we expected to meet the enemy in force.

At Chownkwa, we built mat and straw huts, and established a very large camp, with some of the King's Own Scottish Borderers, the 2nd, 4th Ghurkhas and Madras Infantry and Sappers.

The General went on with the Advance Guard to Taungtek, and next day I walked there with 3 Ghurkhas and took a survey of the road. I enjoyed this walk through the enemy's country with the cheery little Ghurkhas more than anything in the whole campaign.

At Taungtek, where the General had left a small camp on a saddle between pine-covered ridges, I learnt that the night before, a Ghurkha havildar (sergeant) had been shot by Chins creeping round the camp at night. A few days later, Foster of the Scottish Borderers (a subaltern) and two doctors were out walking near camp when 3 Chins, I think, crept up and fired a volley at a couple of yards distance, hitting Foster in the neck and killing him on the spot. One of the doctors fired his revolver back into the bush but saw nothing to aim at. The Chins are better stalkers in jungle than even the Ghurkhas. The Ghurkhas, however, made splendid covering parties which the Madras Infantry did not! Alternately, day by day, we who were making and laying out the road, often with clinometers etcetera, were protected by a covering party of Ghurkhas or Madras Infantry as the case might be. We walked along the native path whilst the covering party got along in the jungle-covered hillside as best they could! On the Madras Infantry days you heard now and then a slip and a crash, and some sepoy had slid down the hill over the rotten timber, rifle and all. They positively could not keep their feet on these hillsides! We were always

Boring the augur holes

ahead. But when the little Ghurkha Highlanders were our covering party, they were well ahead and a real protection. Some of this country was very beautiful, especially up among the pines as you neared Taungtek; the pines were very tall and thick with red stems, and they had been felled across the path by the enemy to prevent our baggage mules coming along. They had been felled by thousands of little dah-cuts. We blew up any trees close to the new path by augur holes and dynamite, and a very interesting piece of work it was, as the forest used to resound for a long time afterwards with the crash of falling timber and the stumps were left like shaving brushes about 3 ft. high. Trees, say 4 ft. in diameter and over a hundred feet high. Very exciting.

Sometimes we got some fish for the men by dynamite – the dynamite (red earth form) was thrown into the water with a bit of Bickford's fuse attached and almost directly it had sunk, a huge column of water would be thrown up, some Manipuri coolies or Burmese would be extended ready across the shallows and catch the fish as they floated down, stunned, and throw them ashore.

At Chounkwa Camp, the time arrived for our leading detachment to advance, following the General's advanced party to Taungtek. But of our Company, Hutton and I were at the last moment found to have had fever so long that the medical officers in medical charge of the camp would not allow us to go on. They told us we should die if we tried to go on and told the General to have us sent down – so down we went! It was a great grief to us. We had been very happy at Chounkwa – and I had made a mess table of split bamboos, and large garden seats, in my spare time on the fever days.

We had formed, at the early stages of this Chounkwa Depot, an officers' camp about a quarter of a mile to the front, on the enemy's side, on a breezy plateau. Above us, in front, was a small Ghurkha picket of 20 men, kept there night and day, to protect the camp. As the detachments went on, their baggage carried by hundreds of naked Manipur coolies, who grunted in time as they ran (most amusing fellows), the officers' camp became gradually deserted till only Hutton and myself and our two Madras servants were left. There we sat disconsolately by the deserted mess table hoping that perhaps the doctors would relent, and let us get on to our work (U.W. Evans had gone on with most of my Company). We wanted to get into the highest mountains by Yashon Gouna, where we heard it was healthy, apricots and grapes grew etcetera – and spent each day in hoping. Meanwhile we were very weak.

One day, towards the end of our stay at this deserted officer's camp, I had ordered 5 Madras Sappers to come up at 3 p.m., and build me a new hut, as the rain had demolished my old one. I must explain we were only allowed 40 lb. kits and *no tents* and it rained nearly incessantly during the 2 to 3 months I was on the campaign – so when we were halted long enough, we built huts.

Suddenly at about noon, we heard shots fired and echoing among the hills ahead, along the new Sapper Road. The day before, the General had sent back our Ghurkha picket and the camp remained absolutely unprotected should the Chins get in on the General's line of communication. However, we thought it was only the General's force in action, so we simply sat outside our huts and listened to the dropping shots. Hutton was in pyjamas, I in uniform. I was not so bad, on the whole, as Hutton, who could not really stand properly without staggering.

The shots resounded through the narrow gorges, and seemed to be fired in a most irregular fashion. There would be two together, then a pause, then two at long intervals apart, another pause, then a regular fusillade of 5 or 6 – and so on. Then a very long pause and four quiet shots – 21 in all, as we counted carefully. Hutton and I looked at each other and had to think what to do. If it should not be the Chins, it would be no use alarming the camp below by sending for troops. If it *should* be the Chins, they would come along our road and there would be no escape from the unprotected Officers' Camp. Finally I sent a message down by Monisamy, my Madras boy, to say the 5 Sappers were to come up at 12.30 (it was that very nearly) instead of 3 p.m. to build my hut as I had changed my mind. Also, I added they were not to come in fatigue working dress, but to be sure to bring their arms and accoutrements with them.

Meanwhile Hutton and I got our revolvers and sat down to await events

– the arrival of the Chin enemy, and our Sapper friends, whichever should turn up first. Hutton was too weak to dress and remained in pyjamas.

In about twenty minutes time, up came the 5 Sappers to make the hut. I told them of the shots, which they could not have heard down in the camp below – the

Watching the Sapper Road

coolies, of which there were 1,200, always made such a cackle – then I marched them up the Sapper Road past the picket post to Point A, and extended them across the saddle of the mountain. We had knelt there some minutes when the pounding of a multitude of naked feet running at full speed sounded round an angle of the road, and we all raised our rifles to our shoulders prepared to put in a volley. Then round came running a host of some 200 naked Manipuri coolies, laughing and drawing their hands across their throats (we could speak only by signs) to signify the Chins were cutting all their throats and were behind them! It was a most exciting moment! We let them go by and waited. Three more gangs of these flying coolies passed us (they had been taking rations to the regiments in front); each time, thinking it was the Chins, we prepared to fire. At last there was a long silence and we waited. Nothing but the enemy in front now! Soon, the news having got to camp behind us, two doctors came up, a commissariat officer and an apothecary, and two or three Madras Infantry. We all advanced along the road for about a mile and this is what I found - the naked, headless body of a brown man, evidently a native of India, lying across the path, eight bullet wounds in him – one through the heart, several in his stomach, chest and back and his stomach protruding on the path. His head had been cut off with a blow of a dah. One or two of the wounds were scorched and blackened with gunpowder showing they had been fired nearly touching the body as he lay. Then we examined the path and the grass near, and the hillside around the track – it appeared that about a dozen or more Chins, creeping round the General's line of communication to reconnoitre Chounkwa Camp, had come upon this unfortunate coolie (who it afterwards turned out had been coming to me from Taungtek with a letter about a lost mule, or something) and had chased him – a running hunt, killing him at last and these were the dropping shots we had heard. He must have had a four-minute run for his life, judging from the sound of the shots. The brass bullets were made of bells looted from the Burmese villages by these

The loss of a Mule

mountain head-hunters. On the whole, it is lucky for Hutton and myself this reconnoitring party had not come on to Chounkwa Camp – at any rate, we should have had a pretty stiff fight on our hands, up at the deserted officers' camp. I never heard exactly who this coolie was except that he was bringing a message. His head having been stolen prevented identification.

There are several incidents of the upward march which I have left till now. One incident I well remember was the death of a mule. I was being carried in a 'dhoolie', being too ill with fever to walk, when I head a shout and a crash and a squeal and got out to find that one of the Sapper mules had been led by a stupid muleteer too far along the Sapper road where it ended in the hillside, being unfinished at this spot. Seeing his mule had got on to the ever-narrowing ledge of a precipice, he let go of the bridle – just in time, for the mule crashed and rolled down 400 ft., covering the hill with carpenters' tools. Some Ghurkhas were sent down, who reported his neck broken. Little of the contents of his load, part of the Sappers' equipment, was recovered.

There are a thousand trivial incidents crowded into that exciting time, we lived in that two or three months through as many incidents as in two years of ordinary civilisation, and those days, despite fever, were as enjoyable as the days in the jungle – whether in Africa or Asia!

I ommitted to tell how Sergeant Major Bean took up a coolie straggling along the Sapper Road and carried him for a mile or two till he heard a sigh – the man had died on his back – and Bean arrived later in the Camp, only to return several miles with a party to bury the corpse.

Another incident was when the General's lunch went off on a tame elephant which had broken loose and followed a wild herd. Also a dead elephant we passed on the way – a horrible sight as it had lain there many days, poisoning our line of march – a tame Commissariat elephant. How these elephants cut up our road across to Burma from Pokkokku to Kan!

Then my lunch with cousin Eddie – when the greatest luxury I could offer was bacon fat, sugar and pancakes of native flour! – or Evans' mule, which rolled over and over him twice on the hillside and Evans turned up much shaken from under the mule with his pipe still in his mouth!

Hutton and I went down to Burma together, Oldfield having very kindly given us the use of his pony, one of the very few the Force were allowed to bring up to Chounkwa – most useful in the 45 crossings of the stream in the Chounkwa gorge.

I remember I was able at last to buy some chocolate from an enterprising Parsi who had come to Kan. Chocolate had also been a medical comfort issued to the men at Chounkwa, and lately it had run out, so there was a great deal of quiet grumbling if they thought others had got it and not they.

I was happily sitting on a bank munching my fairly paid-for prize when two Tommies passed along the top of the bank near. I heard one say quickly in a whisper, 'Why, there's a b——y officer a-eating chocolate!' and the other giggled! Another saying I actually overheard later on, as my draft was punting in Burma canoes down the Myitha River, 'We've 'ad a bad time one way or another – one got shot, one was drownded, and fever's got a lot out of the way, or goin'. That Bill yesterday, now 'e says to me: "Jack, Ahm a-goin' to die." Bill, I says, It ain't no bloody use 'a-talkin' to me, you may b——y well go and die for all I care, Ahm a sick mon myself.' Truly the Britisher does not wear sentiment on his sleeve!

I found our little village of Kan grown much bigger by reason of the huge base hospital that had been built to receive the unusual number of sick. There were a large number of deaths from fever, I think, at this camp, all contracted in the neighbourhood of the Chounkwa Gorge, as Kan itself seemed healthy enough. Some of the roofs of the mat hospital huts were too thin, the hot sun getting through the chinks.

After a short stay at Kan, I was sent down with a sick draft of the Scottish Borderers. The 13 Tommies and I and my Madras boy got into the flotilla of Burmese boats – very like Kashmere doongas – and we were paddled and poled down the lovely Myitha river for some 40 miles to Kaleywa, where there was a hospital hut and *fresh* milk. I never saw such lovely scenery as in this little Myitha River: the beautiful river of clear water running over the golden sand or brown rocks, the high walls of bright green grass and background of high jungle, the red and gold pagodas. On that journey I was very ill with weakness; extraordinary. At last, I think at Kabura, we were taken out of the country boats and put into clean Irrawaddy Indian marine flats – merrily we ran down the Chindwin, 'jumping' sandbanks, having an occasional shot from deck (in spite of my weakness) at duck, and *eating, eating* constantly with the intense hunger of the convalescent! How healthy the air was!

At Mysangi, I spent a week or two in hospital and then went on in another steamer (I think it was steamer all the way but I am not certain) to Rangoon. I soon went before a medical board there. As I had taken a month to come down I was nearly well, but as the campaign was more than half finished and Burma fever returns, I was ordered off on sick leave. 'Darjeeling or Simla,' said the Board. 'The hills in Southern India,' said I – ah! they thought, he means Ootacamund, the fashionable station – I was *thinking* of the Fajun Valley, the most feverish jungle in West Mysore, and of John and Chris Silk and their hospitality on the Baba Buddums. So I said 'Southern India Hills,' without specifying, for I had one panacea, the Board another. The Board wished me to lounge at a hill station – I thought differently. 'Three months sick leave' was the verdict – I ran out of the Board Room as fast as possible from the frowns of stern be-uniformed medics – to the Telegraph Office over the way. Click-click-click went the Morse code. John Silk, Santavori, Kadur District, Mysore. 'How Sambhar horns now' – reply: 'Sambhar horns right to the end of April. Come!!' In May they have all dropped off. I got an Indian Marine passage, I think, to Madras, and then passed through Bangalore on my way eastward. At Kadur, I got out and rode with my 2 chestnut country ponies, my boy Monisamy and my bullock carts to Santaveri, and was welcomed by the two brothers, the kindest hosts I had ever had the luck to received an invitation from.

And so we will leave this campaign. General Symons had some fighting but not very heavy and marched into Yashon Gorma. The Lushai Column from Chittangory meeting there after preliminary joining of hands over the mountains by heliograph. Major Henry, my chief engineer got, I believe, promoted to Colonel, and I think a CB for his services. I got the old Burma Medal next year – it took some time coming.

While making this road to Chounkwa we saw bears sitting on our Sapper Road (at least some of us did), and we saw countless tracks of miltrum and tsine (two kinds of buffalo or bison) but we were too busy for sport, though I carried a 'Paradox' the whole way; all the memories are glowing, though at the time with ever-present fever, they were not so agreeable. I must not omit to mention an old friend's kindness at Rangoon – he put me up at a friend's house and for a month it was due chiefly to my kind hosts I got well again.

Chapter 20

A Shoot in Mysore, India
May–June and July 1890

"Go and buy a crutch!"

I SCARCELY know how to begin the account of this trip. If I start rhapsodising upon it, it will occupy too many pages, but it was such a jolly trip it is almost impossible not to rhapsodise.

The first note of importance is dated Gemmay – Doddi Khan Public Bungalow, Mysore State, May 2nd 1890, and complains of a terrible fever contracted in Chin Land, Upper Burma. But a bit of air on the mountains was doing me a world of good. Out came the old hat, knife, and spy glass and I began to creep about as of yore after the wild beasts. Day after day I went out after the sambhar at Kalhattipui (6,000 ft.) to no purpose. The country was very beautiful. Green turf clothed the top of the hills and the shallow open valleys – 'sholas' or narrow strips of dense forest choked the deep ravines leading down to the country below. In these 'sholas' dwelt the sambhar, and if I got to the top of the hill early enough, I would sometimes sight one a mile away with some hinds, or solitary, creeping along the top edge of a dense piece of 'shola'. I worked very hard, in spite of the terribly weakening effects of the Burma fever. I will put my experiences down from a letter written at the time from Baba Buddum Hills themselves.

2nd May 1890

Karlhutty Camp

Now that I am handling my rifle telescope, I am beginning to think that I am in my youth again, instead of an old man of thirty winters! But the sambhar know better! They stand and greet me with a hoof stamp and sharp grating call; well within easy range, (the unshootable ones) they make round eyes at me – as to say 'go back to bed, you old wreck, sell your rifle and buy a crutch' and then of course I feel my inferiority, get nervous and miss.

I hope in a few days to be at the bison, when I shall feel better. Bison are bigger, and so easier to hit than deer. One can't miss a thing as large as the side of a house.

It is very pleasant among the coffee plantations, the only disadvantage, which one discovers after a few months of it, being that in the home life of the planters' bungalows one seldom meets a lady. There is one lady but she lives at Chikanagabir, 30 miles away. People go on expeditions once a year or so on purpose to talk to her. There is another coffee planter's wife about 75 miles south in Goorg, but *she* is only a *woman* – not a *lady*, there is a difference. But really I am having a very good time of it, staying about among coffee planting friends and going shooting parties in the hills around their estates. My hosts are the Silk brothers, John and Chris. There is Oliver near, and Dunne – and others. We have unlimbered the camera and done a group lingering over the midday meal under some wide-spreading shady fig-tree! Then sometimes we 'cave it'. We take our traps – carried by one coolie apiece – to some cave or grotto in a torrent bed buried in the deepest forest, to shoot sambhar stags before it gets hot; and at noon sit down to currie and rice, made as only a good willing Madras cook can make it; and we mingle the purest mountain water from the stream, whose rippling cadence echoes through our vaulted dining hall – we mingle it with deep draughts of the purest mountain dew of Glen something or other, generally in white bottles with the legend 'Robertsons' Whisky' writ big on the label. Then we bathe (downstream from where we dined) in the clear pellucid waters, and at eve we hunt up some fierce old boar, the father of the mountains, and drive him out of a shola with a gang of beaters and mob him with our rifles as he comes out – not without danger to ourselves from flying bullets. Then evening the meal and the sleep of worked-out shikarring humanity – preparing for another day in this free, careless, happy hunting ground. This is all done at a height of 6,000 ft. above the sea in what they tell me is real Scotch scenery with pure air calculated to drive out fever if anything is!

These were happy days on the broad swelling mountain top, a green sea of sloping downs here and there cut up by high tree sholas; each having trickling through the centre of its shady ravines a crystal stream from where the forest is thickest and moss and maidenhair fern struggle in rivalry, each plant trying to outdo the other in luxuriance of tropical growth, the stream ever singing to the dome of blue and green above an everlasting note of harmony. Round the mountain top the velvet ground falls suddenly in steep precipices to the coffee plantations below. Each rivulet here becomes a waterfall 200 feet high, or a silver cascade, slipping down, white and frothy, over the black sheet rock to reappear below in lovely reaches of reflected greens and blues and browns, where the water passes under the deep shades of the quiet coffee plantations – expanses of dark, low, blue-green bushes growing under a canopy of enormous forest trees, called 'shade trees' which have been purposely left standing. But be careful how you walk through the lower coffee ground, where the rivulets are – for leeches rear up and come at you and crawl onto your ankles, get into your boots and when you take them off you will find them full of blood. No, take instead the path of red gravel that winds through the centre of the estate, past the drying-grounds, where 'lumbani' or gypsy coolies, men and women covered with bangles, handsome Cleopatra-like women, are lazily picking the coffee into baskets and laughing and chatting in a ray of sunlight in the open path and they don't hide their faces, the lumbansi' women, as do other Indian women when a stranger passes.

Go on till through the vista of trees framed in blue-green, you come to the dainty whitewashed walls and great brown expansive roof of the coffee-planters' bungalow. Your host will meet you on the broad stone sweep of the verandah with smiles, the personification of hospitality. But look at the walls of the main room and all round the verandah! What horns these are! Every foot of wall has its trophy; bison and tiger, leopard, sambhar and

Tiger

spotted deer, bear and pig face you at every turn; you are in a mine of wild creatures, with bright glittering beady eyes, they fascinate you from the dark corners. Now sit at the hospitable tablecloth, graced with all the dishes which Madras alone can produce; drink down the sparkling cider or the deep soothing draught of Glen something or other! and look across at the man himself – only Great Britain could produce such a man – if they are guests, a ringing laugh peals up now and then, frightening the sparrows in the roof and echoing into the glens below, to tell the crouching sneaking tiger hidden there that the planter burra Sahibs are merry!

Talking of tigers, *I* saw my first tiger

on this trip in rather a curious way. I had returned from the usual unsuccessful sambhar stalk and was climbing down the steep grassy semi-precipices on the brow of Kalhattigiri. Below, a long slope of debris led to the edge of the deep shady forest of the next estate to that of my host. The line of trees following the contour of the hills was well defined, and the blue-green floor of coffee bushes, though there was no fence. A few small bush-choked nullahs led across the line into the coffee, nullahs streaked down the hill in strips and beginning above with miniature Guribach waterfalls. All at once I saw what I thought was a spotted deer get out of a patch of shola. There was no time to fire – it was an enormous tiger, he trotted along the path within 40 yards of a long line of lumbani men and women picking coffee, whom he had probably been stalking. I rushed down to cut him off at a rock which overhung the path, but by the time I got there the tiger had passed on and escaped into the jungle. A week later my host shot the tiger close to his bungalow.

These were pleasant days, but the planters themselves were such good shots that the game was scarce and shy. In the two months I was there I saw very few sambhar on the hilltops (above) and spotted deer (in the forest below) and I determined to spend the last days of my leave in a celebrated jungle called Lakwalli Forest where bison were said to be found sometimes.

Chapter 21

Lakwalli Forest, Mysore State, India
June 1890

Forester's hut

(Extracts of a letter to Lt. E.L.E. Swayne (Harald's brother). June 12, 1890, Tarikive traveller's bungalow, Mysore State.)

WELL, I THINK at the end of the last letter, I told you I was going into Lakwalli Forest for a few days, but I had had such a good time there and such royal sport that I scarcely knew where to begin for fear you shouldn't believe me. The following menu of entertainment will induce you to read this letter through. Please put 'seen and approved' on the letter before passing it on to the family, if you think there are no lies.

1st Day: Evening – got a bull bison.

2nd Day: Morning – saw 3 bears, wounded and lost one – (this one charged but turned off), and while returning home got charged *unprovoked* by another and killed him when 8 yards away.

3rd Day: Blank.

4th Day: Put up 2 bull bison, fired a snap shot at one of them and lost him. Killed a barking deer.

5th Day: Blank. Elephants within 100 yards of the forester's hut – saw them everywhere for two days. Went to photo them but they got my wind, trumpeted and skedaddled, if you can use such a disrespectful word for such a ponderous beast.

6th Day: Whilst stalking bison 8 miles from camp, in the middle of the day, smelt something, and ran across two tigers eating a dead sambhar, they were tiger and tigress, measuring 8 ft. 6 in. and 9 ft. 6 in. respectively – shot 'em both, on foot at 30 yards with one bullet each. Bodies lay 20 yards apart! Skinned 'em both. Benighted, and slept in thick jungle on hillside – no food, no water.

After this, I think you will read my letter through for the sake of the shikari therein contained. I have a good mind to inflict it on *The Field*. To begin, then, on 31st May I went to Mayanhalli, a small forester's hut five miles from Lakwalli. This small bungalow stood in the centre of a tiny glade carpeted with very green grass; and bamboos rising 50 ft. high all round, and teak trees 100 ft. high. All round the bungalow, tracks of spotted deer and deep footprints of elephants squelched into the mud of a nullah 30 yards from the bungalow. The last traveller along the track had left his pugs everywhere in the soft places – a big tiger. I found this hut quite unvisited since last season.

On the evening of my arrival, I went out in open tree jungle (grass burnt) to look for chital and found a bull bison quietly grazing along across our front, at 80 yards distance – dropped him with a solid bullet from the .577 Express which missed the liver and injured the spine, and finished him with another one or two expanding bullets and a solid one fired at 10 yards from behind, between the horns as he seemed to be rather sick and unable to

A good 24 hours bag on foot

run. Horns 2 ft. 5 in. (bend to bend) – a moderate-sized bull, according to Mouarily's herds in *Bon Natural History Journal.*

I photographed him next morning as he lay, with his own jungle as background, and then went to look for more to the westward in the deep nullahs where they lie up during the heat of the day. At 11 o'clock we were quietly mooning along, stooping under the bamboos, when we heard a plaintive cry repeated at intervals – bears. We left the bison tracks we were on and followed the sound, which led us half a mile, for the bears were travelling, now and then feeding about on fallen fruit, etcetera. All at once they heard us, and we got a sight of them scuttling along the hillside above us. I fired at the biggest and he straightaway left the others and giving a roar bowled himself downhill at us (he was 50 yards away when I fired) but the jungle was so thick that the only chance he gave me was while the breech of the rifle was still open, and as I snapped it he turned off in a bit of thick 'jig' undergrowth which grew up to where I was standing; I fancy his heart failed him, or he couldn't make us out, for we had been standing perfectly still. Then we picked up his tracks, which were marked by a little blood, till a drizzle came on and eventually we left him.

Going home, Iman, my Mahommedan shikari, pointed at a cave 20 yards above us on our left on the steep hillside, in thick bamboo cover, and said '*Dusera reench*' (another bear); I looked, and there was a big black bear *framed* in the entrance of the cave, a living picture, looking at us. The next moment he gave a grunt and promptly came for us! I waited till he topped a big rock just above me, then I could get a good view of him, and lost no time in firing at the white on his chest, toppling him over backwards! and it was just as well, for the 'jig' where I was standing was so thick I had not much room to get out of his way. I measured the distance afterwards from where I was standing to where he lay a black furry mass with his feet in the air, dabbled in blood – and *eight yards* was all it was! When he had stood in his cave he had looked for all the world like an old gentleman waiting at his own hall-door for the rain to stop, before taking a stroll! A cross-grained old beast; and one of his teeth was broken short off; a good skin, which has unfortunately been spoiled by the rains.

As we found no wound upon him, I can't account for his charging like this, unless he belonged to the family party I had disturbed two hours before, and thought his retreat had been cut off.

Next day being blank, we marched 3 miles deeper into the forest, and in the evening near the new bungalow where I took up my quarters, we heard elephants squealing. On the way to this ground, at midday, we had seen a bull bison 20 yards away – sitting head on to us, looming through the bamboos – and while exchanging the .577 for the 4-bore which the coolie was carrying, I clashed the two rifles together, and the brute got under way with marvellous rapidity and galloped off, getting a snap shot from the four-bore which was no doubt stopped by the bamboo clumps. We lost him after two hours' tracking – no blood. This bison had been on the alert, because ½ mile away I had shot a barking deer at 20 yards distance. The .577 proved too big for this little animal, as we found bits of meat hanging 10 ft. above the ground on the bamboos. Well, the bison had two cows with him, which also we heard lumbering away through the bamboo-clumps. After tiffin, 2 hours later, and near our destination, we put up another bull, which crashed away without our seeing him. It is *very* exciting work I think, this hunting through bamboos in the middle of the day. You come on lots of game, though it is 10 to 1 the bison sees, smells, or hears you first. Luckily, they always bolt *away* from you and not at you! Next morning, before dawn, we started on this game again, round the patches of young grass where the bison feed. Weird and elfish we looked in the twilight as we crept like thieves under the feathery bamboos. Everywhere we could hear jungle cocks crowing, and saw at least half a dozen.

In the evening I went out and tried to photo elephants. We saw them altogether for two or three evenings, standing and feeding about in the primeval forest near the bungalow; but this time we could not see them, and all I heard was the scream of a calf as it went off after its mother, having got our wind. (I had asked for leave to shoot one of these animals a month ago, but was refused leave unless I could prove him to be a 'rogue' which I couldn't, so had to refrain). We didn't see a single tusker. Two men had, however, been killed here in the last two years by rogues. But in this herd on this occasion there was none.

The next day we went far afield, 7 miles, into a bit of hill country almost unvisited by sportsmen, so Iman said, for some years past, but we got nothing; though we must have done at least 15 miles of very rough tramping and climbing that day. The day following was a blank day.

On the 6th (this is the *great* day I have been coming to) we revisited the same place, and were making a final cast before going home, up a rise in the ground covered with scrub about breast-high but otherwise open. We were slowly ascending this rise, and had nearly reached the top, when right across me, full in the midday glare of the sun, I saw passing a row of unmistakable black stripes on an orange ground! They bobbed up and down behind the underbush as this beast quietly slouched along, keeping its back horizontal, only 25 yards off and quite unsuspicious of an enemy so near, 'Mustn't let off a *TIGER*,' was the first thought that struck me, and taking a quick aim I fired for the stripes, though I couldn't see the head, which was held low. *Bang!* The loud 'tell' of the bullet simultaneously answered the report, and with a roar she (a tigress) sprang away down the hill at top speed, tail on end − in fact, this was all we could see over the brush undergrowth. She disappeared near a clump of bamboo and taller trees some 200 yards away (she had charged from the sloping ground above us) obliquely to the growth below and in front. There she roared again twice. Iman said, in answer to my inquiring look, 'It's all right, that went into her and she is pretty sick!' Well, only half of my work was over − for Iman said, 'Walk her up, the Sahibs always do,' − for being a fatalist and not caring two pins about its being particularly thick jungle here, 'Walk her up,' he said; so as I didn't wish to appear ignorant of etiquette in these matters, I placed myself in his hands as he calmly led me along the well-marked blood-spoor!

What more need be said? Why, after 'walking her up' for 200 yards to where we had last seen her, we began to wander aimlessly about and quarter the ground in search of her, and I was beginning to think she might make it pretty sultry for us in this tougher undergrowth (about waist-high here) when Iman pointed delightedly to a spot 30 yards away and said, '*Mur gaiya,*' (she's dead) and there she was, lying dead − blood issuing from her mouth and from a hole a little forward of the centre of her body; either the liver or lung shot, I don't know which, as we hadn't time, in the light of subsequent events, to examine her.

I forgot to tell you that it was my nose got me this tigress − I had smelt something 'high' and suggested a dead bison, and we had been going in search of it, and were drawing close on to the object of our search, even more rank, when we had come upon this tigress, which was evidently on her way back to have a midday snack at the carcass!

What more to say? Why − *lots!* I said aloud, delightedly to Iman, 'My first tiger!' and began at once to skin my prize − allowing Iman to wander off to find the kill, see what it was and whether it should have horns worth taking away.

I had already half skinned the belly of the tigress when Iman came back, looking decidedly queer, and said the kill was a sambhar stag with its horns in velvet and then − that wandering casually up to look at the horns he had almost walked down the throat of a second tiger that was gnawing at the meat! So near he was, he said, he could almost touch this great beast. He shrank back without having been observed and came to tell me. 'There!' he said (pointing 30 yards away between two trees) 'is the kill!'

Well. I dropped the skinning knife with a flop onto the belly of the tigress and taking the .577 with the empty case replaced by a fresh cartridge, I crept round very cautiously to leeward of the spot Iman had pointed out − and he climbed up a small tree to have a look round; I also climbed up a little way; but the bush was so thick I could see nothing, so I got down again and advanced a few yards to a thick tall tree stem on top of a low anthill 35 yards (for I carefully measured all the distance afterwards before leaving the spot) from the kill and slightly above it. But though we from time to time heard the crunching of bones, all was almost an unbroken surface of bush some 4 ft. high, with small open intervals a few feet square. I waited therefore a long time resting the .577 Express against the tree and standing on the ant heap to try and get a view, but without our seeing an inch of the tiger's body, the undergrowth began to move in our direction and we could see by it the tiger's course as he left the dead sambhar and came out into the grass from under the shade of the trees to roll and sun himself before taking his siesta – he must have been then 30 yards away.

For ten minutes the vegetation moved over him in one spot as he rolled over and played about; quite unconscious either of our presence or the death of his mate, whose half-skinned body was lying only 35 yards away; at last getting tired of it, I whistled, expected him to show himself and give me a shot. Then we both clapped our hands, at first softly, then loudly, and said 'Sh!' as if we were driving away sparrows! No result! So then I said, 'Iman, throw a stone at the tiger!' He threw a small one, which fell beyond; 'A bigger one,' I said. This time he heaved a rock as large as a half brick plump onto the exact spot, evidently hitting the tiger, for there was a commotion and up bounded the magnificent animal, and made away from us, rearing high to get the view above the dense cover and again floundering in the grass. I raised the .577 for a running shot at the centre of his back, when he should rise again and give me a chance; then I lowered it again; for he suddenly turned, trotted back a few yards towards me, and then stood, with his head raised, to listen, offering me a beautiful oblique shot at his right chest and shoulder. How superb he looked, with the sunlight on his stripes! Taking the best aim I ever took in my life, I let fly at the point of his shoulder and hit him a loud smack. He sprang up on his hind legs, pawed the air a moment, and fell, biting the place where he had been struck. Then with a roar he blundered heavily away downhill, crashing through everything, and disappeared in the underbrush. Iman said by the way he went off he must be dying, probably already down, but we could not see him; so taking up the bloody lane made by his passage we cautiously advanced, I with the Express rifle held forward ready for use in case of a charge, and Iman holding the 4-bore ready in hand to me in case it should be wanted. We had not to go far however, for after an advance of 40 yards I nearly stepped on to his body, lying dead, shot straight through the shoulder, either through, or close to, the heart.

He was a fat, heavily built, though moderate-sized tiger, and though comparatively young he had perfect teeth. He had a short tail, and as he lay, measured probably about 9 ft. 6 in. (and tigress about 9 in. less). I had only my rifle barrel, which was 26 in. long, to judge by, so don't know the exact measurement. At any rate, they were two decent-sized tigers and if my delight had been great when I got the tigress, much greater was it now as I walked from one to the other of the pair! Under the tigress' lower jaw was a very deep fang mark, piercing the bone, lately inflicted, no doubt, by her mate, and he had many fresh scratches on him.

I now went back to continue the skinning of the tigress, and took up the knife again in a very contented frame of mind!

Both animals were covered with swarming ticks and many days afterwards I had not quite got rid of them! But there was no time to waste, as by the time we had removed and rolled up the skins, which took nearly two hours, the sun stood at five o'clock and we had eight miles of the most difficult steep, hilly jungle-covered country to traverse, without a path, before we could reach camp.

It is extraordinary that, as, when I fired at the tigress, her mate must have been sitting at the carcass no more than 150 yards away, he did not hear the shot; neither did he hear us when we were talking aloud, without reserve, only 30 yards away, as we began skinning her. I measured all the distances carefully by pacing and the only conclusion I could come to is that he must have been stone deaf, or stupid with meat – for his belly was full nearly to bursting.

At last we had the skins with heads and paws attached laid on the grass, and very beautiful they looked. But there was no time to admire, so we did up the bundles and set out. A head and set of paws is a good load and my two men being fully occupied with these, I had to sling the .577, weighting 11 lbs and carry also in my hand the 4-bore, weighing 22 lbs. Well, we got over about a mile of very difficult ground but the sun was sinking fast, and when it began to get dark and it appeared hopeless we sat down with our loads in thick jungle, on the hillside; for to go a step further would have been quite out of the question. We had no blankets or matches, I only had a thin mackintosh and one hard-boiled egg left in my haversack and a quarter of a pint of water, which had to go round – though I finished the egg. Soon after dark we heard wild elephants, half a mile below us, breaking down trees and squealing. There were two small rocks; I sat on one and the two natives perched themselves on the other, and we put down the trophies between.

For the first five hours it simply poured with rain and we got wet to the skin (for my waterproof belied its name). But about midnight the sky cleared and the moon rose and shed a watery light upon the scene; over the unending waves of mysterious forest-covered hill, over the numerous teak stems around us, and glittered on our miserable wet figures (how small and pitiful we looked) – but I was in the best of spirits now, and often cast a glance at my beautiful trophies as they lay with the dead eyes staring at the moon!

The night slipped by, I think I dozed for an hour, but as the rock was only 4 ft. square at the top and sloped down into a nullah 10 ft. deep, I was in constant danger of falling if I allowed myself to sleep. Centipedes crawled everywhere, and I 'snapped' them off with my thumb; they were only inch-long ones and quite innocent, more so than the black ants, and the tiger-ticks which were beginning to bite me under my clothes!

However, there is an ending to everything, and although it drizzled again before dawn, I got up feeling perfectly well, such excellent medicine is a contented mind; better than quinine.

We lost our way and did not get into the camp till noon next day, after having been on the tramp for 30 hours, and I had only had one egg since tiffin 24 hours before; and goodness, didn't I have a bath to get rid of those tiger-ticks! And I dipped the 2 skins into a bucket of carbolic acid and water. I met a friend, a gunner of my acquaintance that day – as he marched into my glade where the hut was, he saw my two tiger heads – 'Do you do this sort of thing every day?' 'No, only every other day or so,' I replied.

All night my boy Monisamy piled hot ashes on the skins, and next day, through the burst of the monsoon, I marched 8 miles to Lakwalli with the skins and in the morning rode to Binur Station, 40 miles, and despatched them to my friends in Bangalore by train to get a chance of drying in the sun – for the monsoon had not got to Bangalore yet. They were never taken out of the cage in which I put them, but dried in it, as till dry it was not safe to touch them for fear of peeling. I got 80R reward from the Mysore Govt. which helped me to pay for this trip and good old Iman. The Silks said my

The trudge home

5 days in Lakwalli was about a record.

This was altogether a *red letter* trip — a bison, a barking deer, a bear and two tigers (with one shot each) all in 5 days' shoot. It was the very end of my leave and I had half decided to give up these last 5 days and not try the forest at all — but it made up for all the previous bad luck with the sambhar — and cleared off all trace of the Burmese fever.

Chapter 22

Somaliland
Dolbahanta & Habr Toljaala Survey
Feb & March & April – 1891

(See Route Plan R7 – Appendix 7)

A Herd of Aoul

(After his return from India and Burma, Captain Harald Swayne was sent back to Aden and ordered to place himself at the disposal of the Resident at Aden to reconnoitre trade routes in the Habr Toljaala and Dolbahanta tribal areas to the south-east of Berbera in Somaliland. His younger brother, Lieutenant Eric Swayne (who years later became the British Commissioner for Somaliland) was deputed to assist Harald in this work. On the way back, after many adventures (which are fully described in Harald's book *Seventeen Trips Through Somaliland*), the party was divided into two separate caravans at Huguf. Eric's caravan made its own way back to Berbera after ascending Wagar Mountain and other peaks to take observations, and Harald's caravan headed north for Karam.

Harald's notebook picks up the story at this point: "There only remains to be told how I got down from Huguf to Karam and then on to Berbera.")

A FTER crossing the Huguf Plain, we plunged into the barren mountains to the south, between the Huguf Plain and Karam. They were chiefly

In the valley of Tug Der, we found water. A sketch drawn by Eric, the author's brother

peaks almost buried in long slopes of soft sand, and almost a desert. Most extraordinary shapes these peaks, red, yellow and black presented, coming up out of the yellow sand. In this beautiful Migid Pass I took several photographs and a sketch. It was here that my men – my half of the caravan – made a group for the camera, and I sat myself down amongst them, Adam Yusuf, the half-caravan leader, taking off the cap of the lens. Long will this photo remain as a souvenir of a pleasant, eager, sporting lot of followers – black but not uncomely in themselves – for the photo scarcely does them justice.

Adam Yusuf, Abokr, Awaleh Yasin-Hassan Midgan and many a man

The author with Somali followers

whose names, in my ingratitude, I can't remember – willingly they worked – the trouble they gave me infinitesimal. They worked hard – which they were paid for – they tramped hard daily over the hot rocks – which they were paid for – they greeted one at every meeting with smiles and chatter pleasantly along the road and they were not paid for this – gave their society voluntarily in a cheerful, manly way – without the slightest sign of inequality, yet without the slightest undue familiarity.

This trip to Dolbahanta Country was one of new discoveries, a pure exploring trip, and no white man had been in front of us – there was enough risky adventure to take away the dullness of the dry 'Filal' season and just enough game to kill, though we were not very lucky.

The most exciting sporting adventure was in the Waredad Plain – I got news one morning of fresh lion tracks and followed them over the sand. After some distance we came to a single thorn tree in the open, with a small thicket of grass under it, and my men, poking about looking where the tracks had gone into the grass, suddenly beckoned me to come in a very excited way – then they pointed below the little dark umbrella-topped bush, and there lay the body of a sleeping lion. I could only just see the withers and spine and one massive shoulder, flattened out, rising perhaps two inches above the low grass. I was fifteen yards away, standing in the open, took a quiet aim with my 12-bore 'Paradox' and fired! Out came a huge lion — all paws in the air and rushed towards me while I was looking aside under the smoke — that when he was ten yards away he swung round and galloped away at full speed and I was so astonished, I only fired the left barrel at his tail and missed! Here was a pretty mess! We followed him till the evening, lots of blood from the first shot, which must have missed the spine, but at sunset we saw him galloping away over a hill half a mile away — we followed till dark and gave it up, and with a shower of rain coming on at night it would have been no use trying to track him in the morning. Had I gone right up and put the muzzle to his ear I might have done better.

At Karam, I tried to blow up an Egyptian fort with some powder Welsh sent me from Berbera, but the 20 lbs. or so he sent was not enough. I had a bad day at Siyara under a sandstorm — and so on to Berbera.

Chapter 23

My first big bull Kudu
Golis – August 1891

This was a short trip of less than a week, undertaken soon after my convalescence from the lion bites[1] and in order to perfect my recovery, with the healthy exercise and mountain air of Golis, as a change from the hot Berbera Plain, before starting on a third survey trip with Eric. I took a few followers – Geli, Hassan and I think Kalinli – and roughed it under a sail stretched on sticks. We climbed about the upper slopes of Golis a good deal, in the back gorges behind Mandeira – at last, near the side of Mur Adorya (the Hill of Kudus), in Mirso, I came on the lair of an old bull near a small spring, in heavy cedar jungle, at some 5,500 ft. We were poking about looking at the tracks in the sandy shore of the spring when one of my men pointed up and I saw him! I sat down – the first shot since my bites – and with the Martini-Henry brought him down. He galloped heavily to a ravine and fell, and running across we found him dead – over 50 inches round the curve of the horns. This was my first good kudu – for the one

1 This refers to the incident described on page 106 of Harald Swayne's book, *Seventeen Trips through Somaliland*, when he was attacked by a wounded lioness, and his life was saved by his brother, Eric, who shot the lioness dead. He received eight deep fang wounds in his right arm and shoulder. He said later, 'Although at the present time I am not much inconvenienced by the wounds, my right arm and shoulder are deeply scarred.' In later years he would show these deep scars to his grandson and granddaughter, who, needless to say, were much impressed!

A lioness attacking the author

I got in Sheikh in '87 was a comparatively immature bull – I came back to Berbera much stronger!

Volume II
1896–1902

Chapter 24

Kashmir in 1896

AIMÉE AND I, with the baby (18 months)[1] and ayah[2], arrived at Rawal Pindi (on leave from Lucknow) about 15th April 1896. We went on to Murree by tonga[3], the lower or foothill part of the journey being through glorious highland jungle (but below the pines) and having great variety of trees. It was I think about 30 miles. This first rise from the plains is a great change; no heat – no dust – water about – clean green jungle.

The rise to Murree is the usual pine scenery – to be seen at this height (7-8,000 feet) – anywhere in Simla, Darjeeling or any other hill station. The hotel life was the same and little to describe – though, as usual, a change from the Plains past all description.

There are grand views to south and west from Murree – over great upland wildernesses of snow peaks and plateaux, hundreds of miles of inaccessible country, the valleys alone being inhabited and they are hidden thousands of feet below the grey curtains of mist. From the west towards evening a burning glow comes from the setting sun over these snow peaks, and floods the little tidy walks and terraces of Murree with colour. Every local colour is exaggerated tenfold in the clear air – you are walking on a red gravel walk with brilliant green grass at the side. The effect is quite unnatural but very beautiful. These Anglo-Indian hill stations are just widely extended groups of scattered villas, no native city – for there is little trade. They are merely the bungalows of white people – dainty little walks, English churches and red soldiers – and 'Glen May', 'Loch Katrine', 'Step Aside', 'Pekoe Tip', 'Woodville' are typical names. Very little impression these tiny white spots of houses make in the immensity of the Himalayan ridges if you go a few miles from the station.

In the station all is intensely English: nursemaids and children, soldiers and a bandstand, toyshops, and a few miserable hill-coolies about – go away 3 miles and you are on the native ridge with caravans of sweating ponies and strings of heavily laden route porters.

To describe the 2-days' journey in a galloping tonga to Baramula, sliding

---

1 Harald Swayne married Katherine Aimée Holmes on 10th February 1894. They had one baby girl, Helen Mary, who was born on 23rd April 1895.
2 Ayah = Indian children's nurse.
3 Tonga = Light two-wheeled horse-drawn vehicle.

HGCS and followers – Kashmir

here on the edge of nothing, plunging there into a deep valley, here skirting a rushing torrent, would without the aid of my notes be impossible. There are staging houses (Dak bungalows) – this whole distance being I think about 150 miles or so – but I forget.

At Baramula, we got out of the tonga, took to doongas (Kashmir native gondolas) – one for ourselves and one for the kitchen and servants' quarters. A day and a half of gentle poling up the Jhelerun in lovely reflected scenery, sliding under wooden bridges, and we reached Srinagar and passed upstream through the huge crowded city, the dirty Venice of the East, but very lovely, and moored by the Poplar Avenue at the Munshi Bagh (Winter's Gardens), where the married people are supposed to camp.

We pitched our tents next day under great chenar[4] trees. Aimée had a few days' fever and I got her into Dr Nevis' care. Meanwhile I made my preparations for my 6 weeks' shooting trip to the distant ibex nullahs over the Passes – some 260 miles away. Aimée and the baby and ayah with the servants were about to stay camped in the Munshi Bagh till I returned. Several other ladies were in the same case.

When Aimée was sufficiently convalescent to allow of my going, on 26th April 1896 I dropped downstream in a doonga at 11.30 a.m. with my shikari Gaffur Bux, my second shikari M'Handu (Mahommed), and we were to pick up 13 coolies in Monasbal 6 hours downriver. We floated through

4 Chenar = The Oriental plane tree.

Srinagar, calling on the way at the house of Bahar Shah, my 'banker' and agent, for a belated suit of 'puttoo' clothing, snow spectacles, grass-shoes, and such kit. We got here an alpenstock[5] and a rope and ice-axes. The alpenstock was not iron-shod as it is not done for the game nullahs[6], the clink against the ice and rock being likely to put up game. It is merely plain wood, and not to be depended on not to slip, like an iron-shod stock would be.

To describe the great beauty of my night mooring on the Manasbal Lake outside my shikaris' village would be quite impossible.

A full moon, a rippling

Coolie with Kilta

lake, with black rocks capped with snow peaks reflected in the still water – broken only by ripples; the lap-lapping against the side of the doonga; snores of my men; the little fire basket with its flickering flame, kept for warming the interior of the doonga; the singing of mosquitoes; the starlit deeps away from the reflections of the moon; and the anticipation of at last getting into the sportsman's paradise of an ibex nullah with my shikaris and my good rifle and telescope, and grand trophies for a reward.

We woke with the dawn, and Gaffur Bux had already gone ashore to the village to get his coolies and soon they were standing at the boat picking up my line of loads. My loads were made up in kiltas or hill baskets.

We marched (on the whole of the journey, I was on foot) to Kangan in the Sindh valley – halfway to Sinamaya; 20 miles was the day's walk. Being soft from the plains, I arrived very tired and found the white tents and a long hammock chair ready for me. These were left behind by a Mrs Deardre.

It was at Kangan that I heard of the Deardres but their camp was at Sambal.

On 28th, we broke up the joint camp and made 2 marches – 22 miles in all, to Sonamarg. This is reputed, and rightly so, to be one of the most *if*

5 Alpenstock = A mountain traveller's long spiked staff.
6 Nullah = A ravine, or watercourse

not the most, beautiful valley in all these beautiful mountains. In summer
there are lovely velvet slopes with tall straight dark pines rising up in lines
and groups to glorious serrated rocks crowned with snow peaks – the whole
landscape aglow with colour – blues and greens and glittering white. But
now the whole country was unrelieved white, and black rock. Crocuses
were just beginning to appear above the snow and Sonamarg, though very
beautiful, was frost-bound and covered from top of the peaks to the broad
valley itself with white sheets of snow.

We climbed by tiny paths over enormous avalanches and slips of snow
– fifty to a hundred feet thick – sinking deep as the sun rose in power and
softened the surface.

It was rough work for a lady. There are at Sonamarg remains of a village
and a few half-frozen people were living there and the remains of the old
log chapel – now in ruins.

On April 29th, we had still stiffer work – 12 miles along the upper reaches
of the Sindh Valley to Baltal – the stage from which the midnight start is
made to surmount the Tojila Pass (between 11 and 12,000 feet).

We passed through forests torn by windstorms and avalanches, trees
tumbled in heaps or shorn clean in strips of forest a quarter of a mile wide
the whole hurled down far below, leaving great belts of bare rocks, earth
and debris.

Between Sonamarg and Baltal the Upper Sindh is a gem of Kashmir
scenery at ordinary times, but when we traversed it, this first time, it was
all white.

Then we got to the flat-roofed low storm hut at Baltal – full of coolies
lighting pungent, suffocating fires to melt the snow inside and I told them
to make less smoke but they said, 'We shall be cold and die,' so getting a
little put out, I remarked, quietly and without heat, that being rank unbe-
lievers and bad Mussulmen, they would go to Jehannum when they died
and they would be warm enough there. Relations became later less strained,
and we retired early. Deardre and Mrs and I on the mud floor of one room
surrounded by fire baskets, scores of coolies in the other room.

At about midnight, to get the advantage of a hard frozen snow path with
the light of the moon to guide us, we started to attack the Tojila (11,000 feet).
The first few hours the path (shown by the footsteps of infrequent post run-
ners) led up the bed of a torrent among crevassed snow and glaciers. The
torrent running (ice-bound at night) far below. One of our coolies carried
a rope to haul anyone out who should be so unlucky as to fall into a crevasse.

We reached the summit at 4 a.m. and waited in the full moon for the
coming of dawn (30th April 1896) and we had a bit of food to get the life
into us – food or drink – I forget which – even this ascent which had been
all hard climbing in the yielding snow and slippery ice would have been a

fine performance for a lady, but there was more to come. We were only at the beginning of our troubles.

Before dawn came, I think, we continued on our way. It was very cold and a wind arose, blowing the snow in our faces. Balaclava caps, snow spectacles and treble wrappings of clothes, double-thick socks with separated big toes, and thick-soled grass-shoes, and swaddlings round the ankle and calf became of service now.

The beauty of the ghostlike silvery needle peaks, as we were waiting in the moonlight for the dawn, we shall never forget. The huge mountains round us, all white as was the upland plain on the edge of which we stood, rose like ghosts into the air, blotting out the thickly clustered, brilliant stars with pencillings of white ice slopes and vague black rock points.

Then when the red dawn came, tipping the highest peaks with a crown of gold and magenta, standing out from the grey misty snowfields below, the light broadened and we could begin to see more clearly the new world into which we had climbed.

We could see nothing of the plains below – we were hung up in the air, in a new world in a white basin with jagged peaks for edges and one deep snowfield for centre. Above was the deep blue sky and that was all – but a blue that is only seen with an entire setting of white. Visitors to the white

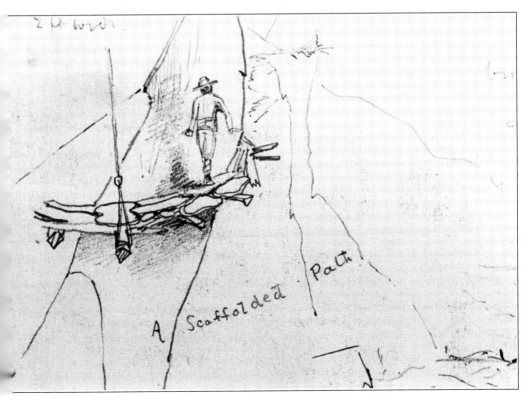

marble Taj at Agra will recall the same blue of this sky as seen against the white stone. It was piercing cold, and a wild powdery drift of snow began to impinge on our faces driven by the rising wind. A little terrier of the Deardres' hid behind us, cowering with fear and cold. In these high altitudes the presence of the wind can be seen from scores of miles away by the little white wisps driven up into the air. I have seen the same being lifted from the shoulder of Everest, when I myself was under Kilimanjaro, 40 miles distant.

This snow drift and the accompanying cold is the worst thing a traveller can face, and this wind prevailing makes the Tojila, though a low pass, a dangerous one.

By endless toil, sinking to the knees at every step as the sun softened the snow, we made the march of several hours to a rest hut halfway to Matigan – full of snow, but the roof of which had been fairly well cleared. It was overhung by a very shaky mass of snow. On the roof of this tumbledown stone shanty we pitched a small tent. The path had been made inexpressibly filthy by past coolies, and to step off it would be to be up to the waist in snow.

We stopped here till the afternoon for a much-needed rest, Mrs Deardre being for the time quite done up, and neither Deardre or I would have cared to go a step further.

After we had spent an hour, sitting with one side of us baking under a noon sun, the other side freezing in a cutting wind, trying to coax the water to boil, we made tea, and we were just going to partake when the tent durrie moved – I was the culprit – and over went the teapot. 'Oh, my precious tea,' said Mrs Deardre and made an effort to save it, but too late. Then we brewed another supply and sat and watched the avalanches, released by the melting snow from the hot sun, sliding down the long white mountain slopes, with a long roar on one side of the mountains or a low rumble, as of an earthquake, if the avalanche occurred on the invisible side. Every quarter minute these avalanches occurred – some which we saw opposite us, a mile away, being very grand – taking about a minute to sweep from top to bottom – the front of each slip a moving rolling mass of snow, ice blocks, snow dust and rubbish. Sometimes three great avalanches were going at once, an extraordinary sight, best seen, no doubt, towards the end of April, at the melting of the winter snows.

In the afternoon, we awoke refreshed from a short nap, and pushed on for Matigan. The walk was as hard as ever – for from Sonamarg to beyond Dras we had in all 70 miles of snow – but towards evening Mrs Deardre forged ahead leaving us two men half a mile behind. We got into Matigan post hut in the evening (a large serai of stone – half blocked with snow) and we slept on the roof – in intense cold – we had climbed and waded 24 miles on foot from Baltal since our midnight start – a fearfully tiring march.

I slept in my little bivouac pup tent built 3 ft. high and 6 ft. 6 in. long

Hill Girls of Kashmir – Kistwar

– made of waterproofing material all of one piece – so that by shutting up the entrance, leaving a slight hole for ventilation, and lighting a lantern inside, I was quite warm, though it froze hard all night. When we got up in the morning we found our water jugs – enamelled iron – frozen hard and Deardre had to put his onto a coolie load without melting the ice – my hair and moustache hung with icicles. By this time, the skin of our faces had peeled and we looked pretty dirty.

Another day of hard snow work and we got to Dras – 16 miles – very bare rocky hills devoid of trees like all the hills on the Baltistan — Tibetan side of the passes. We were, I think, about 10,000 feet here and as we got lower, we began to see rough grass and scanty bushes here and there. Bulit seemed a miserable, snow-bound, iron country. The people on this side were Baltis – miserable people of Mongolian aspect and long-haired and very dirty.

We broke up our combined camp next day, May 2nd, as I was to go to Baltistan, while on the next two marches, the Deardres would branch off to Landlak where they intended to attend the Leh 'devil–dance'. Moreover, I was marching faster, so forged ahead.

On waking at sunrise at Dras, I found a heavy fall of fresh snow had occurred in the night and after striking my own tent, I crossed to the Deardres tent and beat the heavy snow from it, to the surprise of the occupants. I feared their tentpoles would break with the added weight. Then I started for Tasgain, 17 miles, and reached there in pouring rain. The Tasgain camping ground was, so far as I remember it, under a beetling cliff from which very large rocks, as large as houses, rolled from time to time. There were several all round my tent, some as large as a cottage, which had fallen, rolled down the slope and bowled some distance over the plain. There were hundreds of sizes, some old, some recent, with wet clay sticking to them. The men did not seem to mind, so I preferred not to make myself ridiculous by questioning the safety of camping here between the fallen rocks. Sometimes at night I started up, thinking the rocks were coming, and spent an uncomfortable night, wet and cold and rather long after leaving my fellow travellers.

May 3rd to May 8th

May 3rd Tasgain to Memoshtary 28 miles; Memoshtary to Baghacho 25 miles; Baghacho to Karmana 18 miles; Karmana to Kiris 23 miles; Kiris to Dagwena 24 miles; Dagwena to Khappalu 12 miles. Khappalu was my goal for the Ibex nullahs.

Of this Indus march, familiar to all the far-roving English shikaris, there is little of good to be said. The Upper Indus is a terribly hot deep valley in the treeless hills on the Ladak side of the passes – from Dras one soon descends to 9 or 10,000 feet, into the hot regions. In May, it is terrible going from 25 to 30 miles on foot – out of sight of one's coolies and supplies all day. I took with me a tiffin coolie, and brewed a dish of tea whenever I felt inclined – but meals there were none; I saw nothing of my coolies and cooking pots from the start at 6 a.m. to the halt in the next camp at 6 or 7 p.m. Curious country this – sheer desert, hills desert, like the hills bordering the Red Sea, but ten times as high and steep. Far worse than Sinai. The path every three or four miles would touch the steep-cut side of the river and rise from 2 to 3,000 feet over a 'paras'[7]; there being no room close to the stream, the footpath is carried up the bare face of the precipices on wooden beams hung on stanchions let into the rock; a rough contrivance and you look down between the thin loose planks and flat rough-hewn stones to the rushing Indus a hundred feet or more below; to step on the balanced edge of a stone or plank would be instant death, and a healthy head and precipice eye is required, though there is no real danger, for one is *very* careful; sometimes, rounding a shoulder of rock, the path is only 2 ft. wide. Sometimes the path was broken and we had to climb down into the river and wade in the shallows hugging the bank and then a step out of one's depth would be death in the rapids – but we were *very* careful – and apparent danger can be avoided with care.

At Kiris, I think it was, we took to rafts and crossed the river – or rather, on the way to Khappalu, we floated down some miles towards Dagwena – the rafts were merely timbers loosely tied on floating goatskins.

At some of these halts, we came to fans of land – beatifully irrigated by rivulets from the torrents brought down from the melting snow – you left the desert and plunged into a paradise of running brooks, poplars and fruit trees, the sound of ice-cool running water everywhere; and were hospitably entertained by the natives. After a hot tramp through eight miles or so of horrible desert gorges it was delightful to rest upon grass under the shade of trees. These villages are a marvel of irrigation and artificial beauty.

We had a nasty sandstorm at Dagwena. Here the valley opened out, and snow mountains showed their peaks all round – those of the Karakoram – 'The Golden Throne' &c of Conway's *Climbing in the Himalayas*! My nullahs were ahead, beyond Khappalu, in the Lower Shayok River (the Upper Shayok is in Ladak and makes a great drop here). I passed the Dushe, a good ibex nullah, and got a grand panorama of majestic needle peaks of rocks, powdered with snow.

On May 9th, I began my hunting experiences – I marched to the Lunkar nullah, 20 miles, and took up my quarters there for a day or two, intending to try the nullah first and having disturbed it, to go further in to Tinkar nullah. Both were mere deep canyons, so steep and narrow it was a day's work to get from the edge of the snow on one side to the edge of the snow on the other side. I was too late for the good shooting nullahs.

May 10th

---

7 Paras = suspended footpath(sketch on page 129).

Lunkar nullah. A very precipitous one, with a little village on an irrigated fan at mouth – slept in a garden, people very civil. This nullah is narrow and high and goes straight up into the snowline in 3 miles, instead of creeping along for 50 as some nullahs do. The bed of the nullah itself was at a very steep angle and required good climbing, let alone the sides.

We started early in the morning at 5 a.m. and went 3,000 ft. up the nullah, hunting all day.

We at last saw 5 female ibex and 3 small males and one 30-inch male; (length of horns). This was not good enough; so we watched him all day; and in the evening tried a stalk in the hopes of finding a bigger one hidden somewhere near the herd; but, a snowstorm coming on, the ibex moved up to shelter, and could not be found when we made our approach to where they had last been seen.

I had very numb hands and the snow flying in one's face was blinding, and at dusk we came down to camp, which had been moved some 1,500 feet above the village of Lunkar. I had not tasted food since 9 a.m., when I had left the tiffin basket at the site of the proposed new camp.

People reported 3 big male ibex on the precipice 800 feet above this camp; and in the evening, just as I had removed my grass-shoes, we saw an apparent 40-inch ibex on the rock above, looking down at us. It was too dark to shoot. They say there is a way up; shall try tomorrow, if I find it safe and practicable.

May 11th

Climbed the precipice above camp; only one seriously difficult place, but got over it all right without the help of a rope.

We found the ibex at home in the hill – I arrived 200 yards across a gorge from a big buck (apparently big) and wounded him somewhere too far back; and giving orders to have him searched for (as he had retreated to an impossible precipice) I climbed down to camp.

Letters arrived from Aimée dated 28th. I sent off a dak coolie to Khappalu. This evening he should reach Skardu, 14th, noon and return Zinkar Camp noon, 17th. In evening went out again and saw nothing.

May 12th: morning

Sent my 'chota' or second shikari, named M'Handu (Kashmiri for Mahomed) after the wounded ibex with a rope and a dog and 2 junglees. I myself marched up to the top of Zinkar nullah (opposite Lunkar, in the same Shayok Valley). We reached a cave and camped just under the snowline; very cold at night. Heard news from Shikar Gaffur Bux that eagles had been seen hovering about, so I expect they will bring my Lunkar-wounded ibex tonight or tomorrow morning; I like this cave camp in Lunkar nullah – it is safe from hail-stones, lightning and falling rocks, and within easy climb of all ibex ground. It is just at the edge of the snow-line, and there is grass below and snow fields just above us. The ibex stayed all day on the crags among the snow and came down to feed on the grass slopes at 3 p.m. The new grass and crocuses are just coming up after the melting of the lower snows.

May 13th

I mounted the crags above our cave camp, and on reaching the top slope of the mountain (half covered with snow), we saw, up a gorge a mile away, 8 ibex bucks, 4 does, and one young ibex; all the 8 bucks having apparently good horns. There were probably a 42 inches, a 40 inches, two of 37½ inches and 3 of 35 inches – a very fair lot. We lay out all day on the slope, telescoping them, but they were quite inaccessible. We returned late, in a snowstorm, and climbed down to the Cave Camp.

M'Handu had arrived and brought in the head of *my first ibex* from Lunkar, the one wounded yesterday. A thick horn, but only 35½ inches long. M'Handu got to it by being let down 120 ft. of scarps with a rope, according to his own account.

May 14th

Same work exactly as yesterday. Watched the big herd all day with the telescope and returned in the evening; the herd is evidently frightened by a snow leopard whose tracks we have seen; and hence it sticks to the precipices and will require a lot of circumventing.

May 15th

Remained in camp making all arrangements for tonight's march and sleeping out. Cold cooked food for 4 days &c (as we cannot light a fire: it would smell of smoke and the ibex would leave the nullah). I sent Gaffur Bux and the Junglee up to watch the herd today – the third day of watching this herd. I will then rejoin them in the evening when my preparations are completed.

In the evening, I did join Gaffur Bux on the high slopes – we must have been about 17,000 ft. at this watching game (and one had to draw every fifth breath deep into one's lungs owing to the rarity of the air) – and we descended into the deep glacier gorges far below the place where the ibex had their perch on this day. Having reached the bed of the nullah in which, higher up, was the glacier, we bivouacked in a small cave, about 9 ft. long by 5 ft. high by 3 ft. into the rock.

At 3 a.m. May 16th we mounted the nullah, about 4,000ft, to the snow-line; going by way of the glacier, which half-filled the gorge. We found the ibex in an inaccessible place (a very cold wait on first sighting them at dawn). We had a difficult bit of rope and precipice work trying to get nearer; we watched them all day, but they would not move to a better position and in the evening we decided to give up and, glissading down long snow slopes, came back to the small cave bivouac.

I had not quite given it up, however, as I knew it was my last chance of ibex for many a year; for I had no more days of leave to spare, except

The author with the magnificent black bear shot near Gulmarg

a day or two which I intended to devote to shapoo (mountain sheep) and bear on the way back to Kashmir.

One last fling, therefore, at the ibex – inaccessible – long-range – I determined to shoot – hit or miss and then give it up.

I therefore sat down at a slight approach from the spot from which we had been watching them all day, adjusted my sights to 350 yards and opened with the Lee Metford. There was a good deal of scrambling up the precipices on the part of the herd, but the result was that one ibex fell where he had stood and one came rolling, sliding head over heels down a long snow slope, picking himself up at the bottom and limping away into a deep gully.

We came down the mountain in the dark, had lots of falls and snow glissades and I nearly got my hands frostbitten and my nails badly cut. At night I organised a search party of Kashmiris to climb to the body of the dead ibex and look for the other. Myself *May 17th* – I marched to near Gortse 8 coss (16 miles) on the first homeward march. We left Khappalu on our left, 4 coss off. We stayed on the beach near Gortse all night.

May 17th and May 18th

On the morning of 18th I went up this promising grass hill here for shapoo. We saw some small herds of these long-legged wild sheep, and at last one with a decent head, standing 320 yards away. I fired 6 times with the Lee Metford and twice sent my ram sliding down the grassy slopes. I left him finally and made for camp, putting men and dogs on his track. I remained in camp for the evening, sending 'the mullah' to help find the shapoo. The slippery grass hills had been very tiring.

May 19th: Marched to Dagwena, 24 miles – on the way called on the Rajah of Khappalu who was most hospitable. He entertained me and was a most civil host – Khappalu is a beautiful fertile oasis. He sent me grapes and raisins and dried apricots when I left.

From 8 p.m. to midnight I made a moonlight march of 9 miles and lay on the soft sand of the river bed at Kunlis.

May 20th: We marched on to Kiris and Sirinik – say 23 miles. We found the shapoo nullah at Sirinik occupied by Captain Knox of the Royal Artillery.

May 21st: We marched to Agasin 12 miles, and in the evening went up the nullah by the torrent bed, much swollen every afternoon by melting snows above.

May 22nd: Had a terrible hunt after shapoo – saw nothing and in the evening made a moonlight march of 9 miles.

May 23rd: Arrived at Bayhucha 22 miles (met Major Moreland).

May 24th: Arrived at Gungum beyond Memoshtang – say 30 miles.

May 25th: Marched to Tasgam; last night's camp was among rocks and sand. Saw Moriarti across the Indus on the way – tried to communicate by throwing notes wrapped up with stones, but failed – met him at the bridge further up. Last saw him in Victoria on outward voyage. He had a 41-inch ibex.

May 26th: Marched to Dras. Saw Phelps Bros. caravan coming in – they were going on a 1½ years' trip by Garkand. I went into Matigan.

May 27th: Marched from Matigan over the Tojila Pass to Baltal, Chonis; went looking for bears in the nullah at Baltal in the evening. I saw nothing and it rained. This nullah is the most lovely scenery I have ever seen in any country.

May 28th: Stayed in camp during the morning, sending out boys with telescopes and field-glasses to watch for brown bears. ('Red' bears or 'snow' bears.)

In the evening I went out with Gaffur Bux and the tiffin (lunch) coolies. '*Lal Bhaloo, Sahib!*' (red bear) and then he pointed out a big female, looking light gray through the glass.

We made that stalk, my grass shoes coming off as I climbed the steep slope, and I finished the approach in my socks. Just as I had fired at the big female, I saw two partly grown bears jump up, roused by the shot; and as they were the first brown bears I had ever seen, or was likely to see again, I shot at them also – a right and left; and then I opened with the Lee Metford as they made off. At the shots, the big one rolled and scrambled downhill and I knew she was as good as bagged. The other two bears bolted uphill and I emptied the Lee Metford at them at rather long range; but they escaped to the top of the cliffs.

Leaving them, I followed, in my socks over the pine needles, the track of the big bear, downhill, through bush, open meadow and forest; and at last after an hour's tracking (lots of blood showing), I saw her scrambling over a rock 30 yards away: let drive and her head sank, and she slid dead from the rock she had just been passing over.

We rolled her great soft brown carcass down the hill to save labour in getting her to my camp in the valley and she fell some two hundred feet over two precipices with sickening thumps; and we descended to examine her and finally carried her to camp, slung on a pole. Very thin she was – mostly masses of brown fur – for a former occupant of the nullah had fired at these bears a week before and they appeared not to have fed since.

May 29th–5a.m.: Climbed to the top of the cliffs after the two younger bears. The coat of the bear removed yesterday was good reddish-gray and very long, and I am glad I tried in May instead of later. Yesterday completed 8 days' shooting – being 5 at ibex, 2 at shapoo and 1 at red bears.

I left Baltal Valley (the prettiest I think in the world) noon 29th May and arrived at Sonamarg (12 miles). From Sonamarg to Monasbal is 50 miles, Monasbal being in Kashmir.

The beautiful Wular Lake, Kashmir

In a House-Boat

May 30th: Marched to Goond – saw a distant black bear up a tree in the evening, too late to go for him.

May 31st: To Repor. Stayed here 1st and 2nd and arrived Srinagar on June 3rd, having seen a second black bear up a tree at Repor (I was sitting up at night on a rock). Both the half-grown red bears were brought in to the Munshi Bagh Camp by M'Handu – so I had bagged the whole family of them.

Of subsequent sport during this 6 months' trip in Kashmir, the following were the details:

Repor about July 1st. I came down here from Gulmarg. Saw a black bear at dusk up a tree and shot her. Got her after 2 days of following up by man and dogs.

Gulmarg about July 20th. Went to tea with Aimée 2 miles from our hut; and after tea Aimée got on her pony to go home; I went down the hill with the Goojur (our man) and we were just choosing the tree behind which I was to stand and watch for bear at 6 p.m., when a magnificent male black bear (see p. 136) with a good coat appeared in the long grass below me in front, coming up the hill. Aimée had only been gone about 10 minutes. He walked straight up to my tree and when he was 30 yards off I shot him with the .577. We brought him in by torchlight with 10 coolies to our hut and we skinned him next morning on our grass plot, a little girl aged five next door helping with great glee to skin him. Many visitors came to see the body, as it was unusual for the body to be brought into the station.

But to return to the beginning of June, which found me just returned to Srinagar after 6 weeks in Baltistan after the ibex. I found Aimée and little Helen and the ayah still in Camp in the Munshi Bagh under the big trees – all well (shortly before I left in April, Aimée had fever).

They had not been much bothered except by heavy rain and a servant with fits, who used to knock himself about.

Soon after my return, Aimée and I went up the Yakht-i-Suleiman above the Munshi Bagh 1,000 feet (her first mountain) whence we got a lovely view over the city of Srinagar. Shortly afterwards we dropped down the river in doongas, (Kashmir gondolas) and then marched to Baba Manichi to Gulmarg – where I had had a hut built at 8,500 ft. for 250 rupees.

We found Gulmarg lovely – dotted with huts and European camps – there was a pack of hounds (run by Colonel Neville Chamberlain) and constant picnics, golf &c. – a wooden hotel (Nidou's); and one wooden church. A lovely green open upland valley surrounded by pine forests rising to snows above us at 1,000 ft. (Minimay), where we used to go for picnics and bring down the snow. Expeditions after bear and butterfly catching. Aimée always rode a little Kashmir pony. Gulmarg was a most pleasant and unconventional place, the society excellent and constant polo and gymkhanas to watch. A small wooden club. Lots of girls and young subalterns. It was here I shot the station bear, as above described – the station bear of the year; at least, the closest to the station.

Then in August (I think) when the time came to leave Gulmarg, we marched down with Mrs Whary and her little girl (I forget if Whary was there; I think not) to Baramula – on the river, a lovely march; and got into the houseboat which Aimée and I had engaged. In this we went up to a small village close to the Wular lake and made our land march (2 days) to High-Hama in the Lolab Valley. Aimée rode her little pony, I walked, ayah (Doondi) was carried in a dandy by 4 coolies and baby sat on her lap.

Then we got rowed and punted up past Srinagar City, sliding past in the moonlight and on to Islamabad, the other end of the vale, where we saw the old ruins of Martans – Mogul relics, a grand old temple – and we saw a garden with gold foil, very sacred to the natives, and they worried us with beautiful carvings and furs and copper work and silver work.

Finally in October we returned to Lucknow, after a glorious six-month trip.

The Kashmir is a grand country to tour in. Ladies travel about in couples without escorts lording it over 50 coolies and pitching their tents where they will. We saw two American girls doing it!

The scenes in Kashmir one will carry in the head as long as one lives. I shall never forget the Baltal valley where I got the brown bears, the great straight Derdars, sunny smiling valleys, rushing torrents and blue background of precipices and velvet-like green slopes dotted with grand pines. The lovely shadows cast everywhere, lengthening down the slopes and above all the pinnacles of rock, thousands of them, rising into the blue sky with dazzling sheets of snow caught in their crevices. It is the fairest land on earth; I have seen Switzerland, and yet I think so. The prettiest part is peerless Sonamarg and the Baltal valley. One softens with regret whenever one hears the name, Kashmir, spoken, and wonders when one will again visit those lovely hills and valleys.

Chapter 25

Baroda, India
'Xmas 1897

AFTER THE Abyssinian trip[1] I returned to England, and 3 months later, in the autumn of '97, sailed with Aimée for Bombay and was appointed Executive Engineer Bombay Division Military Works, and later Bombay Defences Division.

For Xmas Captain Cox A. R. at Baroda kindly asked Aimée and self – baby and nurse (Mary Diane) to come and stay with him at Baroda. This we did. I forget exactly the date we left Bombay by the B. B. & C. Railway. We found Baroda a most interesting place – with the old Palace and the new Palace lately built, beautiful public gardens &c.

The stay was in all, I think, 10 days. We had two bits of sport here. First, Aimée and I went out blackbuck hunting with the Gaikwari's chitas (hunting leopards).

We all started one morning in bullock carts and on horseback to a village about 18 miles away (I think) and found there waiting for Aimée and myself two chita carts. These were rough bullock carts – merely bullboards – each with its hunting leopard sitting on it held by native hunters. We were invited to sit, and off we went. Aimée's chita, on her cart, kept trying to knock off her hat with his twisting, wiry tail – and it was pretty close quarters to be sitting jolting over rough forest ground, leaning against a big leopard!

We entered high grass (4 ft. high) and got separated, my cart going forward 400 yards, and we lost sight of each other. Suddenly four or five blackbuck and does jumped out of the grass. The boy who was holding my chita unhooded him, showed him the herd and let him go. He made for a small buck which was wrong, and caught him in 80 yards, giving him a stroke with the paw and the hind leg which rolled him over, he then fastened on the buck's throat as it lay trying to rise. The actual race had been exciting for a few seconds, every turn the buck made the chita followed close behind as if buck and chita had been tied nose to tail. A great pace! Then the chita

---

1 With the British mission to King Menelik, when Harald was appointed to represent the Indian government on Her Majesty's Mission under the leadership of Mr Rennel Rodd, March – June 1887

The total eclipse of the sun as seen by the author at Jeur in India. January 1898

was given the blood to drink, hooded, and put back on the cart. Another buck, this time a large one with 23-inch horns, was pulled down; and when I told them to cut the buck's throat and put it out of its suffering, the callous natives replied: 'Wait till the Memsahib comes – she will want to see the chita suck its blood.' I had then had enough and Aimée's cart came up, and her chita had I think also killed a buck. But we both voted the performance cruel, lazy, and not worthy of a sportsman. No doubt it suits the native shikari. It is a thing to be seen once, being one of the national sports of India. But once was enough.

Then I had a bit of real good sport. I had told Cox I much wanted to get a spotted deer (chital), and he told me that in Raj Pipla, about 30 miles pony ride, after an hour's journey along a light railway, I should find some of these deer.

Cox got me three or four of the Gaickwari's troopers, very fine fellows, and posted them and spare riding ponies along the route and by galloping full speed from the end of the railway line I did the 30 miles in one day – and arrived by 11 a.m. At once at this village (where there was a traveller's bungalow at which I was to sleep the night) I was told by the local hunters that there were no chital within many miles, but a tiger had killed one of a herd of bullocks in the jungle some 3 miles away, three days ago. He had been to the kill two nights already and had nearly eaten it all, but there was just a possibility of his coming the third night. This is rare; but the chance was worth taking, and I decided to have a platform made in a tree and to watch that night as there was a half moonlight, and then, whether I got anything or not, I could return to Baroda next morning. Accordingly, it being then noon, I sent people out to make the platform, not even troubling to go out myself and look at it; and by 5 p.m. I started from the bungalow to walk with my local shikari to take up quarters in the tree for the night. Before sitting up, I had arranged that if I should fire shots at game, and follow them five minutes later by 3 shots in quick and regular succession, several coolies were to come shouting and bringing lanterns – rescue me from my tree and bring me home. I only intended to do this if I should be able to tell for certain I had killed the tiger, as otherwise it would be too dangerous for me to come down, or for the coolies to approach, with a wounded tiger about in the dark.

When I got to my tree, I found it very high and very bare, the machan[2] some 20 ft. above the ground and 30 yards or more from the dead bullock. Just the other side of the dead bullock was grass 12 feet high and thick forest trees – so not only was there a probability of a bad distant shot in the dim moonlight, but a wounded tiger could almost cerainly creep away

---

2 Machan = wooden platform erected in a tree as a vantage point for tiger-shooting.

The fine male tiger, shot by the author from a tree by moonlight. The dead tiger had been carted 4 miles to a traveller's bungalow in Raj Pipla.
28 December 1897

Bathing and washing on the steps of a Hindu temple at Baroda. December 1897

without the slightest possibility of recovery next day by tracking. Nothing but a shikar elephant could have followed him. So it was a great piece of luck that I got the tiger.

What happened was this:

The shikari and I climbed up an improvised ladder into our bare tree and waited two hours, when a slight crack of a stick in the direction of the high thick jungle behind the kill told me something heavy was moving there. The crackling of the grass came nearer, but at last there was a loud rustle of the body moving away. The tiger had no doubt come and got a slant of my wind. Nothing happened for half an hour, then just below me in the grass the cry of a squirrel followed by the growls of cubs. My shikari said it must be a tigress teaching her cubs to catch squirrels. This noise also stopped. Another hour, and the same crackling as at first heard came from the left. The tiger, having been frightened on one approach to the kill, perhaps by getting my wind, was now trying to get at the kill through a high clump of grass seven or eight yards from the kill with only a little bit of short grass and open moonlight to cross. Slowly, slowly, the dark shadow crept across the open – now dark and very solid and plain – I could see fairly well to bring the white line of paper (pasted along the centre rib of my rifle) under his chin onto his chest, and bang! A blinding flash and deafening shot and a whiff of smoke rising towards the moon. He lay stone dead – never moved and after throwing few clods of earth that we kept in our tree for this purpose he still did not move. I fired my three signal shots and the crowd came cautiously up with many shouted questions. Before letting them approach, I climbed down and advanced with a lantern. A Rajput with a sword on my right and a man with a spear on my left – my rifle at full cock. But it was all right – a fine male tiger shot through the heart. Of the tigress and cubs I heard no more and we carried him with torches lit to a cart in the woodland village. I walked home through the high forest arriving at midnight and the cart arrived at dawn – then a gallop and train to Baroda and we all got back to Bombay.

Chapter 26

To Phalut under Kangchinjunga
October 1898

DARJEELING is the Hill Station for Calcutta and also the seat of the Bengal Government during the summer, and all the Secretariat officers come up during the summer months and go down again to Calcutta in November.

At the time of this trip, I was Under-Secretary P.W.D. Bengal, and came up to Darjeeling in the ordinary course of business.

Towards the close of the year, October generally, there is a ten-day 'native holiday' for all Hindoos called the *Pujas* – when they are supposed to pray and do no work, and officials in the Bengal Government get away from their offices. Aimée and I were living at a little boarding-house called 'Step Aside'; it and 'Pekoe Tip' were two bungalows belonging to Miss Sills on the hillside below the Mall, Darjeeling, where the band plays and all the nursemaids and perambulators collect of an afternoon. A year later, in the rains of 1899 I think it was, there were terrible landslips here one night after about 30 hours' rain, and Pekoe Tip and several of the houses, including a school, slipped down into the Valley thousands of feet below. There were a large number of deaths among Europeans and natives and more hair-breadth escapes (see photograph on page 150).

It is from Darjeeling that, on a fine day, the finest view of the snows to be had from any hill station in India is to be obtained – Kangchinjunga, over 28,000 ft., seems to be painted in grey and white on the background of blue sky and the great heaving shoulders of forest-covered mountainside, which lead up to it from what seem bottomless misty valleys, overgrown with dense tropical forest, isolate it from all haunts of man. The Kangchinjunga and Everest region seems to be the end of the world. Nothing beyond, except unknown Tibet and Lhassa, the sacred city of priests. It is here that the highest point of the whole crust of the earth heaves itself up into the blue sky – Everest, 29,002 feet, nearly five and a half miles perpendicularly above sea-level. Below Darjeeling is forest: the most beautiful tropical forest in India called Terai, or the forest which clothes the foot of the Himalayas; from Assam almost to Kashmir. Large trees with giant creepers and tree ferns in a great dark tangle that only an elephant can force its way through; orchids and palms. The railway which runs up from Kurseong and Jalpargini passes through the most beautiful forest scenery – perhaps in Asia – the only thing I have seen like it was in the Harar Highlands when going to Abyssinia.

From Darjeeling there is a little route which runs into the depths of the mountains, and the Govt. has built rest houses or 'travellers' bungalows' at Joripokri, Tonghlu, Sendukphu (11,000 feet) and Phalut. So that with coolies to carry the baggage, and good Darjeeling hill ponies to carry oneself, the marching is not difficult. You get from 50 miles (Darjeeling) to 25 miles, as the crow flies – there or thereabouts – from the peaks of Kangchinjunga; and you are from 50 to 80 miles from Everest itself, and can see it from Phalut and Sendukphu.

Aimée and I hired about 12 coolies, men and women, Phulias, with strong Mongolian features, the maidens with their cheeks smeared with pig's blood, old and

A Bhutia – A general favourite – an old lady much in evidence at Darjeeling

brown and caked, to make them attractive! Just a little native custom in Sikkim and Bhutan! We each had a sturdy pony – mine shied very badly. And we marched along the forest path through glorious scenery in a fine climate, on the edge of the most fearful slopes ('Khuds' or precipices of India); these slopes seemed to go down at an almost upright 'mansard roof' angle – straight, straight down through the dark forest till the stems of the trees were lost in the mistiness of thousands of feet of descent. Of course, the ponies would walk on the very edge of the path – a slip could not possibly have been anything but instantly fatal, and whenever I had to get off my pony, he shied backwards at remounting so I had to be careful only to mount at the places where there were saddles between two rises in the path, the only places where there were no awful precipices. It was an interesting journey; one seemed to be marching to the end of the world, up, up towards the glittering peak of Kangchinjunga; through forests dipping into beautiful

Stepaside and Pekoe-Tip, Darjeeling

gullies wet with the spray of waterfalls, among tree ferns; or on the hill among rhododendrons.

It is grand to leave the station of Darjeeling with the petty worries of office, and plunge into this sea of forest where no man treads. We spent the first night at Joripokri bungalow, and then crossed a deep valley and rose again to Tonghlu. Here we began to get good views of the snow – a fine golden sunrise on the top of Kangchinjunga – but it was cold at night and in the early morning, and the wood fire in the little room in the bungalow at Tonghlu nearly stifled us. The next day's march, on the third day, took us to Sendukphu, a bungalow in a big pine forest at 11,000 feet. Here the view was grand over all the mountains and one had said goodbye to civilization, goodbye to India and the haunts of man.

There was only the little hut nestling in a cosy dell in the top of a forest-clothed ridge, from which a view could be had westwards to Everest and south-east to Kangchinjunga – now only about 30 miles distant as the crow flies. It was fearfully cold at night and all our coolies had wandered to a village 5,000 feet below and got *drunk* there – men and women – so our blankets did not turn up and we only had a saddle and overcoat each

Kangchinjunga (28,200 feet) taken through a telescope

for bedclothes, and a horrible stifling wood fire, and most of the food gone too! But the view in the morning! I got up at 5 o'clock and crunched over the ice, which was lying on pools outside the bungalow three quarters of an inch thick. Gradually peak after peak was touched with a red-hot orange glow as if a signal fire had been lit on the top. The sky grew red-grey, with grey mist and pale white snow below and Everest and the distant peaks, Kangchinjunga quite close, all sprang out and bathed their heaving shoulders in the red glow, and twilight began to search the deep valleys. I was at the top of a little hill – it was freezing with a cutting wind, and in spite of thick clothes and an ulster, I could not keep warm. Over away towards Darjeeling were great waves of black rolling forest-covered mountain ridges, and far away to the south-east was the dim magenta-grey flat – a mere indication of the Plain of India some 7,000 ft. below us and some 50 miles away as the crow flies.

We marched to Phalut, a very up and down march, and had to be constantly getting off our ponies and on again, bad for me with my shying brute. Our drunk coolies turned up smiling inanely. It was impossible to be angry, they were so good-natured over it and pleased with themselves.

We passed numbers of yaks and their herdsmen on the road, dark brown

A view from Phalut (12,000 feet). The end of the world and "God saw that it was good"

cattle with long tresses like a retriever, or rather a Yorkshire terrier, and full tails. We also passed a few tourists, among others the Workmans, climbing in the Himalayas − marching, like us, with coolies and ponies.

We went on to Phalut, where we found more open rides, open green grass slopes with some dead pine forests, which stood in ranks of skeleton stems, shooting up towards the sky. Below lay a dense forest, a likely place for bears. From Phalut we marched on to Singlila, a point very near to Kangchinjunga, and about 40 miles by road to Darjeeling. At Singlila we took out our tiffin baskets, and spent the middle of the day taking some photos.

Looking back from Phalut in the early morning towards India, the whole landscape seemed immense. The glowing snow peaks rising out of magenta seas of cloud, and away towards Darjeeling the rolling brown-grey ridges going on for ever and ever, and the little plains of India beyond hidden by a magenta haze.

What little mites we seemed − a million times smaller than ants − the whole Government of Bengal lived in that little spot called by men Darjeeling, which it was impossible to make out, so small was it in the landscape − though it was on top of a ridge and the houses scattered for two miles.

Two miles was a mere dot in that immensity where we could see a hundred − turning from the little works of man, turning our backs on Darjeeling and on India (whose whole public works and bridges piled together in a big ruin would not make one small needle-point of Kangchinjunga), we looked towards the pale white waste round distant Everest, and there had just then been a puff of wind, for we *could see the snow blowing off in wreaths from the top of the highest peak in the world* − a pin-point of a white smooth down!

Chapter 27

After Stags in Mandla
January 1901

DECEMBER 29TH: We (Aimée and I) plus sixteen pack ponies, Saby – the grey riding pony – (for Aimée), some pony men and servants, got ready in one compound in Jubbulpur (Rest Camp Road) on or about 25th December – that was on Christmas Day – the garden full of ponies rolling with their loads in the grass under the bamboo and a babble of pony men. I was to have had camels but the General got them, having paid a higher figure than I was prepared to give. We sent the caravan on several days beforehand (to cover the 110 miles to Moti-Nala).

So on 29th December we found ourselves in a tonga with two ponies – wretched, but supposed to gallop (which they couldn't) – and another tonga for the 'bearer' – a tent servant (gaffur).

From Jubbulpur the road to Mandla goes south-east for 60 miles, and from Mandla to Moti-Nala (my promised land) is another 50 miles – of very bad road. The whole road is 110 miles of teak forests – the road is a single thread winding through dense cover and crossing small open valleys with a little wheat and hemp cultivation, and a hamlet here and there, and thatched huts standing solitary, their roofs clothed in evergreen creeper training over the thatch. Smiling under the bright Eastern sunlight but squalid when you look nearer; filthy, insanitary, sprung from the soil, made from mud bricks and grass and looking as if it were fast rotting back into the original material, which lies scattered about, untidily, as the builders had left it when they put together the hut in a day or two some twenty years ago, but did not even take the trouble to clear their site of surplus material.

The most noticeable features in the forest scenery on this road are the very large teak leaves, eaten with holes by insects, some still green, some already dry in January, for it is three months since the end of their annual rains which occur in July, August and September. We were already getting the light Christmas showers. The grass stands three or four feet high, of a dull grey or yellow hue; already dying, drooping and falling in a rotting litter, as it is being pushed up by the short young grass. The bamboo clumps which clothe the hillsides in the gaps between the straight black stems of the teak trees are showing light green with fresh young foliage, delicate and feathery.

We did the 110 miles in four days, staying at the travellers' bungalows at Tikaria, Mandla, Thonra (here a mere forest hut) and getting our Camp at Moti-Nala. The only traffic we passed was an occasional grass or hemp bullock-waggon.

At Tikaria we lit a wood fire, cutting away the matting from the front of the hearth for safety's sake – it was a cold and keen night – yet the thermometer was 60 degrees, which would not be thought cold in England.

Our servants went to the outhouses in the travellers' bungalow compound and lit big grass fires to keep themselves cheerful far into the night.

Low flat-topped blue hills surrounded the bungalow, with a pink sunset over the grey-green expanse of forest and bamboos. The carters we passed on the road were brown men of stunted growth of the aboriginal tribes who lived in these Central Indian Highlands – clothed in shreds of dirty cloth – all that is left of their property after last year's terrible famine (1900). Sometimes the merchants themselves, of a lighter brown, better clothed and with better features, walking beside the carts, show the type of the Aryan conqueror of the cities and cultivated plains, as distinguished from the lower forest types, the grass and woodcutting aboriginal tribes whom successive waves of Aryan conquest from the north have left stranded in these Highlands; indigenous tribes, Gards/Banjas/Bhils &c.

The ground round Moti-Nala holds sambhar stags (*Rusa aristolelis*), swamp deer (*Rucerous duvoucellii*) Chital deer (*Axis maculatus*) and the four horned and the barking deer, bear, panther, tiger and an occasional bison – the latter preserved as they are scarce in these forests. The buffalo ranges much further east, but I understand it sometimes crosses the divide between Moti-Nala and Bilaspur.

There are some who go shooting to make a bag (and I am not one of them) and some who shoot for a variety of trophies, and some for the life and scenery and some would even prefer to watch the game with a naturalist's eye and not pull a trigger. The game *par excellence* here is the sambhar – his grand dark head the better and the simpler for only having the six points; there is a simplicity and a directness and purpose in the lines and curves of the fine massive antlers which appeal to the artistic sense more, perhaps, than the confused forest of points carried, for instance, by a reindeer; though every horn trophy has its peculiar grace, and when dealing with stags, nature has left nothing unfinished in grace or beauty. Except perhaps that primeval beast, the moose and yet even he probably has his beauty in his own forests!

30th December. Looking out from the bungalow (I wrote this at dawn at Tikaria) it was like the seacoast – capes of blue and areas of cloud, and in the gaps between the clouds can be seen the wheatfields in the valley –

bright, brilliant, rich green. On the hills are wisps of cloud – a fine day. The usual feature is blue flat-topped hills, caused no doubt by the denudation by water of the plateau of some 3,000 feet of which most of the Central Provinces is composed. The peaks run up to nearly 4,000 feet. It is warmer today. In our tonga drive, we pass large herds of black buffalo and find them bathing in the 'tanks' and village ponds – tended by tiny children – their clothing, short skirts reaching to the waist – their distended stomachs showing the un-nutritious food they live on. They have to eat so much to get any good out of it that they expand like balloons – one can fancy a donkey doing this on thistles, or a horse on damp straw, but it is not good to see children blown out like this.

We stopped the tongas near Chiraidongsi, as there was something stirring in the jungle, and on Aimée and I walking through the trees we saw some chital very indistinctly but no horns. So we did not go after them. On reaching Mandla, we put up at the Rest House (travellers' bungalow or Circuit House) and here we found some friends. (White from next door to us at Rest Camp Road – Jubbulpur.)

Evening 30th December. At Mandla Dak Bungalow. A fine specimen of a Dak bungalow, very park-like scenery in the middle of Mandla — a civil station and capital of a District – about a dozen Englishmen live here. A lovely banyan grove in front of the bungalow in a bit of open park — large and shadowy – under which our tonga men have put the tongas, picketed the ponies and made themselves comfortable for the night by lighting grass fires. The banyan grows by throwing down shoots from the larger branches, perpendicularly like stalactite and stalagmite in a cave – the roots hang like creepers till they touch the ground. As the tree grows larger, because of the longer branches, the further out these descending pillars fall. An old tree has a wide (circle within a circle) grove of pillars; and the very oldest trees begin to rot at the centre, branches fall and the pillars are left – a very ancient tree may take the form of a rotten stump and a circle of pillar trees – a beautiful shade a good banyan tree affords, for an army or a flock of sheep.

Mandla is a very pretty, quiet, 'countrified' place (if such a term can be used in India). On 31st December we started for our third tonga-drive. We had to start from Mandla early, because the tongas had to be got over the river on ferry boats. (The Nerbudda, I think.) We sent them on and meanwhile, White, the Executive Engineer of Jubbulpur, whom we met the night before at the Dak bungalow, showed us with much enthusiasm a pretty little church he had built during his earlier service as Assistant Engineer in the Public Works Department.

The ferry in the early morning was pretty – a bathing ghat – slips with brightly dressed women and girls bathing, old Hindu temples, doorways casting deep shadows, cave-like.

We drove along a 'cutcha' or unmetalled road for 20 miles. I got a blackbuck on the way. We reached a small forest bungalow – a mere mud brick hut with thatched roof at Thonra.

Only one room 12 ft. square, with a small verandah and bath-room built of mud bricks, whitewashed, roof thatched, floor of cow dung stamped hard. We had taken the precaution to have a servant and some furniture here from the pack caravan, which had gone on to Moti-Nala (about 30 miles further on). So next day we got some coolies from a village near to carry these things on to Moti-Nala – on their heads; from village to village, rather; changing the coolies every ten miles. Some of the coolies were women and some small boys. We took our servants on our spare tonga. It was New Year's morning. The dawning at Thonra hut – New Year of 1901 – is another added to the long role of New Years and Christmases spent in the Jungle! We were helped out here by Bhawani Singh, a timekeeper or foreman of works, who was mending the roads with a gang of Public Works coolies.

1st January 1901: We went on the last stage of our four days' journey, to Moti-Nala, my 'Promised Land'. Here we found our camp pitched, the tents almost touching another forest hut like that at Thonra. These Forest Department huts are built of very primitive materials, but, situated in the heart of the jungle as they are, they are uncommonly useful. They are used as 'inspection bungalows' by Forest Divisional officers going their rounds, when they ride fast and don't bring tents.

On the way, I stalked a blackbuck by descending into a nullah and fairly creeping up a long grassy hill the other side, always behind a thin bush; on my getting a shot, he bolted a few yards and fell – and going to look for him I saw behind another bush an apparition of a huge bull nylghai (blue bull) which had been in company with the blackbuck; he was so tame I would not fire, and when he had made me out, he cantered over the plains. These plains are beautiful savannahs well described in Forsyth's Highlands of Central India. Our shooting camp at Moti-Nala (near the forest hut) was among the sal forests of Central India, quite different from the teak forest region. I went out in the evening of our arrival at Moti-Nala to look for spotted deer, and put up, at a few yards in dense forest, two sounders of wild pig; but that was all I saw.

2nd January: I was called at 6 a.m. and went after chital (spotted deer), some having been sighted skirting the outside edge of the sal forest opposite camp – just at dawn: they had spent a night in a field of corn close to Moti-Nala village feeding off the young grain. I went after them and got a young stag – he was so mixed up with a bush behind which he was standing

The author's wife Aimée in 'the tiger's haunt', Mandla

that I failed to notice his horns had not got rid of the velvet. In the evening I went out to the Panari Talas, or Pajara Pool, a great place, and shot a big boar, unfortunately his tusks were no good.

3rd January: I saw nothing in the morning. We had had two days of very bad rain, the whole of the 'light' Christmas rains being concentrated on our first days at Moti-Nala. I went out in the evening, a long tramp through the forests and glades of the river bed (Phen-Nuddi I think) and at last just before sunset, we (my two shikaris – Gords and Banjas and my sepoy orderly and a coolie) emerged into an open plain of rather long grass – over waist-deep, white from the dry seeding grass – and I had got to three little saplings 2 inches thick growing in a triangle, when an apparition of two jet-black bears appeared, begging like dogs on their hind legs, looking motionless at me over the grass – 80 yards of yellow grass separated us. I stopped dead short, and quickly fired at the white 'necktie' of the bigger bear – an old female as her head and shoulders loomed black above the golden plain. The bullet 'told' loudly and she dropped howling to the ground, and both she and her big male cub disappeared from view in the long grass, not from sound though! The younger bear set up a fearful roaring and charged past me, though invisible owing to the grass, at best speed; as he passed there was a dying howl from the grass in front of me where the mother had dropped. I stood motionless listening – on these occasions the ear must guide the eye – or the eye will be too late – anyway, if at the moment of a charge you have some other noise near you – the creaking of a saddle or the snorting of a horse – your ear will be confused and the beast be upon you before you have located the sound. And it's no use locating with the eye – that is little guide if you hear nothing to confirm what the eye sees. Then an amusing thing happened! In front was the setting sun. I looked back, and behind me were my followers, led by the plucky chuprassee, running from the forest as fast as they could lay legs to the ground – they were already halfway across the wide plain. So I was left alone among the three saplings. The young bear, after rushing round me a few times, always invisible, made off in the bee-line for the forest to my right. Then all became silent and I waited. I did not want to be too precipitate in walking up to the old female, which I knew lay only 80 yards away in the grass in front of me. If she were dead, there was no hurry; if only wounded a cautious approach was advisable and it would be better to let her get stiff – I knew she had not made off for I should have heard her stirring.

Meanwhile, I took out my whistle and spent some twenty minutes before I succeeded in getting my followers to show themselves at the edge of the forest behind me. They slunk out one by one, seeing me hold up my hands, laughing. I never saw such a disgraceful case of funk. But when they came near and found I had still to walk up to the bear I had fired at, I could only get the two Banjas to go with me. So cautiously approaching with rifles at full cock, I came on the bear's body stone dead. I was within 9 feet before I saw it and pulled the fur at the back to make sure.

Then we made our way to camp with the head and skin of the bear on a pole carried by two men.

4th January: I made a preliminary reconaissance with Aimée to Mandla to look at the barasingh (12-tined stag) ground at Malunjola. We had a terrible time with our tongas in the mud owning to the heavy rain at night. We passed through Mandla village where we left our tongas and mounted our ponies (at least Aimée had Saby – I walked) and we marched across a lovely wide valley bounded by lofty and dense sal forest – it looked a hunter's paradise. But on 5th and 6th January and subsequent days, though I went out twice a day, I shot nothing and the 11th found us back at our old quarters at Moti-Nala.

11 January: This was a red-letter day. I went out in the morning to Jogmandi forest and came upon barasingh (swamp or twelve-tined deer), 2 does and a small stag and a very large stag. I saw them just in the open valley and had a long, exciting, crawling stalk and eventually got the big stag – but following him up in the long grass my second shot broke his horn (eventually mended by Rowland Ward). Length of horns 3 ft 8½ inches – a very good stag – 12 points.

On getting back to camp at 11, I raised my arms above my head to signal 'antlers' and Aimée signalled back approval, while I and my hunters were 300 yards away. Aimée had seen a herd of chital (2 does and 2 good bucks) crossing from the Jowari patch near Moti-Nala village. This is the spotted deer. I went out after them and got into complicated ravines and long grass towards the Rhen River – found them nearly unstalkable under some large trees in the open long grass – but I tried hard and alarmed the deer. They went streaming off down a nullah at full gallop and I knocked over what I think was the best buck (about 34 in.). He got up and I pursued him into the forest and got him with a second shot – a beautiful buck.

12th January: was a blank day, but *13th January*: I went out to the Halon valley to a tank there – the Kurisari Talao (the Panari Talao on the Jogmandi or north side of this road and the Kurisari Talao on the south or Balughat side were quite the best drinking places for game). Coming at dawn to the tank through the reeds I found a stag bathing – reflected in the water – and shot him as he disappeared in the reeds (a barasingh but unfortunately a smaller one than I had thought and scarcely shootable). I had some fun with a lot of doe sambhar in the long grass at 9 a.m. – put grass in my hat and stalked to 15 yards of them and watched them for half an hour. I had to move before I could make them see me. On the evening of the 13th, I went with Aimée to the Kursini Falls — a beautiful spot, but very little water going over.

14th January: Another red-letter day – went back to Kursini Falls and crossed the nullah and there over a plain was a huge sambhar bolting behind a kopje half a mile away – grand horns. I followed cautiously keeping the whole hill between me and where he had gone and then I skirted round the hill and came down into a bushy valley and suddenly saw 3 sambhar hinds under a tree. I let them get away and waited and waited and there was a rustle under the thickest bush and I saw the sambhar getting up. I floored him when he was a yard from the bush (90 yards range) and he turned out to be a grand stag. Horns 41 inches. My shikari Rohun of Maggasim (a Banja) and Lalla of Moti-Nala were excellent men.

16th January: Another grand day – I went to Kursini again and before getting to the waterfall turned to some likely open bush country – cut up by small nullahs, to the left. Saw barasingh does 120 yards away go out of some bushes. Waited and finally the stags followed – I hit him, followed him in thick bush, and finally got him – 35½-inch horns with 14 points. Coming home I held up my arms, signalling to Aimée I had got a big stag as I had before.

We returned to Jubbulpur, arriving in four days after a most pleasant trip.

Chapter 28

Minor Trips in India
Between 1898 and 1902

IN THE AUTUMN of 1898 I went to Bankipore, Bengal, as Inspector of Works, Behar with 8 big districts to inspect – local works under 8 district engineers and travelled 1,000 miles in three months round Behar – an indigo country.

Went to Buddhgaya, a very sacred place with thousands of images of Buddha. Went shikarring with Maynard on an elephant at Gaya and got a few blackbuck. Also had a try for nylghai in the sugar cane near the Sone Canal with Seawrigho – but no luck.

From Bankipur went to Darjeeling and did the Phalut trip described and then transferred to Amraoth in the Hyderabad assigned districts and went with Aimée 1,000 miles round the villages in bullock tongas in the three hottest months in the famine year 1899 – without rain. Aimée came round with me inspecting all the famine works. I had good sport with nylghai and blackbuck.

Easter 1900 – I was Assistant Secretary Public Works Department Bolamm and got promised by Afsun Dowlah, Commander in Chief of the Nizam's army, to shoot in the Nizam's preserves at Karsamudrum. Got nothing, but a hotter country I have seldom known. Jungle dried up and no game. Aimée was with me, and Pye and Benton of the Hyderabad Contingent – and we would have had a pretty camp if it had not been so hot. Pye slept mostly in banyan trees.

In the autumn of 1900 I was sent to have charge of more famine works to a ghastly place called Basin in Birars, and here got 5 more blackbuck. Cholera was raging and Allen, the Executive Engineer, from whom I took over, was down with it.

At Jubbulpur, besides the Moti-Nala trip, described before, I went a second trip there, alone, in May 1901 and got another spotted buck, a bear and a barking deer. I also went out to Nerree with Balfour for a tiger beat and as 50 beaters had been sitting under my tree all day waiting for us to arrive from Jubbulpur, when the beat actually came off, the tiger came through thick bush to within 100 yards of my tree, then smelt where the beaters had been sitting under it, and broke back with a tremendous roar right through the beaters.

I had another interview with this tiger in January 1902, when I went a 10-days' trip with Aimée to the Nerbudda (with pack ponies along footpaths). I sat up all night for him over a calf he had killed – but returning in the morning I found his fresh pugs, and monkeys chattering ahead, showing he had been loitering near the kill afraid to come on.

While I was sitting up in the tree for this tiger, Aimée stopped in camp two miles away. I had arranged to fire signal shots if I got the tiger.

We marched on to the Nerbudda and I got 2 nice chital bucks at Bunsi in one evening. When we reached our camp at Banyakherra, on this trip, I beat several ginghs with Aimée. At one in particular, Aimée and I sat at the saddle where a path came up a rise and down again, cutting off a large jungle from a smaller one. We were beating for sambhar but nothing happened. Next day I was attracted as I passed the same spot by a chital stag barking, and I drove the jungle, sitting about 80 yards from where Aimée and I had sat the day before (on the ground both times). Out came a quite unexpected tiger and trotted exactly over where Aimée had been sitting the day before. He was gone before I could get a shot and we lost him though we followed him till dusk. It was at this the chital had been barking!

Volume III
1904–1913

Chapter 29

A Reminiscence of Campaigning in Arabia – 1904

(This trip is written from memory, notes having been lost.)

THE DELIMITATION of the British boundary with Turkey in the early part of 1904 involved a certain amount of fighting at a place called Suleik, about 80 miles inland from Aden peninsula. The Kotaibi, I think, were the tribe which gave most of the trouble. The country is very rugged and barren. Going in from Aden you get to the mainland at Sheikh Ottoman, a town depending on the British garrison and their ships in the harbour for its commerce. Then about 27 miles through desert and cultivation to Lahej – the capital of a state, well irrigated, ruled by a sultan. Another 13 miles inland, say 40 miles from Aden, across a barren sloping desert, which can be seen from Aden, the big mountains of Yemen begin, at Nobat Dakin. You march from there up a very forbidding river bed, sandy with a small stream trickling through it, and subject to freshets – say about 40 miles to Suleik (I'm hazy about distances). Even in peace time you take an escort of camel troopers of the Aden troop, mounted on fast camels – splendid Indian Cavalrymen, being Tajputs or Mohammedans from such places as Delhi &c. These are the same men I had on my first survey in the Issutugan River of Somali – but the Lance-Naik had in 1904 become the doyen of the Corps, the Rissaldar Major or senior native officer. A fine figure of a man still. He stayed at Khor Maksar at the cavalry stations of Aden, 6 miles away on the sand isthmus. I had about 6 troopers on the occasion of this journey. Dawes, my assistant in the Military Works at Aden, was with me part of this trip. He was afterwards drowned in the Cavery Falls in Southern India while trying to save a coolie on works there. He was carried down the falls and his body found below. A splendid officer. There was on this trip a military post at Nobat Dakin, where the infantry officers treated me most kindly – they were living in tents, the koppie they were on being converted to a military post. It was at the edge of the high mountains and commanded the route to the interior.

I think it was on this trip, but possibly on a later one, when we passed a steep precipice to the main river bed which ran 40 feet below, the path skirting the precipice at 50 yards distance. A short time before, the GOC's[1] baggage had been raided, the raiders coming up out of the river bed, and we passed the skeletons of about 10 camels which had been shot from the ambush. I was careful to send 2 troopers to look into the river bed as we passed along the path, to see that all was clear.

Lahej is a sort of miniature Egypt, a fan of land kept alive by irrigation from the river which flows by Nobat Dakin. Between Lahej and Nobat lies, as I said, a desert of deep soft sand about 18 miles wide, rising to Nobat and the hills.

I forgot to say that we visited the Sultan of Lahej in his palace and slept at the Dak bungalow which he keeps for European guests; and one way to the desert was through Hi Talim, on the outskirts of the settlement and famous for its chukore or red-legged partridge shooting, and sand grouse and quail. There is also the *Gazella arabica*.

Following up the river north of Nobat Dakin, we had on the campaign placed blockhouses at intervals, and it was these and the telegraph line I came to inspect. The field-telegraph had been put up by the RE to connect Aden with the British regiment camped at Dithala, about 100 miles inland near the Turkish border, at about 6,000 feet elevation, with hills immediately behind rising to 8,000 feet. In a recent fight at Suleik, an officer had been wounded by the Kotaibo and 16 British soldiers killed and wounded and many Indians. I especially went to Suleik to inspect the strong blockhouse there which Lt. Gulel of the Bombay Sappers and Miners was then constructing. I inspected this with Yale and duly returned to Aden, after about a week's trip, and am entitled to an Army List entry of 'Aden Hinterland Campaign 1904' which however I never caused to materialise. I made my report in Aden to General Maitland, the Resident. Besides the sport I have already named, there is some good ibex in the interior of the mountains,

1 GOC = General Officer Commanding

similar to those of Mount Sinai. There is also the little white Arabian oryx beyond the Turkish border.

On the whole a short but very interesting Active Service trip in a country very like our North-West Frontier of India in its most barren aspects. Whenever there is irrigation there is malarial fever – otherwise the country is healthy though horribly hot, and Arabs here who have some Abyssinian blood and are dark, are treacherous by nature. They have matchlocks lit by a suspended burning rope.

Chapter 30

Portuguese South-East Africa
October, November 1904

October 9th: Leaving Aden Harbour – a grey-blue mountain summit, soaring to eighteen hundred feet: a yellow morning sunlight behind precipitous peaks: a lively anchorage of blue water: breezes bearing a touch of coolness after the intense heat of summer.

Aden, the thoughtlessly abused refuge of the white man, standing a bulwark of civilization, surrounded by hundreds of miles of wild sea and hundreds of miles of the most barbarous countries left in the world.

Aden, an oasis of struggling civilization, always gasping for life, threatened by almost every power of nature with extinction by desiccation, artificially upheld by man in spite of the extraordinary conditions. Imagine a couple of volcanoes, a blue shallow bay, bordered by sand and scanty mimosa bush. There is no water and scarcely a green thing. Then put upon it a civilization which has to condense water before it can drink; import all its supplies – meat, vegetables, cows to give milk, fodder for the cows, building materials (except stone which is in plenty); and give it a population of some fifty thousand half-savages from Arabian oases or nomadic Somali herdsmen; add some British and Indian troops and their barracks and hospitals, a harbour full of ships and some coal, and you have Aden.

But on the morning of my departure from Aden all was rose-colour. The anchorage appeared never so bright with glistening water, the hill never so fine in outline. I was going across the water, past the steep limestone-capped bluffs of Guardafui, and turning south, I was to hit Africa in a new place, further south than I had ever visited before; a new world.

Full of pleasant incidents is the start of a wild trip, when you feel the grip of civilization and custom relaxing, and you begin to move at fifteen or twenty knots an hour towards your goal!

We passed the bluffs of Guardafui at a mile distance and then steamed south, to arrive at Mombasa on 14th October, winding up the Kilindini Creek, a pretty entrance. The old entrance is at the town side further north.

How well I remember our difficulties in steering into Old Mombasa in 1888. Our occupation of this 'Mission House', a decayed bungalow overhanging the harbour; the drunken riot of my Zanzibar porters on the previous night, and the aftermath. How I found 9 men in an improvised hospital all recovering from their liquor and cut about the head with swords; and how one great Swahili lay stretched dead on a table in the middle of the room, to show on our lifting the sheet a deep cut from a two-handed sword stretching from the small ribs on the right side, across the back, to cut through the skull behind the left ear.

I remember how we of the New East Africa Company, the first organized body of Europeans (other than missionaries) to land there, took possession of the Mission House and filled it with stores, arms and ammunition. Then there was the steam up the Bundarini Creek and the hauling of baggage up through the mud of mangrove swamps to a patch of dry land overshadowed by forest – no railway then! The people were unsophisticated in those days and used to sing out 'Yambo, Bwana Kubwa!' ('Welcome Great Master!') as they worked in the fields.

How well I remember our theodolite station above the Rabai Hills, the sighing of the wind, sounding like surf, through the coconut trees, the boom of ripe coconuts falling eighty feet into the grass. How well established these missionaries were at Rabai! It was said that at the season of Masai raids they could turn out 2,000 muskets.

Dwellers in Mombasa now can little realise how primitive it all was. It was to a different Mombasa we had come in 1904 – so different that the old appears to be a tissue of lies.

Mombasa had hitherto been my furthest south; and it had nothing but old memories for me. We passed the old fort (Portuguese) which we of the East Africa Coy. in '88 were allowed to enter for the first time as a favour, by the Arab Wali of the Zanzibar dynasty. That was the wicked old Africa.

After Mombasa, I was to steam on through palm-fringed summer seas to Zanzibar, go on ever south and into unfamiliar waters; then we would again sight land, and the South Africa of the books which I had delighted in – not that of the war – would lie in front of me: the Africa of Harris and Oswell, Gordon Cumming of the Majuba disaster, of missionary labour and divers men's graves – the South Africa of yesterday.

To those who follow game by instinct and for love of the forest, civilization is a blot. As we entered the pretty wooded Kilindini Creek I tried not to see them, but there were the inevitable gas-works! I hoped for better things beyond the Victoria Falls for they are not harnessed yet; I hoped to be in time. It was the old, wicked, unregenerate Africa I wished to see, Africa as it existed before this depressing war. Everyone, I reflected, has been on the veldt and the indiscreet Press has torn from it much of its mystery, but everyone has not yet been to the country beyond the Falls. The hunter and the artist hold that many of the most beautiful and most interesting spots on our planet have been harnessed, chained, and in the process defaced, by the Engineer. Niagara, and other places. It may have been the beauty and interest of these show places which first attracted the pioneer, got them visited and noticed and then the Engineer came. But there are many places left that have escaped notice: the Engineer and the grog-shop and the billsticker go along beaten tracks – they cannot spoil the whole Earth; and the world will still be beautiful with vegetation and mountain and ravine when our vulgar, crude, ugly Western civilization has long ceased to exist. The Western European is probably doomed; over-centralization, the crowding into cities; and the Colonies may share the same fate and all will go – the shams, the lies, the injustices caused by the inequalities of money which attracts money and leaves the poor without any; with civilization may go drink and disease; and as there are no races to replace this civilization – unless it be the Mongolian – nature may get back her own, as she has often done before, and cities buried in jungle will be the sole monument – the Trafalgar Square lions and the Arc de L'Etoile peeping out of the jungle, serenaded by the fox under a watery moonlight – Nature will laugh at our puny attempts to deface her permanently, as she has laughed before at every race which has preceded us. The buried cities of Central Asia, the ruins of Italian cities, the ruins in Mashona Land and in South America, in Ceylon, and such a sight as the miles and miles of ruins of the ancient City of Delhi show the weight of her hand.

But when Nature gets back her own, and the forest, the prairie, the mountain and the desert (the best and most holy temples ever used for prayer) have returned to their original purity and the sea has taken back her privacy, will all the beautiful forms of animal life still be there – the zebra and the kudu, the deer? Let us hope so. Curiously enough, it is the true sportsman who preserves. The pheasant, for instance, would be extinct in England today were it not for the sportsman.

Suppose for a moment a world run by electricity, till every living thing but man has become useless and electrical, then for a few ages destroy all civilizations till a new one arrives – in the interim what an uninteresting world it would be without the animals!

On 15th October we left Mombasa at 5.30 a.m. – the surface of the Kilindini Creek was bathed in silver dawn with black forest behind, the African bush which is always so pretty in silhouette against the sky. This bush was glowing.

I had landed the day before and presented letters to Judge Calor and to Bowring, had met Gedge of my old caravan, had noticed the splendid flower-gardens which surround the bungalows of the British officials, and the general air of prosperity and business, had noticed the small tramway by which people get about the place, and had taken a walk through the old Arab town by the old harbour (where we landed in '88).

On the German East African Company's liner, which had carried me from Aden (I travelled second), I now found we had shipped some Cape farmers from the south-east of the Old Colony, returning from Nairobi after looking round the districts near the Uganda Railway. They described the land as very rich; the climate much better than anything in South Africa. They said if you put a walking stick into the ground, it would grow. But I cannot, in picturing future farms, help thinking of the lusty native tribes and that there may be fighting in these districts at some future time. There are the Masai and Wa-nandi for instance; such fighting races are liable to bubble up now and then.

These farmers told us that things are bad in Cape Colonies – low prices, lack of enterprise. They talked of cattle and their diseases – falling prices at the Cape; the splendid climate and soil of the higher parts of British East Africa; 'the further one went the better it was' until the drop towards Uganda. They talked moreover of living luxuriously on a rupee a day – you could not starve, they said, in such a country; you and your friends would live like fighting cocks – fresh meat, milk, eggs and vegetables; but no market for surplus produce unless some staple product, like cotton for instance, is found to succeed. Of course, a staple product will be found, for anything will grow. These big, stout, well-to-do British farmers are no dreamers or poets, with their big heads, loud strong voices, blue eyes and red necks. They seem to talk solid sense, and to hear them and see them brings to me visions of thriving colonies at five, eight, or even ten thousand feet, where white men can keep the strain strong through many generations; and I see Mombasa, already beautiful with flower-embowered bungalows, growing, a beautiful city, round the edges of the Kilindini Creek, with mosques and domes – there are some pretty golden minarets already.

The situation of Mombasa is superb. Rich tropical vegetation, with a steamy climate, yet with rain – soft temperate rain at times; but one can always escape the heat by going a few hours up the line to the higher regions.

We reached Zanzibar on Sunday 16th October – or rather the evening before, after two days' fairly heavy rain. Since the direct sailings to Bombay, Indian hawkers and Japanese and Singalese have swarmed into the place – it was not so in '88, when the strangers one saw were mostly Beluchi soldiers or traders of the Sultan's army or the bazaar.

On Thursday, 20th October 1904, at 8 a.m., we landed at Beira. I had several introductions one way and another. Varian, (who was on the ship) introduced me to Strand, and he to Cameron, Secretary of the Club, and I got put down as a temporary member. Then I met Colonel Arnold, Inspector of Exploration, Mozambique Company; also I met Findlayson, who had been shooting where I was going, the Tando di Gorongoza.

I went to two 'At Homes'. At the Portuguese Governor's house I received much hospitality. He had been a Major in the Portuguese Engineers. Greville, the British Consul, helped me to get some of my mules and lent me a camp bed, which he said was absolutely necessary if I wished to keep in health in this country. Greville and Colonel Arnold had some fine buffalo heads and there were some good ones at the Club. Colonel Arnold lent me a 'machila' and a demi-john bottle for boiled water, and gave me voluminous and most useful information about his camps on the Tando di Gorongoza, or Gorongoza flats. Then they gave me introductions to officials in the interior – Esparde, Commandant of Bamboo Creek, up the Salisbury Line; Picardo, Assistant Commandant, Mazamba (near the above river flats).

But I am going too fast. From the ship I landed at Beira with Varian of the Cape-Cairo Railway Construction. Mrs Benson, wife of the manager of a bank in Johannesburg, was also a passanger whose acquaintance we made on the voyage and she went on to the Cape. The arrival at Bamboo Creek is worth recording – the night in the train from Beira to Bamboo Creek was a bright moonlight one and as we could not sleep we foregathered at the back of the train, outside, and he told me stories of the building of the Railway through the plains of Fontisvilla, which was a veritable 'white man's grave' owing to malaria and other poisons. We went through splendid bush like the Indian Terai. Buffalo were plentiful in those old days of the building of the railway before the great epidemics of rinderpest nearly wiped them out all over Africa. He told me of having been held up on a bridge-parapet by one. It was an enjoyable talk accentuated by the big and thick forest scenery we were steaming through.

At Bamboo Creek railway station I got out, and Varian, I think, went on to Rhodesia. This Bamboo Creek was only a siding, nothing more, with a tin and wood store and a bar. Kept, I believe by a Greek. The engine driver of our little engine got off, and when I leaned out of the window and asked him if this was my destination, he most kindly took me over to this store or 'hotel'. There were half a dozen men in shirt-sleeves and a bar-tender and the engine driver chucked a couple of half crowns (or thin Portuguese equivalent) onto the counter and stood me a whisky and soda – he was gone before I could return the compliment. The men in the room looked on me evidently with suspicion because of my 'boiled shirt' and collar, but I managed to get into conversation, and seeing I was neither a cut-throat nor an idiot millionaire, they soon became more communicative.

The talk was mostly of 'pegging out'. If you don't drink whisky you 'peg out'; if you take quinine for blackwater fever you 'peg out' – always keep up your spirits by imbibing some spirit &c &c. They told me that you have to take a machila (or litter), or if you 'peg out' where you are – there is no moving as you are too weak to walk, and there are no ponies. This was their melancholy way of looking at it. I stayed all next day and soon discarded my white collar which would be looked on as 'swank' by the engine men and stokers and we all dined together (about a dozen white men) at a table covered with American oil cloth, and sitting on long benches.

Then I engaged my men. At first, it appeared I could get nobody in Beira. I wanted civilized servants to begin with and here Zanzibaris (Swahilis) are the best, being more enlightened than Kaffirs. The Kaffirs do your carrying and hunting (or rather 'do guide' when you are shooting).

As caravan headman I got Ali, a cheery Swahili from Zanzibar, who had been in the Salisbury 'Black Watch' Scouts. Asked what pay he wanted, he said £3 a month. 'Three quid, Baas,' was what he said. He knew English well, knew Mombasa, Uganda, Somaliland. Mahommed was my second caravan leader; this man and Ali I took out hunting alternately, and used alternately as interpreter in camp.

Mahommed was a French Swahili from Madagascar – £2 and food. 'Seabreeze' – a most invaluable cook – had been Captain's servant on the *Racoon* and gave one a navy salute. He spoke navy English very well and did not seem to care what pay he was given – he said 'About £2.' He also was a Zanzibar Swahili. The Shikoti was a sort of Kaffir – transport leader £2 and food, and a useless man I found him. He was 'Capitao', a headman of coolies. Colonel Arnold and Greville helped me to engage these men, and the first three were a great success.

I was to get my porters or carriers, all Cheringoina Kaffirs, from Commandant Espardi of Bamboo Creek, my jumping-off place a few hours up the line. Also my machilieri or litter men – of whom more later. But to return to Beira; imagine the mouth of a large river, and in the estuary a few islets of sandbank – on these sandbanks Beira is built. The sand is loose and easily lifted into your eyes and ears by the wind. It is also sharp and cutting. The sea has to be kept out by a sea-wall; yet the profits of Beira, as the port of Rhodesia, have been such that the town has rapidly grown and now contains many grand streets; a modern town of clean houses, with its light hand tramways, its telephones, hotels and shops. I will leave to the return journey the description of the railway between Beira and Bamboo Creek; and the Commandant at Bamboo Creek.

I left Bamboo Creek on Monday 24th October at 8 a.m., marching to Mutushima, the first stream, for tiffin, 7 miles. I spent several hours over this march, for no sooner had I got 3 miles from Beira than I chose a big tree, many of which were scattered over this open plain, for target practice. I had brought several 2-ft. squares of white glazed calico and some drawing pins and paper bullseyes. I fired 35 shots at this tree and got a good idea of the throw of my rifle (450 high-velocity double rifle by Holland). I only had one rifle. Marching in the afternoon, I went 17 miles more to Macuire. I had 12 porters and 8 'machilieri' or litter men.

There were some grand trees overlooking the deeply cut river at Mutushima – it ran under an avenue of them, between high banks choked with undergrowth – all dark rich green and very restful after the glare of the hot march (for October is very hot). There were three rivers between Bamboo Creek and Macuire, of which the Mutushima was the first.

The arrival after nightfall at Macuire was interesting, as it was my first view of the village and people of the interior. Bamboo Creek is only a railway settlement and cosmopolitan. I ought first to mention that between the last two rivers I shot the bull of a herd of water–antelope in some marshy ground. This was the first game bagged by me – horns about 26 inches.

We crossed the first river by dug-out canoe – left there as a ferry. The second we waded as it got dark and walked up the bank into the clearing which is the settlement of Macuire. This is a Mozambique Coy.'s station, the Commandant being an Italian, Signor Morelli. The station is surrounded by plantain groves. I called on Signor Morelli, but he was reported by a very dirty-looking European subordinate to be asleep, so I had to defer seeing him till next morning. I put up in an empty rest house, partly used as a storeroom for plantains.

There was a bad thunderstorm early next morning which stopped us marching from Macuire till about 8 a.m. Whilst waiting, I saw about 20 Kaffir women with hoes being driven along by a black Portuguese Kaffir, with a pruning knife in his hand, a most ferocious-looking ruffian. They were evidently slaves by their furtive, gliding movements and general dejection.

My Swahili Ali said they had been sent to S. Morelli's house to work in the garden, but they had been sent back again as 'It was raining, and an Englishman being camped here, he would be ashamed to work them in the pouring rain!!!' Ali seemed to know all about it. He said, if I had not been there, they would have had to work, rain or no rain!

25th: marched from Macuire to Macaiya – 15 miles; Macaiya to Serapanya – 9 miles. *26th:* Serapanya to Macopute – 12 miles. *27th:* Mapokuti to Mazamba – 20 miles.

But Ali was a character and I must allow a little for his wishing to please me as an Englishman! Ali was an old sergeant of the Salisbury 'Black Watch', a body of scouts used in the Matabele wars. He was a Swahili but had travelled much. He showed much intelligence and spoke a comic kind of broken English. 'Bwana – your English Island, Sar, I Zanzibar Island where I born – oh; yes Island people are best people but these Cheringoina Kaffirs are very bad people no good making spears, carving sticks, nothing – and forgetting which side dey scratch 'emselves like the monkey.' Once when

I had told him I would not shoot female antelopes, he showed me a herd of hartebeeste and said: 'One big man Ingondonga run 'way, three gal she stay behind.' This Ali knew snatches of Masai, Waganda, Arabic, Zulu &c and had been in the Soudan. He said that when a small boy, he used to rub two sticks together to make fire; but that now all African races, however, remote, have matches brought from Europe.

These marches seemed to have been much understated by previous travellers and sportsmen – anyway, they were very long and tedious ones. The only interesting things were the really fine tropical woods and the actions and cries of the machila men, of whom I had eight. They sing in cadence as they run – a set of words expressing kindred ideas. The front man says the word and the others grunt in acknowledgement. Thus (in Kaffir) 'Table–huh! Chair–huh! Footstool–huh!' or 'Hartebeeste–huh! Kudu–huh! Sable antelope–huh!' or (in Portuguese) 'Captain–huh! Major–huh! General–huh!' or 'England huh! Portugal–huh! Germany–huh!' I was very much amused at all this, and the play of their bronze muscles, under the heavy fifteen-foot-long machila pole, was a sight to see; they were many of them well built, all muscular and some of them were like living statues. They were sweating and shining under a bright sun through bright green forest. On the whole cheerful, in this country which has no horses and where, in that respect, journeys are usually melancholy. Then the machila, but for these men, would be melancholy, a litter suggesting sickness.

On the 26th I marched from Sarapanga (where I came on impala buck) to Rogue, and on 27th morning to Assistant Commandant Picardo's shooting-box at Mazamba, and on the 27th, I had an adventure when the

The cries of the Machila Men

Portuguese black police were tying up an old woman to the flagstaff in order to flog her. When they saw me they all fled to the bush, old woman and all, carrying the cat o' nine tails with them. She must have been fifty-five at least!

On 28th I started at 6.30 and marched 6 miles to Colonel Arnold's Camp in the 'tando' or river plain of Zangwi. Here I found a sportsman, Captain Warwick, in possession. I saw a little game; that is, two herds of hartebeestes (Lichtensteins) and one of zebra, and then one of sable. I got a couple of Lichtensteins bulls (ingondonga) among some ant-hills, and pitched camp at noon. It was very hot walking in the open 'tando' or plain at midday. I was glad to rest at some forest which jutted out into the flat plain.

29th October: Finding the tando at Colonel Arnold's first camp shot out, I marched 14 miles to my tando 2nd camp, passing Warwick halted in his green Willisden canvas tent; and I went on, passing the main river. There were a very large number of hippopotamus tracks near Warwick's camp. I got a sable bull and hit another. While marching along a valley where there was a lot of low flat thorn bush and many fresh tracks of black rhinoceros, we suddenly got a glimpse of two magnificent black-maned male lions on the further side of the stream about 150 yards away, moving off as they had evidently seen us. I fired for the ear of the hindmost, but evidently went too high, for the lions cantered off and plunged into a nullah to their left. I was not after lions, but followed the tracks till we lost them in dense thorn thickets in the nullah.

In the evening, I got a water buck.

Among the other servants, 'Seabreeze' was my cook. The name has been given in all ages to the 'seedy boys' or Sidi Bhais (Hindustani) (no doubt a Lascar name), the black stokers in the Navy. He was a Swahili like Ali, and Seabreeze had formally been valet to the commander of a British gunboat. Whenever I said it was good dinner, he would pull a lock of hair on his forehead and say: 'Yes Sir, thank you Sir,' so I always replied: 'You were servant on a Man-'O-War weren't you, Seabreeze?' and he invariably answered anxiously: 'No Sair, not sarvant Sair, to sailors; *Kaptain's* sarvant, Sar.'

I had now got back my 'thieves' feet', the slow, questing, untiring glide which comes to me after a few days of the forest country. One has to be so careful about every stick or large leaf which may break under the feet and disturb the jungle, which is as silent as an empty church.

Warwick had a shotgun and I heard many shots in the distance. They seemed an indiscretion in this silent wilderness of leafy glades shut in by high trees, which was a living 'zoo' if one could only have seen all that was in it. One of the men got a glimpse of a lioness and cubs as they bounded away into the bushes.

1st November: I shot a warthog boar in the forest near Jirimaji, and then I doubled back in my course to Captain Warwick's tando camp and put up my tent there in the evening. I was glad to get a yarn with him again, and a comparison of sporting luck.

2nd November: In the early morning I got a grand stalk after a bull eland in the open. It was too clever and it was spoilt by a reedbuck jumping up under its nose and scaring it away.

3rd November: I went to Magamba and on to Chief Matondo's village. Old Matondo very decent. He was thirsty and we sat on a log together and I let him have a drink from my water-bottle, so I won his heart. He gave me a good hut, and chickens for dinner.

I remember this Camp well, for I was here some days off and on. Opposite my hut door, a young woman sat with a child on her back, pummelling corn in a big stone 'pestle and mortar' arrangement. She kept singing a monotonous refrain, the baby's nose banging against her back. Would many generations of this produce the negro flat nose? I wonder! How is it that some of these Kaffir women in Cheringoina are so uncomely? In a really primitive society perhaps, where the general law of the beasts and birds holds good, the male serves to be more beautiful and attractive than the female. In civilized life he puts his limbs into cloth cylinders! The crowing of the cocks in Zambezia woke one up at two separate times − 4 a.m. and 5 a.m. − in Aden they crow in the afternoon in order to wake people up after their noon siesta. At the first crow in Zambezia you wake your cook, at the second you wake yourself.

4th November: I tried for zuka (eland) and pala pala (sable).

5th November: I tried for zuka again and got a nice bull 2½ miles from Matondo's. I looked for a good kudu deal on these hills − a very nice place. In the evening I marched to Nyama (meat) and the hippo-pool 4 miles south of Sabuca.

It was nearly sunset by the time I reached the group of pools − which formed a section of the river here, pools strung out like pearls in a necklace, being the deep places in a continuous river which was shallow in places. These pools were sunk deep down in the soft alluvial soil and screened around by reeds, thorn-bush and grass which was growing along their margins.

We left the narrow, winding track which ran parallel to the river in the upstream direction on its left bank and a mile from it; the single footpath, which is six inches wide, the width of a man's feet, is the main track of African travel between village and village. It was crossed by minor tracks to side villages, the main track differing from these by being continuous, while they are often lost in savannah of coarse buffalo grass, thorn thicket or swamp. We left the main track and walked a mile before reaching the pools, not attempting to fire at a startled bushbuck or any other chance game, for I was intent on the hippopotami which old Matondo had promised I should find, and as we crossed this tando of grass or forest-glades we had to approach the pools in absolute silence. Soon we struck the line of high tree jungle which marked the line of the river.

Now the sun, shining straight and low into our eyes, was just preparing to make the final plunge behind the trees on the opposite bank of the river, into a sea of glowing yellow flecked by filmy grey clouds. Under this big clump of trees in front lay, so said our guide from Matondo's, the pool, many miles long, where we should probably come upon the hippopotami. The pools are part, I think, of the Losema River. What little wind there was blew straight to the front from the back of our necks; so to better this, to us, unfavourable hunting condition, we made a wide detour, following the downstream direction so as to strike the long pool at a point where, we had been told, we could find some high spreading thorn-trees under which to camp. We found a flat green sward, and heavy fallen limbs of dry trees for firewood, ready to hand for immediate burning. A comfortable site for camping – what memories those dry trees bring back to me of distant camps in many climates!

My tree having been chosen, and a much larger tree for the men, and the blue floor-cloth of my little tent pinned down so that the tent, when pitched, should face so as to have from the doorway a pleasant view of some magnificent white-stemmed trees, probably the giant mahobo–habo, I left my Kaffirs to prepare the night camp, first giving instructions to Ali as to being quiet in speech, the knocking in of tent-pegs and the breaking off of firewood for burning at night; and above all, silence when going down to get water. Then I took Ali and the two hunters (cacciadore) and the Cheringoina and Zambezi boys, with the waterbottles and spare cartridges; and we started for the evening hunt, pushing through the high grass, still hot from the blazing summer sun of the late afternoon – the sun now setting redly and still warmly in the west. Now we turned north, upstream, for the deeper mysteries of the great pool, my 'promised land'.

As we advanced, between walls of high grey thorn-trees, and also great forest trees, along a winding path pitted deep with hippo tracks in stiff clay – as we advanced the trees grew higher. A white ibis screamed and darted into a great gulf of space above the deep bed of the river, the bed of the latter being closed in by the long grass, sloping almost perpendicularly, which commenced a steep fall to the opposite bank, ending in a deep thicket just over the water, which itself we could not see. At our feet, on our side of the river, a dense thicket hid the low-lying water 40 feet below, and into this dense overhanging thicket our path, made by the hippopotami in going to drink, plunged in a perpendicular chimney, as it were, a sort of ventilator shaft, made in the black tangle of dry brushwood by the enormous bodies of the hippopotami forcing their way through in their nightly wanderings.

Glad we were to get out into the evening light below, and to straighten ourselves out on a green lawn of damp swampy grass a few feet from the water's edge, after our plunge, in constrained stooping posture, through the thickets and lianas. We were now on an edging of short grass, thirty feet wide, an inch or so above the level of the water. The river eddied silently at our feet, mirroring the sunset glow; and across, there was a plunge of some small body slipping into the water by the opposite bank – a water-rat, perhaps. A tremendous silence prevailed, as if all nature were waiting for the sun to set.

Directly opposite, on the grass on the other bank, was something which made me concentrate my attention – some presence felt. A gap in the thick bush brought down a small hippo-path – continued on this side by the one through which we had scrambled – and there I saw fifty feet of dry clay, and on it a long straight dead branch – *branch*? It was the Father of all the Crocodiles, the largest, not that I have seen, but that I ever believed possible – 25 feet long at least, I shrink from saying 30 feet but he looked like that – a wet and shiny raw umber – horribly alive, his muscles all flowing and rippling and undulating as he woke to life, and imperceptibly changed to a fast gliding mass soon to slip swiftly under water. He had lain snuggling under the opposite bank, so that had we been coming down from that side, instead of from the side we actually travelled, we should have dropped through the tunnel of brushwood right onto his very back!

Magnificent he looked as I brought my field glass on to him when I first saw him, motioning the men to be still. Of course, I could not have fired as we might see hippopotami at any moment.

Just as one of the hunters pointed upstream, remarking that sabuca lay in that direction, a ripple appeared on the shining surface of the river a mile away, and fixing our eyes on this as it slid nearer to us on the glassy surface – it spread into two ripples – it then became two heads and eyes of two hippopotami swimming down towards us. Hunch! They had yet several hundred yards to come and we waited without a move. Nearer, nearer, the ripples came – nostrils now, eyes and ears perhaps, shining in the yellow light, then underwater again leaving always a floating eddy. Would they see us and dive? As the leading one appeared for two or three inches above the water for a moment, I fired for the ear – instant disappearance and a commotion, then a head half above the waves at which I fired – disappearance again. The eddies calmed down and scarcely was the echo of the rifle over before the stream was as calm as ever, not an eddy or ripple. No, a new ripple appeared – the leader, for some unexplained reason, diverted its course and swam under water straight to where I was standing, and having reached

The big bull hippopotamus after being dragged to the bank by the Zambezi boys

within 3 yards of the bank, close to my feet, began disturbing the surface
but nothing could I see – I sprang back a few paces and fired into the water
where it was most disturbed, and all was still again. The reeds stopped
moving!

The worst of hippopotamus shooting is that you seldom know the result
till several hours later when the carcase floats. It is too haphazard as regards
target and results to be satisfactory. However, besides the natural history
specimens, it yields a quantity of excellent meat, which is a great boon to
the inhabitants of the villages around, and which can also be exchanged for
flour for one's men.

There was nothing further to be done, as it was rapidly growing dark
and we had a difficult way back to camp. But next morning we came up
to the river and saw at once two huge bodies floating, one at the spot close
to where I had stood and fired into the water at my feet, and the other
near the centre of the pool. It was caught by snags and held or would have
floated downstream. The latter was a very fine old bull hippo. Leeches about
ten inches long were crawling over the bodies, and they twitched and rolled,

tugged at by a circle of small crocodiles under the water. Our Zambezi boys and the villagers at once plunged in waist deep without the slightest fear, making a great shouting and splashing – a thing I would not have dared to do, and I think few men unaccustomed to these rivers would dare to do. In a twinkling they had made fast a rope round one leg and rushed ashore with it. Luckily my great crocodile which we had seen the evening before – the 'King of the Ford' – was not there. They dragged the big bull close to shore, and spent some hours cutting them up, while I went back to camp. Along all the paths leading from villages buried in the jungle, some miles away, men and women came running all the morning to our camp and to the water's edge, till at least a hundred people were collected, and the trees round the camp were hung with festoons of biltong or drying meat. I also set up a bartering place under a tree and changed meat for flour, which my men wanted as a change of diet.

My leave now being near its end, we marched back to Beira and the hospitality of Colonel Arnold and the British Consul, Greville – I felt like Alice just back from Wonderland, into the everyday world of hand-push tramways, the cars shoved along by splendid Shangans (related I think to the Zulus) with hair standing straight up in a brush on their heads; where coloured people have to walk in the deep sand of the streets while Europeans walk on the concrete side-walks; where the wind cuts your face with sand at the street corners. The Shangans are moving bronze statues. Outside the bar, a top-heavy German passenger liner with funnels striped like a croquet ball (of the Deutsch Ost Afrika or WoermanLinie) rides at anchor, the smooth water full of her reflections or reflections of the heavily wooded banks of the inlet.

I met with the Commandant Eapada and Assistant Commandant Picardo, who gave me every assistance, and I dined with Espada and his French wife and clever young daughters who played the guitar after dinner. They showed me their farm and I found Madame an adept with a full-sized rifle which she fired at a mark on a tree. The Commandant's port wine, neither heady nor over-alcoholised, flies straight from Portugal to one's heart, and memories of it are mingled with the flavour of Portuguese hospitality and the kindness of old Matondo, who practically presented me with two hippopotami for a drink of water! I have the semicircular tusks still!

The Custom-house at Beira is not all pleasure. An Anglo-Indian, however, feels curiously at home there if he has had many dealings with the Custom-house at Bombay. What this feeling is, is not apparent till it strikes him that many of the officials must have walked straight out of Bombay or Goa and taken appointments in Beira. The same slight figures, dark complexions, grand names, restless, ambitious expressions of the 'Portuguese' we are accustomed to see in our Indian station in minor positions of trust – club, bandsmen or cooks. What would some Anglo-Indian communities be without them? But here they are in higher position, clanking swords and saying goodbye in the Colonial way: 'So long!'

I had had only 10 days' real shooting and 14 of marching and questing – all the game eaten by men or changed for flour, so none wasted and it was a godsend to the villages near. The game encountered and bagged was: 2 reed buck, 2 water buck, 1 hippo bull, 1 hippo cow, 2 Lichtensteins, hartebeeste bull, 2 hartebeeste cows (meat for villages), sable bull (1 only), 1 cow sable (by mistake), 1 impala buck, 1 eland bull, 3 bushbucks, 1 do. doe (for men's meat), 1 duiker buck, 1 warthog boar.

I only kept the following trophies:

1 sable head, 1 eland do., 1 Liechtenstein do., 1 impala do. and 2 hippo tusks.

I had only to regret that I had to come out without a 'nyati' (buffalo) head and a really good sable. For the Cape Buffalo horns are the prize of these regions, and the sable I managed to secure was a poor one. There is no doubt that Cheringoina and Gorongoza are a natural zoo with lots of forest for cover. But the country is unhealthy at certain seasons. I had received nothing but kindness from the Portuguese officials and special kindness and hospitality from Colonel Arnold, Captain Greville the Consul and other English in Beira.

Chapter 31

Lahej and Nobat Dakin, Arabia
August 1908

THIS WAS a blazing hot trip – and only occupied three or four days. The Resident at Aden sent me up to Nobat Dakin to look into the question of an anicut[1] for irrigation. We had our water-supply scheme for Aden, getting the water from near Lahej; but someone (French I believe) had put forward to the Sultan of Lahej the idea that the water would be wanted for an irrigation scheme for Lahej territory; this, of course, if carried out, would have blocked the Aden water supply scheme. So as Chief Royal Engineer Aden, I was sent to Nobat, in the hills 40 miles from Aden, to enquire into the feasibility of the Sultan's anicut scheme.

As luck would have it, two tribes were scrapping with each other in the desert of 20 miles which you have to cross to get to Nobat Dakin, bang across the track I would have to cross. So the General decided I would have to have an escort of 20 Aden troops.

We started in the heat of the early afternoon. It was about 100 degrees in the shade, August being the hottest month in Aden, where there is no rain from year's end to year's end except for a shower every 2 years which fills the celebrated ancient 'tank' reservoir in the heart of the crater of the volcano – the latter 1,800 feet high.

We arrived in Lahej one evening in a dust storm with thunder and lightning. I had to extend the men with their ponies at open intervals in the sand-dunes, because of the lightning. Rain had fallen in the hills and the river in front of us was reported by the guides to be quite unfordable so we had to off-saddle our camels and sit down by the river from midnight to daylight.

At 6 a.m. we forded the river. I was in the centre up to my waist with a dangerous cataract a hundred yards below, and just then a freshet began to come down, the river rose several inches and I felt lighter and was nearly swept off my feet. The river was about 90 or 100 yards wide. Then a camel was swept off its feet and men had to run down the bank and get a rope over it, and dragged it ashore just in time to prevent it being swept over

1 Anicut = A dam (Tamil).

the edge. This was a very nasty place. However, we got across without further mishap.

I rode with the escort, keeping our scouts well ahead and on the flanks, for 20 miles across the desert, and spent the remainder of the day surveying the site of the proposed anicut, a great reservoir wall to be built across the Nobat Dakin Gorge. A most romantic canyon among savage treeless mountains. We kept our cavalry scouts on commanding points while I was exploring the river bed. The survey completed, we rode back the 20 miles to Lahej, getting there at nightfall after riding some 50 miles, twice fording a river and taking a lot of angles and work on foot. Needless to say, I was dog tired, but met a man coming the other way from Aden, at the Dak Bungalow, and sat up till 1 a.m. discussing the education bill, neither of us knowing anything about the subject.

Going over my notes next day, I discovered to my horror that the whole of my survey depended on an angle which I had taken on the instrument but had forgotten to record in the Field Book. So we rode back, with the thermometer registering about 100 degrees in the shade, to Nobat Dakin and back to Lahej, a distance of 40 miles as on the day before, and I came back with the treasured angle. After this strenuous x-chasing I spent a second night at the guest bungalow. Then 3 hours sleep and a ride at dawn of 30 miles back to Aden, taking advantage of the early cool – 4 a.m. to 9 a.m. The irrigation scheme was by later calculations proved to be too expensive for Lahej State to undertake.

Chapter 32

Europe

THIS WAS one of our best trips, (Kitty[1] and myself), which we made during our Indian service. A wonderfully successful trip, cheap, and it took in so many delightful things and it was all on the way Home on 8 months leave from India.

We left Mhow on 7th February 1910 and took passage in the Italian mail-boat, the Flori Rubattins liner from Bombay, going on board about 10th February 1910.

Among the passengers were Sir Edward Buck of the Agricultural Department, some American missionaries and their wives, two young subalterns and a young Irish doctor and a Montenegrin-Greek prince. As usual we touched at Aden, Suez, Port Said and then we stayed a day (February 25th 1910) at Messina — to discharge and take in cargo. We were more than 6 hours off the quay, and spent the day ashore going over the terrible ruins, as it was only 18 months since the great earthquake in which over a hundred thousand people were killed.

We went ashore at Messina in a shore boat, and landed on the quay among hundreds of barrels of lemons. The facade of every house on the quay front was standing but the houses themselves were empty shells inside, right back through the thickness of the town. It was just as if a solid mass of houses in London, in the space between Pall Mall and Oxford Street and from Park Lane to Kingsway, were entirely gutted. In every house the inside partition walls, stairs, landings and bedrooms had all fallen to the ground, just as water runs out through a bottle, the bottom of which has been knocked off. All these things were lying strewn inside the houses in high mounds; mattresses, bedsteads, pictures, clothes, mortar and rubble, and skeletons of men and women and children, all looking like a heap of stones with rags flying in the wind. A terrible joke of the Almighty, of nature or of a Devil — one wonders which! The good gone down with the criminal, the innocent with the guilty! I have never seen a sight which so impressed me as the ruins of Messina after the earthquake.

---

1 Harald's first wife, Aimée, sadly died in January 1905, and was buried in Aden. (The grave was still in good condition when visited by her great-grandson, Paul Winder, in 1994.) Harald later married Amy Christina ('Kitty') Swayne, a cousin, in 1907.

The English chaplain's house, occupied by my father some years before, facing the quay, a five-storied house, of which he had the third flat, so far as I remember, went down with the rest and I understand the chaplain and family were all killed.

Great marble pillars and capitals were strewn about, and military working parties were picking at the high heaps of ruins. The day of our visit they dug out the corpse of an old man, a type-writing machine, and a safe containing securities to the value of £20,000. Standing on the apex of the larger heaps of ruins were double sentries, soldiers or policemen, with revolvers, rifles, belts and service kit, and ball cartridges. I believe that after the dust of the earthquake had begun to settle but for a few hours, criminals and thieves had already been looting the ruins, and a regular revolver battle had raged for days while killed and wounded were being carried away in litters from under cellars and rubble. One man was buried in a cellar next to a candle factory, grubbed a hole to the next cellar and lived for weeks on the candles – there are other stories. A great wave had come in, wrecking ships in the harbour and flooding the ruins while the wounded were there. One ship, even eighteen months later, lay anchored in the harbour, a cargo boat, waiting for the owners to turn up – missing owners, the whole of whose families and accounts and possessions had been crushed into mortar-dust.

On the quay were long rows of barrels containing fresh lemons, grown in Sicily ready for export. Girls, I think, were making 'Roses' lime-juice cordial from fresh limes.

We wandered out to the new American frame town, put up at lightning speed by contract, to which the survivors had moved from the first tents and open bivouacs to which they had fled for weeks after the disaster. Just as in the famines in India, the United States has sent ships full of wheat, so America has stepped in here with a healing hand. This frame town was like an Eastern bazaar, people living in the street outside the frame shacks, making boots and every kind of article out under the sunlight squatting on the ground. Now eighteen months after the disaster, with business going on, and the hot Mediterranean sun flooding the streets, everyone appeared gay.

It was reported a year or two later, in the press, that the Queen of Italy came inspecting to Messina, and was shocked by the small progress made in rebuilding the town. For my part, I estimated it would take 20,000 soldiers and engineers about 20 years to do it, and about 3 years to clear away the ruins!

From Messina we went by sea to Naples, arriving on 27th February, and we stayed in and around Naples till 3rd March. Those four days at Naples were pretty full of marching through the streets, later a great funeral with priests in full canonicals; we went to one of the best restaurants where two big stout men in evening dress, up in an alcove above all diners' heads, sang a song about '*Tante figlie*' and occasionally embraced after each line, pretending to be girls – two huge and dark and hairy men with heavy moustaches – made us all roar, all the English people, but the Italians took it seriously and the singing was excellent. I expect we were very ill-mannered.

We went to arcades and shops and then – Vesuvius and Pompeii. Figure yourself driving through a squalid suburb of the poorer part of the city, a long, long, East-end street like the Old Kent Road for instance, and then think of masses of fruit and vegetables in mud and dust, trodden under foot like Covent Garden market on an untidy day; men lying asleep or drunk, half-dressed or in rags, on the side of the pavements; hawkers; untidy barefoot children begging – beautiful children in themselves, but the squalor! It was worse than an Indian bazaar; I can only liken it to a slum of Dublin. Then through outer suburbs and the open country-gardens full of orange trees and lemons – to a small funicular railway which took us halfway up Vesuvius. At the top, a long ascent on foot up a mule-path through barren brown rocks like the hill at Aden – about a dozen tourists in little knots a quarter of a mile apart or so, according to the efficiency of heart or lungs. At the top, some fearful and dangerous-looking scallywags who forced us to avail ourselves of a short rope to get up the final lip of the crater – charging enormously for their help. They tried to force us to buy their bad wine in filthy bottles and were most threatening – but we kept a stiff lip. One American lady who was alone, and had come up the winding path of a mile or more by herself, complained she was pestered by a couple of tramps who followed her all the way trying to fleece her. But we watched her from the summit and I think she joined other tourists going down. These tramps are in with the railway attendants, and look on tourists as fair game. We encountered great opposition also from Cook & Sons' people, because we had come up with a haversack and sandwiches and would not lunch in the little café at the terminus. Arrived at the summit of the lip, you look down into a circular crater apparently a few hundred feet deep, barren like the crater at Aden, with little jets of smoke or steam rising quietly at a dozen places – we could easily have climbed down to them, but tourists are not encouraged to do this, no doubt there is risk, and no doubt there must be suffocating gases about. My father ascended Vesuvius about 1860 or thereabouts, or earlier, in the very earliest days of continental climbing, and complained of the sulphur fumes then coming out of the crater.

More interesting than Vesuvius was our expedition to Herculaneum and Pompeii. We had a very good guide, a handsome youth with a very Roman face, an excellent speaker, and there were about fifteen tourists, ladies and men – he stopped us at the different points of interest and gave us an open-air lecture at each.

Small narrow streets with single-storey houses – just the empty shells, unroofed but clean-flagged pavements everywhere and splendid pictures on the walls – chiefly figures – looking very eastern, draped with unsewn draperies like the winged Victory and painted or inlaid in the original colours, the dress of Roman days. Deep ruts from chariot-wheels on the paved ways were as fresh as when made; ruts worn by years of use. And workmen with pick and shovel were unearthing paintings and inlaid pictures before one's eyes, clearing off rubble and ashes from surfaces that had not seen the light for about two thousand years. They were mostly men and maidens dancing. On the way home we saw the lower edge of an old lava flow where it had engulfed a village. Back past walled gardens, orange and lemon groves and beautiful children turning somersaults and begging and offering fruit and flowers for sale round our carriages.

From Naples we took another ship and went on to Genoa about 5th March, and saw the sights of the place and chiefly a beautiful view of the town and harbour. And from Genoa, we went along the Riviera railway, through countless tunnels, and past the Italian frontier at Ventiniglia, to Nice, where we arrived on 7th March.

We had very cold and bad weather at Nice – we saw the return from a football match between our Navy and Royal Marines and a French regiment of the Chasseur Alpines. It was interesting to watch the smartness of the marines in their walking-out dress (the spectators) and to see the laughing Jack Tars climbing onto trams chock-full of French men, hanging on by the skins of their teeth, and all a good-humoured laughing crowd. We went to see the gambling tables at Monte Carlo; American poppas and thin girls brushing against awful-looking roués and sweet old white-haired ladies, constant habituées, sitting with piles of gold five Napoleon pieces in front of them, croupiers sending rainbows of gold over the people's heads as they tossed streams of gold pieces across the table to one another. The walls of the great halls were covered with great classical paintings of nymphs &c. It all seemed very orderly and well arranged.

From Nice we went on to Tarascon and St Remy de Provence. Gabriél and Dagmar[2] met us, I think, at Avignon, and drove us in their motor the 20 miles to St Remy. Afterwards they motored us to Nîmes, Arles, the cave town of Les Beaux, built by the Huguenots for defence in the mountains behind St Remy – they showed us the Roman triumphal arch behind St Remy. My mother was I think there at the time. We were at St Remy from 11th March and stayed with her and Gabriel, she sharing the house with them. All this Rhône country is the most exquisite country in the world – irrigation canals, cypress wind screens, great fields of vines and crops

2 Harald's sister, married to a Frenchman, Gabriél St. Reny Taillandier

let go to seed for the seed companies in England (like Suttons), and when these crops are in blossom it is a wonderful feast of different masses of colour. It reminds me of Kashmir in spring. There are ancient Roman aqueducts I think, and Druidical stones which Gabriel showed me. You can get lost in the hills behind St Remy, and there are wild boars. The Roman Arena at Arles is a Coliseum with all the seats, animal houses, ticket offices, all standing intact as they were built, all of lasting stone. We went on to Lyons, Basle and Lucerne and spent (17th March) a day in Lucerne but found the beautiful lake lifeless and cold so early as March.

We reached Aix-la-Chapelle (Aachen) on 19th March 1910 and stayed till 28th March – with Jack Harston and my sister Georgie. A queer old German town, and we saw a regiment of infantry recruits and some fat NCO's and bandsmen marching, and we saw a wonderful griffin or dragon fountain and splendid bathing houses. The forests round Aachen touched the frontiers of Germany, Belgium and Holland, and the French and Luxembourg borders were either there or very near. The forests here are an Alsatia in themselves, a resort of criminals from all the five frontiers and from the towns – a butcher had a few days before enticed a young girl into the forest and cut her up with a meat chopper! Mountain police were galloping up and down the endless rides or fire-lines, patrolling the forest as we took our walk.

That was a delightful time at Aachen – but I went to a German dentist who hurt me cruelly with boiling water and iced water alternately on an exposed nerve! Nephew Harald had a boy friend who was continually boasting how Germany was going to beat England (this was a few months before the Agadir incident in Morocco which nearly ended in being the beginning of Armageddon; to be stood off there, but to break out in earnest 3 years later in 1914). How little we knew when we were at Aachen, Kitty and I, that four years from the time of our visit Aachen would be the gate through which the German hosts would swarm into Belgium in their first rush, and would be a great German base throughout the 4 years' war. At that time the Germans, superficially, seemed to like us!

Waterloo (30th March 1910). We went to Brussels (29th March) and after a short time in the trains, we got out at a small railway station and climbed countless steps and high grassed pyramids surmounted by a lion in stone or bronze (I forget which) and a railroad observation post. I cannot remember the exact date of our visit, but it was a few days after leaving Aachen. This pyramid has been erected since the Battle on La Haye Sainte plateau, the headquarter position of Wellington. It is of this lion that Wellington said, on revisiting the field – 'They have changed my battlefield.'

From the top of the mound we were shown the whole battlefield by a British sergeant, who had also as an audience a party of young American college ladies. I soon made the acquaintance of this sergeant as an Anglo-Indian; for he said, pointing to Hougemont Farm: '. . . and then both sides took and retook it and finally it was cannonaded and all "went phutt".' (Hindustani for 'went to pieces!'.)

He showed us the wood through which Blucher's Germans dragged the guns at the critical moment of the battle, reinforcing Wellington's left. He showed us the monument over the Duke of Uxbridge's leg. The Duke, I believe, got home to England.

Then we went to Hougemont and visited the farm and enclosure full of bullet marks and holes from round shot. The old Farm is now inhabited.

We went back to a museum on high ground near the station and saw relics picked up from the field — among them a skull with a bullet sticking between the eyes! What a feast for a healthily constituted boy of 12!

To think that Wellington and Napoleon were only about 1,200 yards apart and could with Lee-Enfield rifles have shot each other today! The battlefield, which was one great shambles, was only about 1,500 yards across and about 1½ miles between the right and left flanks. Open, undulating ground now covered by peaceful crops beneath which the dead sleep sound!

In 1820 and the years before and after, crowds of visitors went touring to the battlefield and collecting trophies.

We saw churches at Antwerp (1st April), cathedrals and murillos, and were home (Harwich, 3rd April) for King Edward's funeral on 10th May 1910.

Chapter 33

India – Durbar Days

A T SECUNDERABAD in 1906 we had a visit from the Prince of Wales, now King George V, and all lined up on the railway station platform to meet him. There followed a big review, processions of State Coaches, and a big dinner. On this visit the Prince had great tiger-shoots in Hyderabad State. There was another big Durbar at Secunderabad when viceroy Curzon came and also did some tiger-shooting.

But the great Durbar was at the Coronation of King George in Delhi in the cold weather of 1911–12. I was serving at Lucknow as commanding Royal Engineer of the 8th (Lucknow) Division under Lt. General Mahon (now Sir Bryan Mahon), who was sent up to Delhi with troops of his division and his whole divisional Staff, as escort to the King. There were other troops there – in all 50,000 men on parade – but they were for the Delhi manoeuvres before the King. It was the 8th Division which was responsible for the safety of Delhi during the Coronation and later in Calcutta. The Divisional Staff had very little to do, so we had ample time in which to observe everything that was going on. The first question was expense. General Mahon had an official Divisional Staff Camp and as there were a great many guests the camp had to be kept suitable to a standing camp, with every civilized luxury. Some of us were given the choice of joining this camp, which was rather on the cavalry scale, or camping as private individuals; and as I had my little shooting tents, six small tents of the 'Kabul, double fly 80lb' variety, I elected to have my private camp. After a bit of bother, I was shown a plot of ground near the old Badli-Ki-Serai fort, a brick ruin, near the main Cavalry Division camp. This settled, I had with Kitty to settle what furniture, crockery etcetera we should take, cooking pots, servants, carpets etcetera. Eventually we had everything ready, and long before Christmas I was hiring a whole railway truck for carriage and tents and baggage, and a horse-box for the carriage-horse. All these preparations were ready by about 25 November 1911.

I hired the whole railway truck for the journey from Lucknow to Delhi, containing the phaeton (shafts removed and axles taken from under springs), tents, furniture and baggage. My horse went in a horsebox in the same coach with the GOC's horse. This rapid goods train took about a

The method of tiger shooting from a tree used during Durbar time. This photo shows Lord and Lady Curzon (in centre) and Miss Leiter. Taken near Secunderabad, S. India

week, and the horse had to have his syce[1] with him and food for the journey.

Kitty and I must have gone to Delhi on about 25 November 1911 by

1 Syce = Mounted attendant.

The author's 2nd wife Kitty

passenger staff train. We took seven servants in all, all men. Cheyt Singh Chuprassi 'did ayah' for Kitty. I had my old bearer. We took one cook and cook's boy (washer up), two khitmutgas (waiters) and one sweeper (sanitary man).

I was very glad to have chosen to put up a private camp, as our expenses were for the three weeks or so of the Coronation Camp only 5 R (7/-) a day each. Whereas the GOC's staff camp was to be £3 7s 0d a day per head all told – tents, furniture, messing etcetera – so for three weeks (the minimum period allowed) it would have cost Kitty and me £50 a week or £150 for the camp in all. With my little shooting camp it cost only £15. There was to be, however, it is only fair to say, a rebate of 10 R (14/-) owing to a Government grant to staff officers on duty at the camp. In the event, with our little shooting camp, Kitty and I were comfortable. There was to be a huge camp of 50,000 troops alone, for the march past, and no doubt about 50,000 visitors! But we weren't quite prepared for the immense canvas town, covering miles of ground, with great streets laid down with road metal and oiled daily. The organisation was superb. We had never been in anything quite like it before. Great water-supplies, electric light, power house, sanitation, all on the enormous scale of a large town.

Besides the other divisions employed on the Delhi manoeuvres, our 8th Lucknow Division, commanded by my own General, consisted of about 11,000 horse, foot and artillery; and additional troops for Calcutta numbered about 5,000. So my job was Commanding Engineer for 16,000 troops. But there was nothing to do, as our Division was at Delhi merely for garrison purposes, lining the streets, both in Delhi and Calcutta, etcetera, and some of the Staff had next to nothing to do, my own work (looking after all military works, water supplies, sanitation, housing of troops and camping) being all done by a special Camp Staff independent of the Division, with companies of Indian sappers and miners to help them.

Our 'shooting' camp was most comfortable. I put up four Kabul tents for No. (1) – which was practically our house. I pitched two tents (80lb. tents) in continuation of one another and two more parallel but a few yards away. Then I got the four outer flies on the inner side and joined them into one roof; the space underneath this canopy we turned into drawing room and dining room. Other Kabul tents were used for cook, kitchen, servants and a little tent d'abri three feet high for the sweeper, who was not allowed to live with the better caste servants. Our camping ground at Badli-Ki-Serai (the scene of an old battle) was very conveniently situated for the Review and the great Durbar or Coronation enclosure, i.e. Durbar amphitheatre.

The various ceremonies and visits were one continual excitement and delight. We had our phaeton, also I had a bicycle, so we could get about. The Camp roads were always crowded with bright colours – a most cosmopolitan crowd from all over the world. British, modern Americans, with representatives of every nation in Europe and our Colonies, Dependencies and Dominions; Bhutanis, Tibetans, Arabs, Chinese, Japanese etcetera. All in their very best clothes. We had a Military Tournament, sports of all kinds, visits to the great Durbar tents of Bhutan, Kashmir, Baroda, Hyderabad etcetera, visits to people we knew in the Lieutenant Governor's camps from Indian Provinces and regimental messes from all over India.

The first event was, of course, the entry of the King into Delhi on horseback with every kind of staff, also on horseback, through the narrow streets, crowded on every vantage point. And then the procession to the Ridge. We all, officers of the Civil Service, Army and visitors, assembled on the Ridge (the famous Ridge of Delhi, from which the Siege was carried on in the Mutiny). The Procession was chiefly motors and carriages, with some escorting troops.

An amusing incident, though annoying to more than one person, no doubt, occurred at this ceremony on the Ridge. About five minutes before the King was due to arrive, a trooper of the Viceroy's Escort cantered up to the Ridge to announce that the King was in sight, as a warning for the Salute and various formalities. Where the King's motor (a carriage) was to stop there was a red carpet similar to those put down in London at weddings. On either side of this carpet, standing stiffly at attention, were two splendid officers – of our Pathan or Afghan Levies I think, both most distinguished dark gentlemen, very fine and manly, covered with medals and orders, black whiskers brushed up etcetera. Well, the orderly trooper (an Indian) had only one idea in his head, and lance standing up from his right stirrup he cantered up to report to the Viceroy, I think. Anyway, he never noticed the two fine Indian officers, and promptly knocked over one just like a ninepin on to the red carpet, the horse leaving his hoof marks on the carpet. The officer picked himself up, purple with rage, and out trotted Lieutenant Governors of fifty to sixty million people, Commissioners and all the hierarchy of the Indian Civil Service, and began violently dusting the red carpet. They only had three minutes. It was beautifully done, and when His Majesty arrived a few minutes later he could little have guessed the scurry as he got calmly out and walked along the red carpet. But I often wonder what the Colonel of the Viceroy's bodyguard said to the trooper at Orderly Room next day!

There was a review and march and gallop past of 50,000 troops, some 8,000 cavalry, British and Indian, and British Horse Artillery galloping past, much of the cavalry being Imperial Service Native State Cavalry and Bikanir Camel Corps.

One small boy Raja, I fancy Bikanir, led his Camel Crops trotting by on a huge camel, and another boy rode on a charger and led his cavalry. There was a nasty spill in the gallop past of the cavalry in successive lines, and one unhorsed trooper was seen to run hard across the front of a charging line, hoping to get out by the flank, but they were coming on too fast, and when he had got about twelve horses' widths from the end of line, they were upon him. He faced them calmly at the last moment, stood to attention and saluted, and two files opened out at the gallop and just managed to avoid knocking him down. It was very coolly done on his part.

We had a great day when the King went to see the Polo Match. I forget what the match was; I fancy my General had brought a team, being one of ten leading Polo lights of India. My General was I believe, generally called 'The Mahout' in the Polo world and was a well-known character and a first-rate all-round sportsman.

At this Polo match we seemed to meet everybody we had ever known; and at the turnstile I met Ali, my Arab chuprassi (commissionaire) of Aden days – he was of the Subeihi tribe behind Aden, but had come in the retinue of the old Sultan of Lahej, who, had come to lay his sword before the King. I knew the old Sultan well, and went often to see him at the Lahej Palace, thirty miles inland from Aden, and in those days took photos of him. He

was killed accidentally by British troops in the Great War (about 1915 or
16?) where there was an invasion of Lahej by the Turkish troops operating
against Aden. He had gone on the roof of his palace to see the fighting and
being mistaken for a Turkish officer, he 'stopped one'. He was a dear old
man, most popular in our Aden community.

Another most interesting function was the inspection of old Indian Mutiny
and other veterans, European, Eurasian or Indian. Shaky old men with a
variety of medals. They came up to the King and Queen who sat in their
motors (at least Queen Mary did), and they said a few words to each. One
I noticed had Lord Napier's Abyssinian medal. I was told the King went
to the top of the ridge (really a very low rise in the ground and not a hill)
with old Ghurkha veterans who defended Delhi in the mutiny, and that
they described to the King on the actual ground how the mutineers came
up to the attack and were shot down before they could reach the guns of
the defenders, of whom the Ghurkhas were a part.

In Delhi Fort, after passing the celebrated Kashmir Gate where Hume and
Salkeld had defended themselves while they fired the powder (vide the picture by Mrs Butler), and then jumped down into the ditch, the King sat out
on the rampart, about fifty feet above the plain, while we had a great garden
tea-party inside for the King's guests – Europeans, Civil Service, Army and
visitors and distinguished natives. In front of the ramparts two million of
the natives were collected on the great plain and could all be seen at once,
occupying a space of about a square mile. This was called the Padshahi
Mela, or the King's Fair. Booths and dancing and singing. The King and
Queen sat up on the ramparts in Coronation robes enjoying the scene.

We were present at the function of the receiving of fealty from the great
chiefs. The King and Queen sat on a raised platform at the top of a long flight
of shallow steps and Gabriel of the District Colonial Service – who appeared
to be Master of the Ceremonies – conducted each chief in turn up the steps
and presented him. The Chiefs observed varied ceremonies. The Garkwar of
Baroda had his peculiar way of making his obeisance, just walking up in
white walking dress with a cane – the subject of much future official com-
ment. The Begum of Bhopal went up thickly veiled. The Indian Rajas laid
their swords before the King for him to touch. The Raja of Bhutan (half
Mongolian and nearly Tibetan) unrolled the folds of a white handkerchief
which appeared to be endless, and laid it fold after fold at the King's feet, the
'handkerchief of peace'. Tall Indian civil servants or venerable political officers, in frock coat, led up the most wonderful little ruling princes or cadets, in
turban, jewels and aigrette, to do obeisance to the King. Some little princes
led about by Commissioners were only about eight years old by the look of
them!

And then the Coronation in the Amphitheatre; that was the sight of

sights! We were all assembled in the great Amphitheatre or temporary grandstand in the shade of a Colosseum of immense size, each in our ticketed seats.
Thousands of school children dressed alike, like blue or mauve or green buds
of flowers, showed beautiful masses of colour. The King and Queen were
on a raised dais, with little princes in aigrettes and jewels and robes holding
up the royal trains. The King wore a heavy gold crown (the sun beating
hotly down on it), and now and then put up his hand to ease its weight.
It is said that when the King and Queen had left at the close of the ceremony
the crowd broke rank, rushed in and kissed the ground where they had
stood – for they believe in the Divine Right of Kings! A breathless moment
had been when the King made his own speech and suddenly announced
the transference of the Capital and Viceroy's winter seat from Calcutta to
Delhi. It had been quite unexpected, and the secret unusually well kept.

We had electric lighting all through this white city which was a huge
city of tents, and there were one or two terrible fires, terrible in their
suddenness! We were walking towards the camp of the Lieutenant Governor
of the Punjab when I suddenly saw a light at the top of the large tent –
and then a huge flame – the distance was only about 200 yards or so, but
Kitty and I ran to see what was up. By the time we got there, the tent
which had caught fire was a heap of black ashes flat on the ground mixed
with a mass of broken china in small pieces. A crowd was collecting, and
a camera operator putting up his instrument. It could not have taken two
minutes for us to reach the spot and I had seen the first glimmer in the
roof! All the other tents had instantly had their ropes cut and were round
the burnt annex, all lying prone. They said that a dinner table had been
laid with expensive service for a hundred or two hundred guests and it was
shortly before the evening dinner hour. Almost-priceless Persian carpets may
also have been burnt with the huge marquee.

But we had also a much more dangerous fire later on, and had it spread
to the King's reception tent, the tragedy would have been one only rivalling
the conflagration of the charity Bazaar in Paris!

The King's reception tent was very large and very beautiful – of what
material, I don't know. The finest! and it was huge, like a market roof –
upheld by long painted poles as pillars – vistas of these in every direction
– as large as twenty circus tents enclosed all round by walls or 'kanats.' It
would I should say, hold seated in the auditorium about two thousand
people. The stage part of it, more or less on the same level of the rest, was
the Court, and the King was conferring knighthoods on Indian civil servants
and others who had done good service to his Empire. There were hundreds
to receive honours. Then the audience! Every distinguished head of a
Department in the Civil and Military Services of the Indian Empire, and
no juniors. There was scarcely anyone under the rank of Colonel or

King George V and Queen Mary receiving fealty from the great chiefs of India

Lieutenant Colonel. If any Majors, they were ADC's or military secretaries or Indian Civil Service men of the rank of senior Deputy Commissioner or Collector working on some Lieut. Governors' Staff. All the Governors of Provinces, Lieutenant Governors of Provinces, Chief Commissioners of Provinces, Commanders in Chief, Army Commanders, Political Agents, Political Residents to chiefs and the greatest ruling Chiefs – all were there and composed the Auditorium. I was almost the junior, and only there because I was on the Departmental Staff of the GOC 8th Division, as head of the Royal Engineer Services of the Division. All were heads of some Department. I'm only showing the dislocation that would have been caused had there been a catastrophe and the *promotion* the Juniors would have got all over the Indian Empire had there been a catastrophe.

Then suddenly, a bolt from the blue, the excitement happened! The King was knighting man after man with a sword laid on his shoulder, each greyhead knelt down in front of the King and got up and passed on, backing away from the 'Presence'. Then was a quick bugle fire-call thirty yards away outside. We all jumped up in our seats and stood listening. Something exciting, and running about outside. Remember, we knew how these tents practically *explode*. They are so dry and inflammable. They go off like petrol, we had seen the Punjab Lieutenant Governor's tent go up! Well, a few ADC's, cool as cucumber, walked up and down the aisles, saying 'Keep your seats!' 'Sit down,' and we all sat down – not a stir. The King went on knighting the kneeling Commissioners and passing them on. He did it neatly, the only thing one noticed was that it all went still like clockwork but quicker. We didn't know that the Ghurkha Guard were busy with knives cutting the kanats (tent walls) away behind the King and in other parts around the tent. The performance went on. Later, say half an hour later, a lady three seats from me slipped off her chair; they were small chairs and we were very crowded. A dozen people sprang up at this. An ADC said quietly 'Sit down' and they sat down again!

When we all broke up at the end of all ceremonies, we discovered what had happened. Lord Crewe's camp was next to the King's apparently, and beyond Lord Crewe's tent, which was the only tent between the tent which caught fire and the great tent in which the King was knighting people, a man had left a bicycle (it was about 8 p.m.) with a lamp lit leaning against this second tent; that tent had gone up in flames! It was a pretty near shave and if our huge reception tent had caught fire the whole audience of about two thousand people including ladies in the Auditorium would have been stifled under a heavy burning canvas roof. There would not have been twenty seconds to get out; it wasn't a case of exits – only those near the tent walls, with knives in their hands at the moment, would have got out. Where His Majesty was working, there were few people and a smart Gurkha Guard, and it is possible the people there could have been got out, but not certain. Had there been a catastrophe every junior official in our Indian Empire, and many all over the world, would have got sudden and rapid promotion! So much for an incident which ended well and is an example of coolness in the average British official and educated British audience, for there were present all the elements of a trampling panic, had people not kept their heads! Nothing appeared in the Press at the time and those present were careful to say very little about it; it would have been a 'scoop' for some paper!

The conditions of our little camp at Badli-Ki-Serai were often amusing. On the canvas roof of my No. 1 tent, when it sagged after rain, little pools collected in the four centres between supports, and the sparrows used to bathe there and shake out their little wings amid delightful chirpings above our drawing-room!

On another occasion, at 1 a.m., an English cavalry trooper, dead tired and looking for the cavalry camp and perhaps a little drunk, stumbled into the drawing room and tried to walk through the canvas wall of the sleeping tent onto Kitty's bed! I went out and discovered him in the drawing room, searched his pockets and found he was not a burglar, and escorted him across the railway line to his camp. I never heard how he got on. He had been from 5 a.m. the morning before to 1 a.m. on this night on his feet or in the saddle drilling and manoevering, and was dead beat and very stupid.

The rush and scurry of the return to Lucknow from Delhi on 16th December, 1911, was an adventure. The trains were overcrowded with officials returning. We stormed the refreshment rooms and penetrated into the kitchens where I found twenty-five men waiting to get eggs for their wives, early breakfasts, and only fifteen eggs poaching in a saucepan! Captain Gardiner, an official of the Railways, trying to defend the Refreshment Room door and restore order, was nearly powerless! In the train we got our Durbar Medals handed round to us by the senior Colonel of the Division's Staff, and later we were very pleased to hear that our Divisional General was to have a 'K'. The whole of the 8th Division and additional Divisional troops were to be reassembled in Calcutta in about a fortnight's time to look after the King's welfare and safety during the ceremonies and levées at Calcutta.

Our General, Sir Brian Mahon, was to form a Divisional Staff Camp to which visitors from England would be invited as his guests, on the 'Maidan' or Hyde Park of Calcutta, which is a magnificent piece of open ground graced with many equestrian statues and monuments, and the terrible Ochterlony Column to General Ochterlony – a straight high column, like the Nelson Column in Trafalgar Square or the Claude Martin Column in front of the Martinière College at Lucknow.

Chapter 34

Calcutta ceremonies
25 December, 1911 to 8 January, 1912

THESE BEGAN with a great entry into Calcutta, the King and Staff riding with cavalry escorts through the Maidan to Government House to stay with the Viceroy (Lord Hardinge). Grandstands and booths were put up all along the route. The Maidan was well policed but the King often took private rides in the morning very slightly attended. He often passed through our General's camp. One day I was standing in front of our Divisional Office with two other senior officers when four men rode towards us in plain clothes. We said, 'Hello, I wonder who these people are,' but when they came nearer I recognised them and said just in time, 'I say, it's the King!' So we stood and saluted and he passed on and got through the grandstand booths. He was apparently arguing or discussing with one of the officers in attendance as to which would be the shortest way through the grandstand and various timber obstructions. On another occasion, he passed a yard from my tent as I was shaving in the morning – going through the same gap. There is no doubt the King was immensely popular in India, curiously enough, because of his simple ways and the confidence he showed in the Indian people's loyalty, let alone his great pluck and coolness on every occasion. His Staff who went tiger-shooting with him could not say too much of his real sportsmanship and coolness.

At Delhi, I had a story that a motor accompanying the King's motor knocked over an Indian policeman accidentally and that the King got out of his car, had the man sent to hospital (and insisted on a daily bulletin of how he was getting on). It is these little stories which attract the Indian people – they like in a ruler greatness, power – but above all consideration for others and benevolence – above all benevolence and mercy – for in an autocratic country they would suffer so much under a ruler not benevolent!

My own opinion is that King George in 1911–12 did for India what King Edward VII did for France – I have never seen the Calcutta (Bengali) population so polite to Europeans as when the King was down there. There was a great crush at the fireworks on the Maidan, so great a crush that the limb of a tree near us was broken by the weight of the people sitting on it to get a better view. But even though it was nearly dark, the only light being the glare of the fireworks, the crowd always stepped politely aside to let an officer pass. At ordinary times the Calcutta crowd is careless and sometimes intentionally rude to Europeans. We had a mysterious death at our Calcutta camp during the dinner hour. One of the servants who had been waiting at a table was found stood up against the outside of the tent – dead – but I never heard the end of the story.

There was a great levée where we officials and our wives were all presented to the King – at Government House, Calcutta; and a pageant on the Maidan of all the States in India and historical periods, when real medieval chain mail could be seen, mail often used in former Indian battles. Asia was civilized and wore chain mail and chain shirt, I believe, when all Europe was without it, in fact it probably came from Asia originally.

And so ended the Coronation Durbar, a great event in the history of India. It has been represented on the cinemas since, in colour, but it does not give one the hot feel of the sun on one's face, the smell of the dust or the smells of the bazaar, and all the thousand influences which go to make up the memories of India for those who have been there!

Chapter 35

Rangoon in 1912

THIS WAS merely an inspection journey when I went as CRE 8th Lucknow Division to inspect the Military Works Forts at Rangoon, down the River Irrawaddy (Rangoon River), and also to inspect the Rangoon Port Defence Volunteers. I left Calcutta soon after General Mahon's Calcutta Camp broke up after the Coronation – 8 January 1912. I must have left Calcutta on about 17th April 1912 and arrived at Rangoon on 20th April. Inspected the Military Works. Breakfasted with friends at Rangoon on 21st who told me all about the ruby mines. I stopped at the Pegu Club, and must have left Rangoon about 24th April for Calcutta and got back there 27th April 1912.

It was just before leaving Rangoon about 11 a.m., 24th April (my boat left at noon same day) that I had a very curious adventure which would have done for the *Wide World Magazine* and was very like the usual yarn one sees in that periodical. I had an hour or so to wait before my steamer was to leave for Calcutta, and it occurred to me that it might be interesting to pay another visit to the great Golden Shaway-Dagon Pagoda, which I had seen before in 1890 when campaigning in Burma. No sooner said than done, and at the Pegu Club I hired a 'tikka gharry' or closed four-wheeler, and drove out to the Shaway-Dagon. In old days, I had been there in festival time by day and night and the beautiful silks worn by the Burmese on these occasions will always live in my memory. The Burmese are so gay after the rather melancholy Indians! The Pagoda has a magnificent cupola covered periodically with new gold leaf. Leading up to the plinth is a gallery about 150 yards long – rising to the Pagoda by successive flights of steps. The gallery is arcaded over with a roof, and stalls for small curio shops, and booths fill the sides for the whole distance. The plinth is very large – flagged and all round it are other temples. There is a splendid view. All round are green mango trees and palms, a sea of green. On the plinth a generally vivid life is continually going on, people coming and going, families from the country, old people, pretty girls and children come to see the sights of these pagodas, just as families in India come to their festivals on pilgrimages, or we in England take our families to the seaside.

Being for the moment, or for the hour, a regular tourist, I bought a few curios in the arcade, leaving my cabby or 'ghari-wallah' sitting in his cab waiting for my return.

When I got up onto the plinth I saw a rush of people, and three policemen leading off a man who was spotted all over his white clothes with blood, fresh blood, and while two policemen led him in handcuffs, the third carried a sword or 'dak' red with blood.

I walked on to a crowd standing gravely regarding something on the flags of the plinth, and this was the body of a woman apparently very dark (not a good-caste Burmese but more like the people of the small hill tribes of India, or perhaps half Gond, half Burmese). She lay unconscious and apparently dead, in a great pool of blood, with half a dozen sword-cuts bitten into her skull and her left ear hanging down on her neck by a piece of skin. She was soaked in blood from head to foot. The crowd of Burmese were standing motionless watching her bleeding to death. I left the crowd, which evidently meant not to lift a finger, for I think orientals consider it unlucky to touch a corpse or badly wounded person. I was the only European present. So I walked over to a stall and, speaking Hindustani, proceeded to borrow a couple of grass mats. Then I saw another European coming up the steps, a sight-seer like myself, and spoke to him, then I saw an Indian who looked like a Sikh soldier and we took the mat over, lifted the body on it, and we then carried her down the 150 yards of steps to where my cab was waiting. She seemed to be still breathing. It appeared from what I could gather that the man who had attacked her was her Burmese man or husband, in a fit of jealousy. We bundled the body into my cab and I sat down with her head on my knee, saturating my trousers with blood. I had to use both arms to prop her up in this position. The Frenchman went about his business and just then a police NCO, a European, turned up in a hurry, furiously angry that I had interfered and destroyed some of the evidence he would have collected, by moving the body! He went up to the Pagoda to investigate. I told the cabby to drive on. The fastenings were defective and the doors flew open. I had no third hand to keep them closed – so office clerks returning to lunch were interested to see a European in a cab, an apparent murderer, propping up a body of a native girl in a closed cab, the doors of which were wide open.

Well, to make a long story short, near the hospital I met an orderly with a litter and four carriers strolling off along the road to the Pagoda, evidently answering a call, and I felt pleased that I had saved twenty minutes or so in getting her promptly into hospital.

A month afterwards, when back in Calcutta, I got a note from the matron to say the woman had a fractured skull in addition to the sword-cut, but that she was progressing favourably.

I got back to Calcutta in due course, travelling on the steamer with a touring theatrical company, and was soon back in Darjeeling, making preparation for a great project, a long trip to Ladak, the western threshold of Tibet, for the summer. I was anxious to get some of the Himalayan game I had not yet met, notably the aorial (a near relation of the Barbary wild sheep) and the bushel or blue wild ram of the higher Himalayas, found at from 10,000 to 18,000 feet elevation. That trip was to take me up in the mountains to a height of 20,000 feet and over a great many high passes. Meanwhile I was to make preparations for another trip to Burma – after the 'thamin' or Burmese swamp deer called the brown-antlered stag, which trip I carried out the next year.

Chapter 36

To the Taj, Agra
and Fatehpur Sikri in 1912

THIS WAS a beautiful little Christmas trip undertaken by Kitty, Helen[1] and myself at Christmas of 1912, soon after their arrival in India.

We stayed at a hotel in Agra – Lowries I think – and visited Fatehpur Sikri by motor on 26 December, 1912. Of course, I had visited the Taj often before. Its influence is irresistible – it is pure sentiment, just something spiritual, impalpable.

The Taj is built on a high square marble plinth in a great Italian-designed garden of formal and beautiful Cypress trees. It is a square block of white marble with a large central bubble, cupolas, and deeply shadowed great arched recesses. It has four minarets – lighthouse-like – at the four corners of the plinth.

It was built by the Emperor Shah Jahan as the tomb of the wife of his youth, Arjuman Bannu (Muntaz-Mahal) who died in 1629, soon after he came to the throne. The Emperor Shah Jahan was buried at last next to her in this tomb thirty-seven years later. The portrait of Shah Jahan and Arjuman Bannu can be bought, painted on ivory, at Lauries Curio-Shop. They were both very handsome people and one is not surprised that romance clings to this couple. The height of the building from the garden walks to the summit of the dome is 240 feet. The whole building is covered with beautiful coloured stone designs of flowers and inlaid verses of the Koran.

Sir Frederick Heres, in his *The Other Side of the Lantern*, writes as follows about the Taj:

Within the mausoleum itself a high screen of marble trellis-work encloses the monumental cenotaphs of Arjuman Bannu and her King. The lady's tomb is very small, and it lies under the very centre of the Dome. It is so little that it is almost lost beneath the colossal vault; on her right side her husband lies, and his tomb is as great as hers is small. Everywhere on the screen, on the walls, on the cenotaphs, there is exquisite carvings, together with fantastic

---

1 Harald's daughter by his first marriage, his only child, born on 23rd April 1895, was aged 17 at the time of this trip.

work in inlaid stone of many colours. Both the carvings and the tinted designs show flowers and flowers only.

A cream-coloured light steals through the windows, while through the open door can be seen palms waving in the sun. The actual bodies of the dead lie in a low vault in the foundations of the building. The chamber is of white marble, its walls are absolutely plain, and it is approached by a long, narrow staircase. The tombs themselves, which stand within this humble vault, are of the utmost simplicity.

As is the custom with Mahommedan graves, there is carved upon the man's tomb a pen box, and upon the woman's a slate. The pen is active; the slate is passive. It is the pen that fashions the writing; it is the slate that bares its surface to be written on. A ray of light comes down the narrow stone way, but it falls only upon the small marble slab beneath which sleeps the lady of the 'Taj'.

I have often seen the Taj by moonlight – dim, mysterious and cold – against the white marble work of the dome and cupolas the night sky looks very blue! There is something very unsubstantial and ethereal in the Taj as seen by moonlight – something sweetly sad, and one should not miss seeing it then as well as in the daytime.

At the curio shops in Agra you will get coloured stone work, portraits of Shah Jahan and Arjuman Bannu on ivory and all kinds of Indian art. Don't get soapstone models of the Taj as they soon break.

In the Jumna behind the Taj you see river turtles swimming about. We drove on to the Secundra Tomb from Agra, the tomb of the Emperor Akbar, grandson of Barbar the Lion and direct descendant of Tamerlane. From the top of this tomb one sees the Taj Mahal, also Agra Fort, the River Jumna and the Great Gate of Victory at Fatehpur Sikri.

The town of Fatehpur Sikri was built of red stone by Akbar in 1570 for his two sons, but it was never occupied by them, and to this day it stands as fresh as when it was built, the only monument of the kind, I believe, in the world, of a town built but never used. There are great deep eaves making the architecture singularly lovely. The eaves of the great houses and offices are properly decorated. There are inscriptions quoting the word of Huzrut Isa (Jesus Christ of the Mohammedans). We saw the council chamber, the baths for goldfish, the great Tower of Victory with its numerous red cupolas and we saw the place where there were held the combats of wild animals, tiger fights, and elephant fights. We also were shown the great place of public trials and the rings where the execution elephants were tethered ready to trample condemned criminals to death before the vast multitude assembled in this great rectangular Colosseum.

There is a great stone dais, with steps for the Emperor and court.

This wonderful abandoned town stands among jungle and squalid Indian

The Taj from the River Agra

villages of today, and it is interesting to motor out to it (about twenty-two miles) from Agra through the cotton fields along a high road well shadowed with an avenue of trees. The town of Fatehpur Sikri is as empty as when it was built over three hundred and fifty years ago. It was built in 1570 and only occupied a few years. It stands deserted save by the 'jackal and the leopard.'

In the town of Agra we saw people dyeing a large number of saris and other cloths and drying them in the sun.

This visit to Agra and its neighbourhood was one of the most memorable that I made in India. It ranks with the view of Kinchinjunga from Darjeeling, and my trip into Kashmir. It included one of the greatest sights of the Indian Empire. Perhaps among them one should include the Golden (Shway Dagon) Pagoda at Rangoon, the Palace Moat at Mandalay, the Lake Palaces of Udaipur and the Dilwara Temple of Mout Abu; the walk across the Howrah bridge at Calcutta when the city is going home to its food, the Caves of Elephants and the Calcutta Race Course on a big day.

Appendices

(The Route Plans have been derived from parts of Map No.3, Northern Somaliland, shown as the end-papers of the book).

Appendix I – Route Plan No. 1

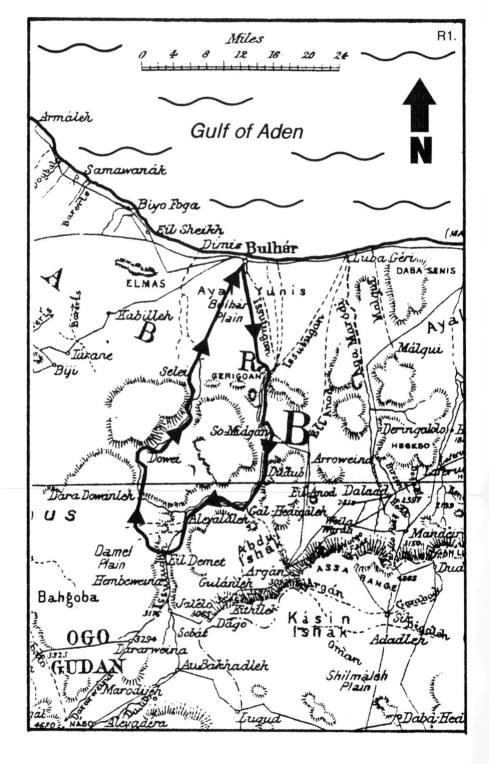

Appendix 2 – Route Plan No.2

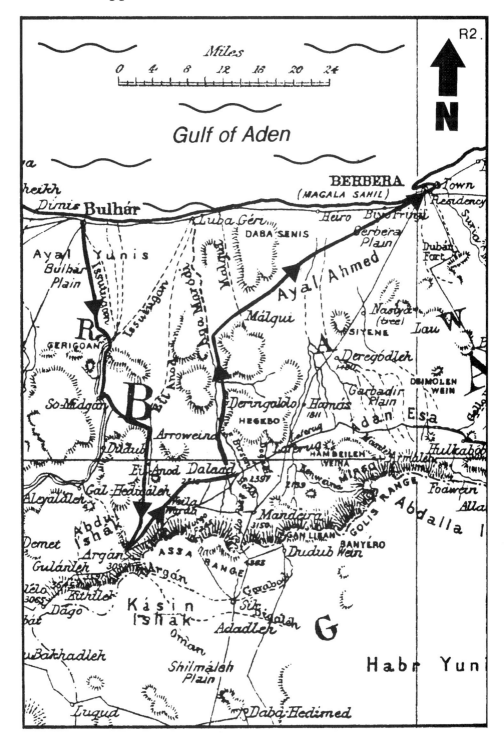

Appendix 3 – Route Plan No.3

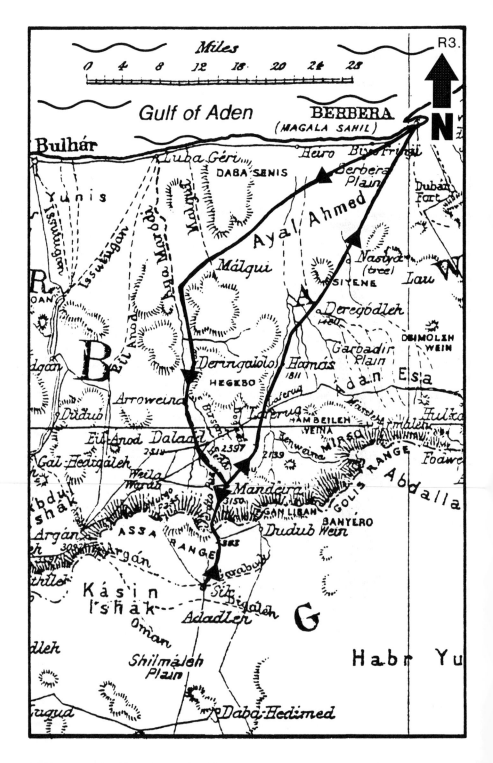

Appendix 4 – Route Plan No.4

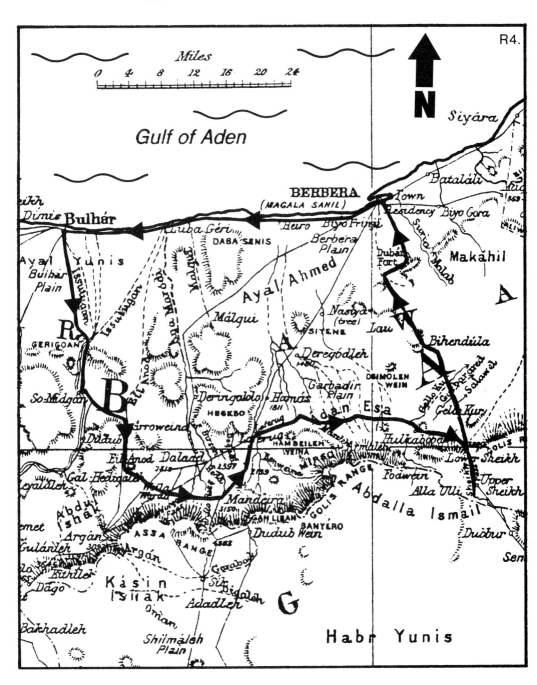

Appendix 5 – Route Plan No.5

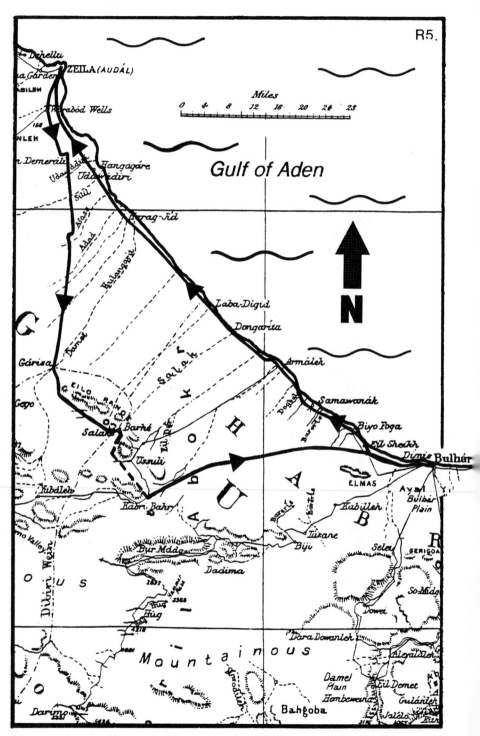

Appendix 6 – Route Plan No.6

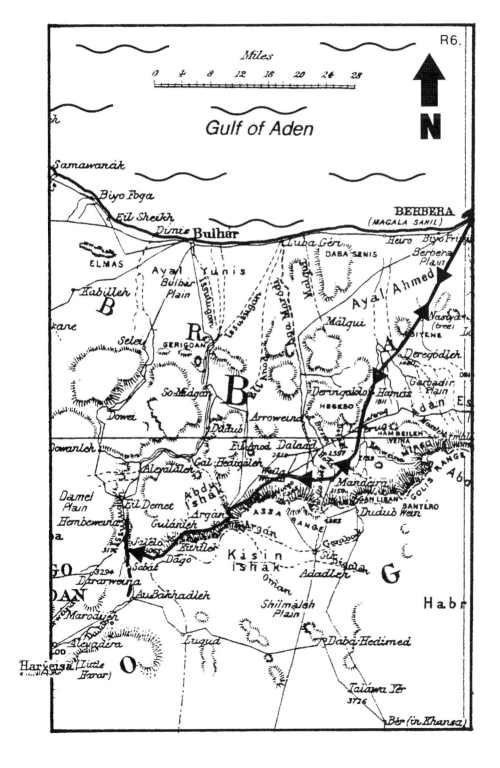

Appendix 7 – Route Plan No.7

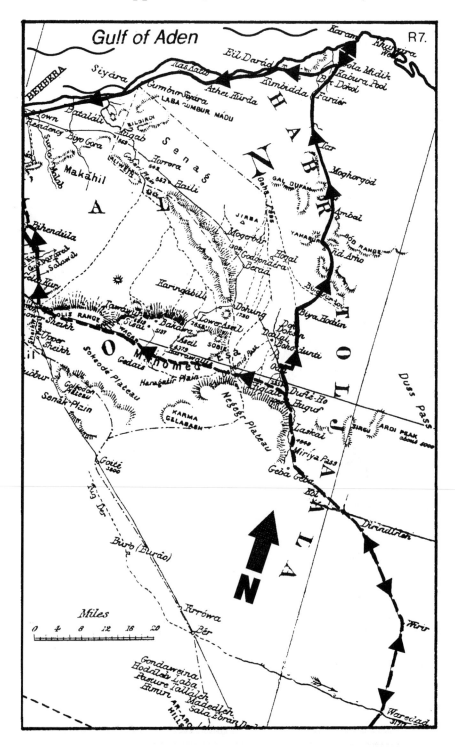

Appendix 8 – Map 2, India, Ceylon & Burma

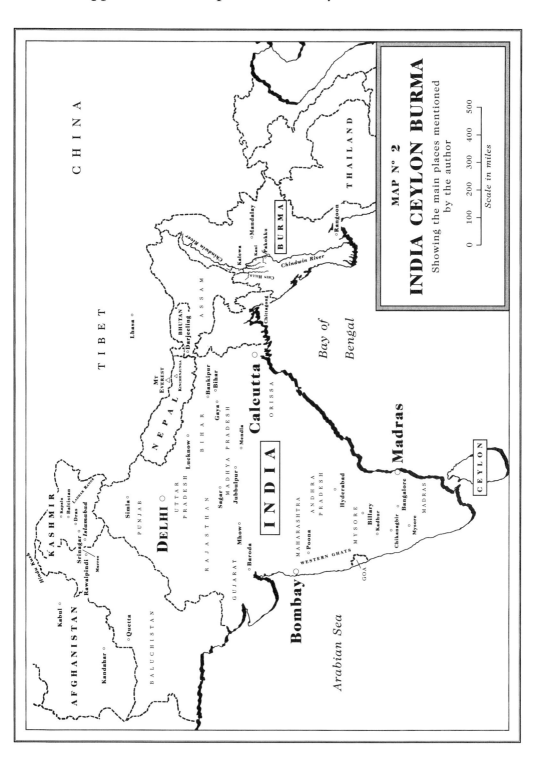

Appendix 9 – An Extract from

The Royal Engineers Journal 1940

The following memoir has been reprinted from 'The Royal Engineers Journal' and provides a valuable insight into the author's life. It was written after Harald Swayne's death by an old comrade and friend and gives a very good summary of the life of one of the remarkable men who helped to make parts of Africa and its wild life known to the modern world.

Colonel Harald George Carlos Swayne, C.M.G.

The name of the subject of this memoir is probably almost unknown to the present generation of Royal Engineer officers, but two generations ago he obtained a well-earned recognition, not only as a sportsman and shooter of big game but as an intrepid and painstaking explorer of the north-east corner of Africa, now known as Somaliland.

Swayne liked to be referred to as the last of the early explorers, in succession to such great names as Burton, Livingstone or Stanley. When he went to the Somali coast in 1884 the hinterland was unknown to Europeans; when he left it for the last time in 1897 the country had been reconnoitred, boundaries fixed and contact established with Abyssinia and with the French and Italian settlements. Further, in the course of journeys covering many thousands of miles of route, he had obtained a personal knowledge of the people occupying the country, and of the physical geography and the fauna and flora, much of which was new to science. He became in time a life Fellow of the Royal Geographical Society and was also a Fellow of the Royal Zoological Society. In 1894 he published a book of his experience under the title of *Seventeen Trips Through Somaliland*, written mainly from the point of view of sport, but containing much detail of the people and the country. When Somaliland came into the limelight by the operations against the Mad Mullah in 1900 to 1903, this book became a standard work of reference and new editions were called for in 1898 and 1903.

In all his trips into the interior, whether official or private, Swayne made a reconnaissance of his route and notes on the people and places, and on his return made reports through the Indian Government to the Indian and Foreign Offices. During all the discussions on Somaliland he was consulted by these Offices and in 1903 Lord Curzon stated in the House of Lords that Major H. Swayne was the leading authority on Somaliland.

Harald George Carlos Swayne was born in 1860, he was the eldest son of the Reverend G. C. Swayne, a Fellow of Corpus Christi, Oxford, who was for many years an Anglican Chaplain in France, Italy, Germany and Switzerland. Swayne was educated at Manilla Hall, Clifton, and in 1878 joined the Royal Military Academy, passing out as Lieutenant, R.E., in February, 1880. Electing for service in India, he joined the Bombay Sappers and Miners and in 1884 was ordered to Aden with a company of that Corps. Up to 1884, the coast of Somaliland on the south side of the Gulf of Aden had been controlled by Egypt, who had also a garrison at Harar, but in 1884 all Egyptian garrisons were withdrawn, and an Arab Emir took control at Harar. Aden was interested, as about half the native inhabitants of this town are Somalis and many supplies for the town are drawn from Somaliland, including about 60,000 sheep each year. The Indian Government therefore appointed Residents in Somaliland and sent small detachments of troops and police to occupy the coast ports of Berbera, Bulhar and Zeyla. In 1885, Swayne with a detachment of Indian Sappers was sent to Bulhar to build police barracks and defences against attacks by the local tribes. These latter were often raiding one another, and although they had no special enmity against the British and indeed looked to us for protection, they resented the attempts of the Residents to stop the inter-tribal warfare. On one occasion Swayne, as the senior military officer, had to lead a charge at the head of twenty-five mounted men of the Aden troop and some police, but these local troubles did not become serious. The country abounded in game of all sorts, while big game, including elephants, lions, rhinoceros and hippo-potamus, could be found in many localities. Officers from Aden began to come over on shooting trips and an article by Swayne published in The Field attracted the attention of sportsmen of all nations. In August, 1885, Swayne, who had been spending his leisure in making reconnaissance sketches of the country round Bulhar, was instructed by the Indian Government to make a reconnaissance of the coast and hinterland. Between this date and February, 1887, he was employed on this duty. At first he had an escort of Indian cavalry, but finding this caused local unrest, he replaced them by an escort of Somalis about thirty in number, whom he armed and trained not only for protection but to assist in the survey work. In this, his first survey, he covered 2,000 miles of route and made many expeditions into the interior, getting in touch with the tribes with whom he soon established friendly relations. In nearly every case he was the first European who had been seen by the inhabitants. He learnt to speak Somali and used it as easily as he spoke English, and developed a great friendship with many of his followers which they reciprocated. In 1887 he returned to India, where his routes, which had been checked by many observations for latitude and longitude, were compiled under his supervision as D.A.Q.M.G. in the Intelligence Office at Simla and the resulting map was printed at the Bombay office of the Indian Survey. Full reports were also sent to England and in these

Swayne is credited with having introduced the term 'sphere of influence' to cover our interests in Somaliland, a term which has since taken a definite place in our Colonial history.

In 1888, Swayne, whose reputation had by this time reached England, was engaged by the Imperial British East Africa Company to lead an expedition to Mombasa to develop that port and to organize an expedition to the Albert Nyanza to look for Stanley, who had disappeared into the interior of the Congo region in an attempt to relieve Emin Pasha. The expedition was to endeavour to drive cattle with them into the interior and for this purpose Swayne secured the services of some of his Somali subordinates. Swayne was given the acting rank of Captain and had a substantial party under his command, which was to include twelve Europeans with 900 armed Swahili porters and two Maxim guns. His second-in-command was Mr. Jackson, well known later for his work in Uganda. Just as the party was leaving London, news was received via the West Coast of the death of Major Bartellot with Stanley's rearguard, and when the party arrived at Mombasa it received the news that Stanley and Emin with a large party had arrived at a port in German East Africa. Swayne's expedition was thus cancelled but he was under engagement for six months with the British company and was employed in carrying out exploration and survey work on the River Tana. This ended in rather a spectacular manner, when Swayne, alone at midnight in a dugout canoe, and pursued by an irate hippopotamus, was rescued just in time by the presence at a bend of the river of H.M. survey vessel Stork, commanded by Captain Pullen, R.N.

At the end of his six months' engagement Swayne, who had contracted fever, did not renew his engagement but returned to India. Promoted Captain in July, 1889, he took part in the Chin-Lushai campaign in Burma, being employed on roadmaking in a hostile country with Indian Sappers. For this he received the medal and clasp. On returning to India the Indian Government asked him to undertake a survey of the whole of Somaliland on the same lines as his previous reports, and offered him the services of an officer of the Indian Marine to assist in the technical work. Swayne was confident of his ability to carry out the survey hinmelf, he had been through a very full survey course at the S.M.E., Chatham, under Major Sir Charles Warren, and Captain W. G. Morris, R.E., and had also, on the introduction of the Royal Geographical Society, taken a series of lessons on navigation from a retired Naval officer, Captain Coles, R.N. He therefore asked that instead of the officer suggested by the Government he should have the assistance of his own brother, Lieut. Eric J. F. Swayne, of the 16th Bengal Infantry. This was approved and during 1891 and 1892 the two brothers carried out a series of route marches at slow camel pace, which covered over 7,000 miles. The methods previously adopted by Swayne were continued and developed, a route by prismatic compass on a stand was recorded each day and this was checked by many thousand cross-bearings, using a large 8-in. transit theodolite, and by observations of the stars by a large telescope, which fixed the latitude and longitude with a considerable degree of accuracy.

In the course of their wanderings, the brothers, while not delaying the survey work, took every opportunity of sport. The country was then infested by lions, and on one occasion Harald Swayne was attacked by a lioness which seized and mauled his right shoulder. His life was saved by his brother Eric, who running in to close quarters shot the enraged animal. Swayne was severely injured but carried on the survey until he had to go down to the coast to have his arm dressed by a native hospital attendant.

The last expedition carried out by the brothers was into the highlands surrounding Harar on the border of Abyssinia. This town, which is the centre of a flourishing area, had been left in charge of a local Emir when the Egyptian garrison was withdrawn in 1884, but in 1887 the Abyssinians under Ras Mackunan, a son of King Menelik, occupied Harar, and started marauding expeditions against the neighbouring Somali tribes. These latter appealed to the British Government, whom they had come to regard as their Suzerain and Protector, so Swayne was asked while carrying out the survey to report on the general situation. His route took him to Gildessa, a small town in Abyssinian occupation, about 20 miles north of Harar, where he and his brother entered the town with some attendants and were soon in conversation with some of the mixed crowd in the market, which included Arabs, Gallas and Somalis. Meanwhile the Abyssinian officer in command of the town stopped Swayne's caravan and diverted it into a central enclosure used as a barrack by the small garrison. As Swayne wrote in his book, it would never do to admit that an English party could be dictated to by any local official whether Somali or Abyssinian, so Swayne at once demanded an interview with the officer in command, while his brother took charge of the convoy, formed it in column of route and detailed advance and rear guards. The local garrison of about equal strength turned out under arms and for a short time an affray seemed imminent, but the firmness and tact shown by Swayne prevailed, and he was allowed to march out to a camp outside the town, where he agreed to wait for 48 hours while a report was sent to the Abyssinian headquarters at Harar and instructions were received from Ras Mackunan. At the end of 48 hours no reply had been received so Swayne, in spite of protests, started on his march to the coast at Zeyla. He was followed by a messenger from the Ras with a cordial invitation that Swayne, as the first Englishman who had visited the area, should come to Harar. This Swayne was unable to do, but he sent a polite reply promising to make a visit at a later date. This expedition, which included a survey of the proposed boundary between British and French Somaliland and Abyssinia, was the last trip made by the brothers and on the receipt of their reports in India they received letters of thanks from the Commander-in-Chief in India and from the Government of Bombay, with a personal note from the Governor, Lord Harris, to Harald Swayne, congratulating him on continuing at work after being attacked and mauled by a lion.

The survey carried out by the brothers was completed on the return of Swayne to India, a skeleton of the points fixed by astronomical observations being prepared and the detailed routes being fitted to this skeleton. The final maps were photozincographed at Calcutta at the headquarters of the Survey of India, then under Sir Thomas Holdich. Although not based on a rigorous triangulation, Swayne's survey was sufficiently accurate for all practical purposes. His maps were at first marked confidential, but when the official ban was removed they became the basis of all maps of the region both at home and on the continent. The total area covered was about equal in area to the whole of England and Wales. Swayne's reports of his various reconnaissances were published by the Government of India in two blue books; these included not only a detail of the work done but an historical summary of the growth of Somaliland from the earliest times, a detail of the many different tribes, each tracing descent from an Arab sheik, and valuable notes of a political nature on the fighting qualities of the tribes and their relations with their French, Italian and Abyssinian neighbours.

In 1893 Swayne became due for long leave out of India and spent this on a project which he had had under consideration for some time, to lead an expedition for exploration and sport from Berbera across Somaliland to the head waters of the River Shebeyli and to attempt to reach Lake Rudolph, which had recently been discovered by an Austrian expedition. He obtained leave for this, though the political department was unable to make the trip official or to give him any direct assistance, but Swayne had just received a legacy of £600 which he spent on the expedition in the purchase of stores, arms and camels. He organized with this what he described as the best-equipped party he had had under him. It comprised 24 men picked from 200 applicants and these he armed with Snider carbines, for which he took 150 rounds apiece. He used 50 of these for preliminary training and taught his little force a simple form of drill and tactics, adapted to the conditions he had to meet. It may be noted here that Swayne never used his little army to force his way into any area against the wish of the inhabitants. His armed escort was necessary to prevent attacks by marauders and on two occasions when he was approaching Harar he had to make a display of force to resist a threat by the Abyssinian armies. But his combination of firmness and tact always enabled him to carry out his plans without fighting and in his case it may be truly said that Preparing was Preventing.

He was the only European with the party on this trip, but his head man and his two hunters were trusted friends on whose loyalty he could rely. In selecting the route he decided to commence by visiting Harar in reply to the invitation of the Ras. Space does not admit of much detail of his experiences on this trip, in the course of which he reached the Webbe Shebeyli or Leopard River, at a distance of 400 miles from Berbera and about the same distance from the east coast of Africa. At Harar he was greeted most cordially by Ras Mackunan and on leaving received from him a gift of a grey riding mule with embroidered equipment, a buffalo hide officer's shield, two spears and other presents. This gift caused great interest at the various places he reached on his march. Time did not admit of Swayne reaching Lake Rudolph but he reached his main objective, the Webbe Shebeyli, at a place called Imé and followed the river eastward for about 70 miles, when he turned north again by a route which took him across a waterless tract of the Haud, the high inland plateau 4,000 to 6,000 feet above the sea, which extends along the south of Somaliland proper. In the four and a half months he took over his trip, he had covered one thousand two hundred miles of route. At many points on the route he was the first European who had been seen by the natives, and when he told them he was English, he heard many complaints of raiding by the Abyssinians and also collected much information of a political nature. At Imé, where he was treated as the guest of honour, the population thronged round him on his departure, beseeching him to ask the Great Queen to arm their country and stop the Abyssinian raids! This was duly reported to the British Foreign Office together with much other political detail and Swayne received a letter of thanks for the report.

On the completion of his four and a half months of exploration he returned to Aden, only to find that an extension of leave he had applied for had been granted, so he at once returned to Berbera and organized a second party of 34 men. With these he again crossed the Hand to the Webbe Shebeyli, with the intention of crossing that river and exploring Gallaland down to the River Juba. With the help of a flying raft he got his whole party safely across the river, but found that the tribes in Gallaland had been much upset by an exploring party from the East Coast of Africa under a foreign explorer, who had forced their way through the tribes. Swayne managed after some delay to make friends with the tribes bordering the river, but the approach of the wet season compelled him to cross to the north bank and he returned to Berbera by another route across Somaliland. In both these expeditions Swayne kept a record of direction and distances, but made no astronomical observations. He made a careful study of all the animal life, finding many types which were almost unknown, and identifying seven new types of antelope of which two were named after him. These were the Somali Hartebeest (Bubalis Swaynei) and one of the little Dik-dik antelopes (Madoqua Swaynei). Later, when Africa House was opened in Trafalgar Square, he gave one of his rhinoceros heads for the decoration of the office of the East African dependencies. On completion of his leave he joined at the S.M.E., Chatham, where he commanded a company and in 1894 was called to the Foreign Office as a witness before the Anglo-Italian Boundary Commission, receiving again a letter of thanks for his services. At the end of 1895 he returned to India.

But his close connection with Somaliland affairs was not yet finished. During the years following his visit to Ras Mackunan at Harar in 1893 the development of Abyssinia had progressed very quickly and this country had come into the turmoil of world politics by King Menelik's defeat of an Italian force at the battle of Adowa in January, 1896. The raids of the Abyssinians into Somaliland had increased the unrest in that country, while the French at Jibuti were jealous of British expansion. The British Government therefore decided to send a political mission to King Menelik at Addis Ababa with a personal message and presents from Queen Victoria to the King. The mission was also to endeavour to arrange a settlement of the relative boundaries of Abyssinia and the French and British spheres of influence. The head of the mission was Mr. Rennell Rodd, C.M.G., then chief Secretary of the British Agency at Cairo, and the second-in-command was Lieut.-Colonel F. R. Wingate, C.B., then Director of Military Intelligence with the Egyptian Army; the other military members were Captain Harald Swayne, who represented the Indian Government and was given the temporary rank of Major, also Captain the Hon. Cecil Bingham, 1st Life Guards, with Captain Lord Edward Gleichen and Lieut. Lord Edward Cecil of the Grenadier Guards. The civilian members of the mission were H. H. Pinching Bey, second-in-command of the Egyptian Sanitary Department, who was in medical charge, and Captain Tristram Speedy, a well-known traveller and big game sportsman, who had been attached to the expedition to Magdala in 1867 and was selected for his knowledge of the country and of the Amharic language. The mission had an escort of 20 Sowars of the Aden troop, armed with carbines and lances, under a Jemadar and of a Havildar and eleven members of the Somali police who were dressed in khaki uniform and armed for the occasion. All the members of the mission carried their full-dress uniform, and Gleichen, who wrote an account of the mission under the title of A Mission to Menelik, noted that except Mr. Rodd and Gleichen himself all the members exceeded 6 feet in height, the average of the whole being 6 feet 1 inch! They were thus well able to impress the natives both socially and physically.

Swayne was entrusted with the selection and purchase of the presents for the Emperor and his family and was also responsible for the provision and management of the transport. To help with this he obtained the services of some of his Somali followers, under the headman who had accompanied him in all his previous journeys. This was no light charge, the expedition started with 185 camels, which had to be changed at Gildessa for local donkeys and again changed at Harar for mules, of which 300 were required. These mules had all to be purchased, according to the custom of the country and were sold again on return to Harar, when a spirited auction resulted in an unexpected profit!

Largely owing to the efficiency of Swayne's arrangements, the mission marched from the little port of Zeyla to Addis Ababa and back, a distance of 960 miles in all, between the 20th March and the 14th June, 1897. Swayne, in the second edition of his book, Seventeen Trips Through Somaliland, gives many interesting details, but the only incident of note was that soon after leaving Zeyla the mission encountered several parties of Italian prisoners, 2,000 in all, who had been captured at the battle of Adowa and were being repatriated. The reception of the mission was most cordial and on its departure it was escorted from the capital by an Abyssinian army of 20,000 men dressed in striking uniforms; the officers wore silk shirts and cloaks, the higher officers carrying shields decorated with strips of silver indicating their rank; while many of the soldiers wore leopard skins or decorations of lions' manes.

In addition to his work on the transport, Swayne continued his map-making; he arranged with Gleichen that the latter, who was the intelligence officer, should make a sketch map of the route and Swayne himself sat up many evenings taking shots of the stars, to fix positions for latitude and longitude, with a large transit theodolite. The position he finally arrived at for Addis Ababa was about 13 miles from the position shown on the existing maps, and he was gratified a few months later, on meeting the French explorer Captain Marchand, who had carried up a similar line of survey, to find that the latter's calculation agreed very closely with his own. Both were within 1½ miles of the position fixed later by more accurate methods. Mr. Rennell Rodd, in his final report, refers to Captain Swayne as 'an extremely hard-working officer who had spent a great deal of time in scientific and astronomical observations.' This report was 'received with satisfaction' by the Marquis of Salisbury, then Prime Minister and Secretary of State for Foreign Affairs, and a copy was communicated to Swayne. Swayne also received the permission of Her Majesty to accept and wear the Order of the Star of Ethiopia, a very high and rare honour conferred on him by the Emperor Menelik II.

This was the last active work done by Harald Swayne in East Africa.

Among the results of the Rennell Rodd Mission, a British representative was appointed to the court of King Menelik and an agreement was arrived at as to the boundary between the Abyssinian, French and British spheres;

the boundary between the British and Italian spheres had been defined on the map in 1894. Another change, which had wide-reaching consequences, was the transfer of the control of Somaliland from the Indian Government to the Foreign Office. This change adversely affected Harald Swayne as when difficulties arose in 1900 with the 'Mad Mullah' the home authorities called on his younger brother, Eric Swayne, to put down the disturbance which had arisen. Eric Swayne, after leaving his brother on the completion of their work on the survey in 1892, had taken service under the British East Africa Company and was employed in the difficult and confused fighting in Uganda which was terminated by the capture of King Mwanga of Uganda and King Kabarega of Unyoro. Eric Swayne was given the duty of escorting the two Kings to the Seychelles and while at Aden, in November, 1900, on return from this duty, was ordered to Somaliland to raise a local levy to deal with the Mullah. As the Home Government would not agree to a permanent occupation of the country, the only course was to try to capture the Mahdi's person. Eric Swayne carried out two winter campaigns in 1900–01 and 1901–02; in the first year he defeated the Mahdi's army and forced the Mahdi to escape into the Haud, the following year he had a hard-fought battle at Erigo, south of the border of Somaliland, but the Mahdi again escaped. Eric Swayne was then invalided with fever but returned later as Commissioner and Commander-in-Chief of Somaliland and later again was appointed Governor of British Honduras and received the K.C.M.G. The next two winters fighting was resumed by much larger forces under Brig.-General Manning and Major-General Sir Charles Egerton, the latter gaining a victory at Jidbali and driving the Mahdi into Italian Somaliland. Harald Swayne was intensely interested in all these happenings, and made several attempts to go on service. He offered to serve under his brother in any capacity, but he had recently been promoted Major and was thus senior to all the officers who were detailed to accompany Eric Swayne, and the appointments in charge of the transport were filled by junior officers. In 1893, when Harald was offered employment, he was incapacitated by fever, but in this year he published the third edition of his book, with a preface explaining the reasons for the revolt of the Mullah. When public interest was aroused by the news of the fighting at Erigo, The Times published a statement that the country had never been surveyed. Actually the survey by the brothers Swayne was very complete and gave ample information, but their maps had been treated as confidential both in India and in the Intelligence Office in London. Swayne got a question asked in Parliament but only obtained an evasive reply, that the work done by the brothers was a 'reconnaissance' and not a survey, but in a subsequent debate in the House of Lords, Lord Curzon made the statement already referred to, that Major

Harald Swayne was the best authority on the Somaliland interior. With this we may leave this part of the story.

In the intervals between his visits to Somaliland and after he left the country in 1897, Harald Swayne was employed in India on some of the many jobs open to R.E. officers. In 1898 he was on plague work in Bombay and later was temporarily Chief Engineer to the Calcutta Corporation and Under-Secretary, P.W.D., Bengal. In 1899 he was employed on famine relief work in the Nizam's territory and in 1900 conducted an enquiry into allegations against an English Civil Servant in that area. Swayne's report showed that these accusations were unfounded and he received a letter of thanks from the Resident for his work. He was C.R.E. of various areas as Major and Lieutenant-Colonel, and in 1911, when he had been promoted Substantive Colonel, he was made C.R.E. of the 8th (Lucknow) Divisional Area, which included the large stations of Lucknow, Cawnpore, Benares, Allahabad and Calcutta. He retired on an Indian pension in June, 1914.

He spent most of his leaves in travel and exploration; in 1903 he marched from Ob station on the Siberian railway into the highlands on the border of Mongolia and was successful in getting good heads of the Siberian wild sheep, the 'Ovis Ammon'; he published a record of this trip under the title Through The Highlands of Siberia; in 1904 to 1907 he marched from Beira to the Zambezi; and in 1910 visited Nairobi in Kenya and marched through Uganda to the German border at Toro.

In 1911 he visited Gilgit for sport, fifteen marches from the railway, and in 1912 visited Leh and the West Tibetan border, twenty marches from the railway; in the same year he was sent on duty into West Tibet proper, crossing from Darjeeling into Chumbi. In 1913 he made his fifth visit to Kashmir, marching and hunting in mid-winter, and in 1914 he celebrated his retirement by a trip to China and Japan, returning via Siberia.

The outbreak of the Great War in August, 1914, thus found him on the retired list, but in January, 1915, he assisted his wife to form a hospital, known as Mrs. Swayne's Hospital, at Cherbourg, under the French Red Cross and worked there until in August, 1915, he was given the Command of the 5th Labour Battalion of the R.E. Pioneers. This battalion was employed in the neighbourhood of Ypres on railway construction; for this work Swayne was twice mentioned in despatches and given the C.M.G., a somewhat belated decoration which, however, gave him much satisfaction. In August, 1917, the strength of the battalion was reduced to one company, and Swayne, after some work at the Ministry of Food, was employed by the War Office after the Armistice in lecturing to the troops in the Army of Occupation. His last duty in this capacity was on the 27th October, 1919.

On reversion to civilian life he bought Burghill Court, near Hereford, where he lived for some years, but he travelled extensively on the Continent and built himself a villa at Alassio, which he afterwards let to Sir Edward Thackeray. He occupied himself in lecturing and writing on travel and geographical questions in various scientific publications and in the press. He had also a gift for sketching and when a young officer, had given up part of his leave to attend art schools in Paris; most of the illustrations in his books are from his own sketches.

Swayne was three times married, first in 1894 to Katherine Aimée, daughter of Sir William Holmes of British Guiana, second in 1907 to Amy Christina, daughter of R. A. Swayne, Esq., of Tillingdon Court, Hereford (she died in 1936), and third in 1940 to Lorna Jean, only daughter of the late David Newman, F.R.C.S., and ward of Major-General Telfer-Smollett, Governor of Guernsey. By his first wife he had one daughter, now the wife of Lieut.-Colonel Winder, R.A.M.C. His third marriage ended in tragedy. The marriage had been arranged to take place from Government House, Guernsey, on the 30th January, 1940, but on the 22nd Swayne tripped over an obstruction in the hall of his hotel and falling heavily fractured the femur of his right leg. He was taken to hospital, where a few days later the marriage took place very quietly. He seemed to be making a good recovery and a house was taken to which he could be moved, but a few days before he was leaving hospital pneumonia supervened and he passed away quietly in his sleep on the 14th April, 1940.

The writer of this memoir got in correspondence with Colonel Swayne in connection with the preparation of Volume IV of the Corps History, when Colonel Swayne supplied a series of letters giving details of the work of himself and other R.E. officers in Somaliland. Swayne was at the time in Italy, but he came to London early in 1939 on his way to the World's Fair at New York, and very kindly arranged to get out of store some of his records and a copy of the map of Somaliland prepared by his brother and himself. The writer then had a very interesting interview in London and discussed many points of the draft he had prepared for the History, all of which had been checked by Swayne in considerable detail. It is not possible after a short interview to give any personal idea of the character of the subject of this memoir, but the short record given above is abundant testimony to the tact and skill he displayed in dealing with all classes and to the respect and affection he earned, not least among his Somali followers, who he always spoke of as his friends.

I may close this record with an extract from a letter from his wife, 'I should so much like some reference to be made to his wonderful kindness of heart and generosity. I have never in all my life known anyone for whom I had a greater admiration or who had such a wonderful outlook on life.'

In his Will, Colonel Swayne included the following clause:

'I desire that a parcel of records comprising documents relating to my

Military Service copy of survey sheets of British Somaliland and astronomical and other documents in connection with the Political Mission to the Emperor Menelik of Abyssinia in 1897 should be sent to the Secretary, Institution of Royal Engineers, Chatham, for the use of the Editor of The Royal Engineers Journal for obituary purposes or the Royal Engineer Museum at Brompton Barracks, Chatham.'

It is hoped that the above memoir will be accepted as a fulfilment of the first of these objects.

W.B.B.

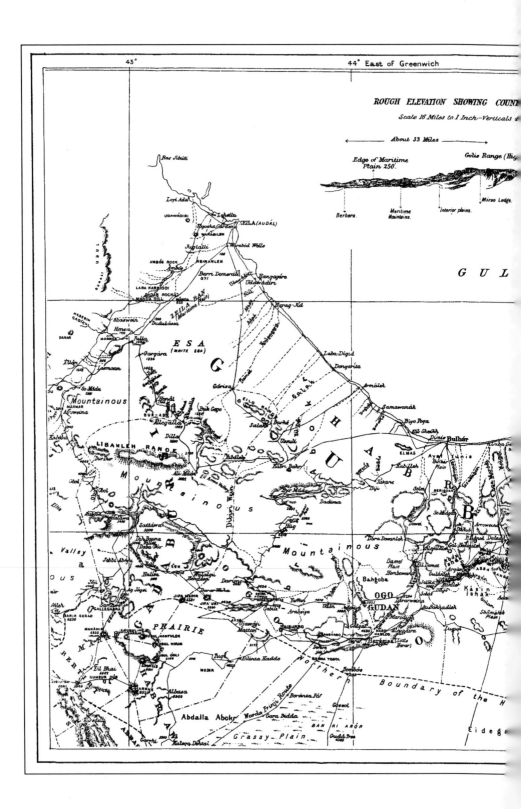